7.50

CONTRIBUTIONS TO
MODERN ECONOMICS

CONTRIBUTIONS TO MODERN ECONOMICS

JOAN ROBINSON

BASIL BLACKWELL
OXFORD
1979

Set by The Camelot Press Ltd, Southampton.
Printed and bound in Great Britain by Billing & Sons Ltd,
Guildford, London and Worcester.

CONTENTS

PREFACE   vii

REMINISCENCES   ix

1 THE SECOND CRISIS OF ECONOMIC THEORY   1

EFFECTIVE DEMAND

2 THE THEORY OF MONEY AND THE ANALYSIS OF OUTPUT   14
3 OBSTACLES TO FULL EMPLOYMENT   20
4 THE CONCEPT OF HOARDING   29
5 THE RATE OF INTEREST   35
6 KALECKI AND KEYNES   53
7 MARX, MARSHALL AND KEYNES   61

CAPITAL AND PROFITS

8 THE PRODUCTION FUNCTION AND THE THEORY OF CAPITAL   76
9 PRE-KEYNESIAN THEORY AFTER KEYNES   91
10 CAPITAL THEORY UP-TO-DATE   103
11 THE MEANING OF CAPITAL   114
12 HISTORY VERSUS EQUILIBRIUM   126

PRICES

13 A LECTURE DELIVERED AT OXFORD BY A CAMBRIDGE ECONOMIST   137
14 THE PHILOSOPHY OF PRICES   146
15 'IMPERFECT COMPETITION' REVISITED   166
16 THE THEORY OF VALUE RECONSIDERED   182

INTERNATIONAL TRADE

17 BEGGAR-MY-NEIGHBOUR REMEDIES FOR UNEMPLOYMENT   190
18 THE NEW MERCANTILISM   201
19 THE NEED FOR A RECONSIDERATION OF THE THEORY OF
       INTERNATIONAL TRADE   213

CONTEMPORARY REFLECTIONS

20 HAS CAPITALISM CHANGED? 223

21 LATTER–DAY CAPITALISM 229

22 SOCIALIST AFFLUENCE 240

23 WHAT HAS BECOME OF EMPLOYMENT POLICY? 254

24 BEAUTY AND THE BEAST 267

PREFACE

These papers are drawn from the work of fifty years. They include contributions to two great intellectual upheavals in economic theory – the Keynesian Revolution and the revival of the classical theory of profits led by Piero Sraffa – as well as some discussions of the formation of prices in capitalist and socialist economies and of international trade.

'Reminiscences', which serves as an introduction, relates the evolution of these ideas to the personal and historical events that influenced them.

The pieces selected are those which have been found most useful for students, but some, especially 'The new mercantilism' and 'What has become of employment policy?', may be of wider interest.

I am grateful to John Eatwell of Trinity College, Cambridge, for encouragement and help in producing this volume, and to Murray Milgate for reading the proofs.

Cambridge 1978   Joan Robinson

REMINISCENCES

1

MARSHALL AND PIGOU

WHEN I came up to Cambridge (in October 1921) to read economics, I did not have much idea of what it was about. I had some vague hope that it would help me to understand poverty and how it could be cured. And I hoped that it would offer more scope for rational argument than history (my school subject) as it was taught in those days.

I was somewhat disappointed on both counts. Alfred Marshall was the all-dominating influence on the Cambridge faculty; the last item in this volume (24) indicates how I took to him. I felt smothered by the moralizing and mystified by the theory; in particular, no one seemed to know what was meant by the 'representative firm'.

When I returned to Cambridge in 1929, they were still arguing about the representative firm (*Economic Journal*, March 1930) but meanwhile Piero Sraffa had turned up, rescued by Keynes from Mussolini. He was calmly committing the sacrilege of pointing out inconsistencies in Marshall, and, moreover, introducing us to other contemporary schools of thought (but they were no better).

My first book, *Economics of Imperfect Competition*, though inspired by a hint from Sraffa, was mainly influenced by Professor Pigou. Pigou seemed to have reduced Marshall's *Principles* to a logical and consistent scheme but there was an obvious defect in it. The whole argument turns on 'price equals marginal cost'. This entails that the sales of an industrial firm are limited by the capacity of its equipment. Short-period profit per unit of output is equal to marginal cost minus average prime cost. Plants that are yielding any gross profit at all are working up to capacity (with rising marginal costs) and the rest are shut down and kept in moth balls.

This was evidently absurd, particularly in the slump when most plants were working part time. With the aid of Richard Kahn, who had been studying actual pricing policy in the British cotton industry, I used the newly invented concept of 'marginal revenue' to show how short-period profits are positive even at under-capacity working.

With this apparatus, we produced a complete restatement of the Pigovian system with various amendments, in particular, the demonstration that, in Pigou's own terms, it is not true that wages are equal to the value of the marginal product of labour.

A few months before *Imperfect Competition* was published, Edward Chamberlin's *Monopolistic Competition* appeared. He was upset by the coincidence and all the rest of his work was devoted to showing that my theory was quite different from his. During his reign at Harvard, it used to be said that you could always get a good degree by abusing Mrs. Robinson.

I recognized that several of the questions that he raised, such as deliberate product differentiation as a means of competition, were more interesting than mine but obviously there was a very large overlap between the two books. I suppose that Chamberlin was annoyed at having to share all his footnotes and reviews with me, and he resented Nicky Kaldor's comment that he went in for unnecessary product differentiation, but there was a deeper reason.

I had been very well pleased to refute the orthodox theory of wages, which had stuck in my gizzard as a student, while Chamberlin refused to admit that his argument damaged the image of the market producing the optimum allocation of given resources between alternative uses. This ideological difference underlay an otherwise unnecessary controversy.

I soon abandoned the field; when I came under the influence of the incipient Keynesian revolution, I realized that my Pigovian book was leading up a blind alley.

First of all, it was all conceived *a priori*; some scraps of observation were introduced into the assumptions here and there but, in general, it was all a deduction from Marshallian assumptions as interpreted by Pigou. Keynes, by contrast, was concerned with an actual phenomenon – unemployment – and was trying to find out a theory to account for it.

Secondly, the whole problem of time was fudged. There is no clear distinction in the book between short and long-period relationships or between the future and the past, though I avoided the horrible neoclassical methodology of drawing a plane diagram showing a timeless relation between two variables and then moving about on it. (This point is raised in the 'Lecture delivered at Oxford' (13) below.) Keynes had instinctively recognized the nature of historical time in which today is an ever-moving break between the irrevocable past and the unknown future, though he did not express the point clearly till after the *General Theory* was published.[1]

[1] See 'The general theory of employment', 1937, *JMK*, Vol. XIV.

My own impressions of my book after thirty years are included in this volume – 'Imperfect Competition revisited' (14).

After passing through another intellectual revolution, I took a more kindly view of Marshall. Though he fudged the problem of time, he was aware of it, and he took pains to avoid the spurious neoclassical methodology. It was Pigou who had flattened him out into stationary equilibrium. When I republished the 'Lecture' and some other pieces (in CEP, Vol. IV) I wrote:

> These essays were written in a hilarious mood after reading Piero Sraffa's *Introduction* to Ricardo's *Principles*, which caused me to see that the concept of the rate of profit on capital is essentially the same in Ricardo, Marx, Marshall and Keynes; while the essential difference between these, on the one side, and Walras, Pigou and the latter-day textbooks on the other, is that the Ricardians are describing an historical process of accumulation in a changing world, while the Walrasians dwell in timeless equilibrium where there is no distinction between the future and the past.

2

EFFECTIVE DEMAND

In the summer of 1930 Keynes was lecturing from the proof sheets of his *Treatise on Money* and the book was published in October. Meanwhile Kahn had produced the first draft of what became his famous article on the multiplier.[2] In the term beginning in April 1931, we got up a circus, as we called it, to discuss the *Treatise*, and from then till the completion of the *General Theory of Employment, Interest and Money* in the winter of 1935, and beyond, I was involved, along with Kahn, in a continuous series of discussions, writings, lectures and correspondence around the development of Keynes' ideas.

It is difficult to convey an impression of Keynes to someone who did not know him. In the world, he was considered arrogant and harsh; this was because he loved to put a pin into any pompous balloon that he encountered. With us in Cambridge he was far from harsh. He had exacting standards but withal he was warm-hearted and generous. He was conscious of being far more intelligent than nearly everyone whom he met, but that was just a fact; he had no need to puff himself up. He had a sense of absolute values; he was willing to argue with anyone on the merits of the case in

[2] 'The relation of home investment to unemployment', *Economic Journal*, June 1931. Reprinted in *Selected Essays on Employment and Growth*, Cambridge University Press, 1972.

hand; he could be ferociously obstinate but it never occurred to him to use his authority and eminence to crush a younger disputant and he was ready to take an interest in fresh ideas wherever they came from.

He was great fun; even a boring committee meeting could be amusing when he was present. At a party, he did not lapse into talking college shop as so many academics do, but entertained the company by enlarging on some striking thesis, such as that the continent of North America cannot support human life.

His mind worked many times faster than anyone else's so that, however much work he was doing, there was always plenty of time in his day. Above all, he was blessedly free from the vice of wanting to have been right. He quickly absorbed the criticisms of the *Treatise* (conveyed to him by Kahn) that were raised at the circus; immediately, his mind began to race towards new formulations.

In those days seminars were unknown. Our circus, first proposed by Piero Sraffa, was organized as an unofficial venture. The main speakers were Kahn, James Meade, who was spending a year in Cambridge in order to transplant economics to Oxford, Sraffa (who was secretly sceptical of the new ideas), Austin Robinson and myself. Only students who were considered up to it were allowed to come.[3]

To understand the argument at the circus, it is necessary to recapture the central position of the *Treatise*. When he was writing it, Keynes believed that 'monetary theory' was only about prices. On the plane of policy, he had supported Lloyd George's scheme to conquer unemployment by expenditure on public works, but in the high abstraction of the *Treatise*, employment was hardly mentioned.

The argument postulates a position of equilibrium at a moment of time when saving is equal to investment and the level of profits is normal. Then an increase in investment causes prices to rise and so profits to increase. Owing to peculiar definitions, this is called an excess of investment over saving. This excess is not reduced by expenditure on consumption, for if part of profits are spent, prices rise all the more; profits are a widow's cruse that cannot be exhausted. On the other tack, if entrepreneurs reduce consumption in order to save more, 'the cruse becomes a Danaid jar which can never be filled up'.[4]

One of the main topics at the circus was the relation between demand and output. Austin Robinson immediately spotted the fallacy in the widow's cruse at a time of unemployment. If businessmen increase

[3] See *JMK*, Vol. XIII, Chapter 5.
[4] Quoted, loc. cit., p. 339.

consumption when profits rise, there will be an increase in the output of goods and services, with not necessarily any rise in prices at all.

This was the first step from the theory of money to the analysis of output which is described in my article of 1933 (2), included in this volume.

A second topic was the amendment of the *Treatise* definitions. Kahn's article was expressed in the language of the *Treatise*, but he now discovered that the saving over any period is necessarily equal to investment in that period. This was described as Mr. Meade's relation, because James had assisted in the discovery.

There was some confusion at this time between an accounting identity that must be true by definition and a causal relationship. The important point was the causal relationship, that is, the manner (shown in the multiplier) in which a given increase in investment leads income to go on rising until it reaches the level where saving is increased by an equal amount. At the same time, what was most shocking to Marshallian orthodoxy, a reduction of expenditure on consumption (with investment unchanged) will not increase saving but only reduce income.

Kahn reinforced the point (unwittingly following the Marxian schema of expanded reproduction) by imagining cordons drawn round the investment and the consumption-good industries and studying the trade between them. The excess of the income of the consumption sector over its own consumption – that is, its savings – is equal to the expenditure on consumption of the investment sector. Thus the sum of the savings of the consumption sector and of the investment sector is equal to the value of investment.

Another point which we took up was the notion of normal profits. If, as Kahn argued, there is a supply curve of output as a whole (given money wage rates) in a short-period situation with fixed total productive capacity, then, corresponding to any given state of demand, there is a particular amount of employment, level of prices and flow of gross profits. There is no one level of profits that is more 'normal' than any other.

It is interesting that Gunnar Myrdal, in *Monetary Equilibrium*, found almost the same way of reconciling Wicksell's theory with the experience of unemployment.

There was one more topic, though I do not remember if it came up at the circus or later – that was the 'buckets-in-a-well' fallacy. Dennis Robertson tried to maintain that whenever there was an increase in saving, more money would be passed to the Stock Exchange and used to finance a corresponding increase in investment. This view arises from the all-too-prevalent confusion between a flow of income and a stock of wealth. A reduction of expenditure on consumption does not increase the total flow of saving if the flow of investment remains the same, but causes income to run down until the new flow of saving is equal to the old flow of investment. At the same time, when net investment is going on, the total of wealth is growing and part of the corresponding savings are made by individual owners of wealth, who may hold them in the first instance as an addition to their money balances and later use them to reduce debt or purchase other assets. The demands for money and other assets relatively to the stocks in existence at a moment of time affect the level of interest rates and the value of shares (common stock), which have only a secondary and indirect influence on the flow of investment.

It is worthwhile to repeat these old arguments, for modern teaching has been confused by J. R. Hicks' attempt to reduce the General Theory to a version of static equilibrium with the formula IS/LM. Hicks has now repented[5] and changed his name from J. R. to John, but it will take a long time for the effects of his teaching to wear off.

Dennis Robertson was sarcastic about the circus, and came to only one meeting. He had an ambivalent attitude to Keynes, who had been a close friend. He admired Maynard's intellectual daring and yet was frightened by it. He clung on to old doctrines, such as that a cut in wages must necessarily increase employment, and he kept up a running fire of criticisms, some of which were useful, though on peripheral points.

As the argument went on, he became embittered. He tried to prevent me from expounding the new theory in my lectures (but Pigou ruled in favour of free speech). Lord Robbins[6] and others have drawn a pathetic picture of Dennis, but it was Keynes who was grieved by his hostility. After Keynes' death, when Robertson had returned to Cambridge as Pigou's successor, he created a lasting schism in the faculty by trying to re-schedule the syllabus so that Keynes' theory could not be taught (if at all) before the final year.

In the days following the meetings of the circus, there was a clear distinction between those who had seen the point and those who had not. Austin Robinson said that we went about asking: Brother, are you saved? George Shackle has given a touching account of his conversion.[7]

All this time, controversy over public-works policy was raging between Keynes (who was supported by Pigou although from a quite different theoretical position) and Professor Hayek, at the London School of

---

[5] Cf. Joan Robinson, 'What are the questions', *Journal of Economic Literature*, December 1977, reprinted in *CEP*, Vol. V.

[6] See *The Autobiography of an Economist*, Macmillan, 1971, p. 222.

[7] See *The Nature of Economic Thought*, p. 53.

Economics, supported by Robbins, who has since expressed regret at having been on the wrong side.[8]

A delegation led by Abba Lerner (then a graduate student at LSE) came to Cambridge to suggest that the young generation on each side should get together and settle the debate amongst themselves. The *Review of Economic Studies* was founded as a forum for discussion (it later evolved into something quite different) and a weekend meeting was arranged at an inn half-way between London and Cambridge.

Cambridge was represented by Kahn, Austin Robinson and myself, and James Meade who had been back in Oxford for a year but was (at that time) in complete accord with us. Abba Lerner brought three contemporaries (none of whom remained in the profession). It was agreed that there should be no appeal to authority; every point must be argued out on its merits.

At the first session, James explained the multiplier; Kahn, who came later, went over it again. Then it was the turn of London. They said that before they could discuss employment they must analyse what would happen if everyone confidently expected that the world was coming to an end in six months time. We went over the ground with them; it would make an interesting tripos question. The point was to distinguish what capital goods could be consumed in six months, by ceasing replacements, from what would have to be left.

At the end of the session James very earnestly asked: Before we rise, could you tell us whether this illustrates the boom or the slump? but none of them was prepared to say. Next day, Abba asked to go over the multiplier argument. With some help, he repeated it correctly and seemed to be convinced. His companions were quite shocked and were seen afterwards walking him up and down the lawn, trying to restore his faith.

On the last evening we relaxed the rule about mentioning names and asked them to explain what Hayek really meant by 'capital consumption', but it was not a success.

Abba came to spend a term in Cambridge. He had been used to being the intellectual leader of his group and he very candidly admitted that he had been distressed to meet an argument that he could not answer. After passing the term in mental agony, he found out that saving is necessarily equal to investment and became for some time an only too fanatical supporter of Keynes.

This volume contains some of the pieces which I wrote to elucidate points in the *General Theory* or draw riders from it: 'The concept of hoarding'(4), 'The rate of interest' (5) and 'Beggar-my-neighbour remedies

[8] Op. cit., pp. 152–5.

for unemployment' (17). The lecture: 'Obstacles to full employment' (3) was one of many which I gave after the war in various European countries to expound and defend the new theory. Reading it now, it seems to have been prescient. It points out that the great unsolved problem of a regime of near-full employment is going to be inflation and it argues that, once the idea of employment policy has been accepted, the question should be changed from: Can governments influence the level of production? to: What kind of production should they support? This is the theme of the first piece in this collection: 'The second crisis of economic theory' (1) which summarizes all the rest. The article written in collaboration with Frank Wilkinson (23) reflects upon the situation as it appeared in 1976.

3

CAPITAL AND PROFITS

Michał Kalecki came to Cambridge just after the *General Theory* was published. This volume contains a paper (6) in which I described our first meeting and mentioned some of the important amendments that he made in Keynes' theory. His work was the most original and important of any in the inter-war years, which is now at last beginning to be recognized, and later he made applications of the new theory to problems of socialism and of the Third World. He did not have, like Keynes, a long struggle to escape from Marshall, but approached his problems directly from Marx.

In Marx's system of analysis, the problem of 'realizing the surplus' – that is of effective demand – is somehow separate from the process of accumulation. Kalecki developed, from the 'schema of expanded reproduction' in Volume II of *Capital*, an integrated analysis. He showed (more clearly than Keynes had done) that profits provide not only the motive for investment, but also the finance to support it, while he emphasized that development does not depend only on investment (the output of Department I) but also requires an adequate increase in the output of wage goods (Department II).

However, his model, in which the workers spend what they get and the capitalists get what they spend, shows the determination only of the flow of profit in national income; it does not discuss the formation of the rate of profit on capital. To define the *rate* of profit it is necessary to define the value of the stock of capital, and that no one seemed able to do.

Harrod's *Towards a Dynamic Economics*, 1949 (expanding ideas conceived in 1938), opened up a discussion of long-run growth in Keynesian terms, but he also lacked a rate of profit. I had innumerable discussions with Piero

Sraffa but they always consisted in his heading me off from errors; he would never say anything positive. Thus it was not till I found the 'corn economy' in his *Introduction* to Ricardo's *Principles* that I saw a gleam of light on the question of the rate of profit on capital. This led to a new upheaval in ideas, comparable in excitement, though not in immediate practical importance, to the Keynesian revolution itself.

The first round was my article of 1953 (8). I wrote about it in 1974:[9]

> 'The Production Function and the Theory of Capital' was met, not only with incomprehension, but with ridicule and indignation. I can understand this now better than I did at the time. In Cambridge, the meaning of the capital to labour ratio in a long-period sense was a well-known unsettled question that Dennis Robertson has left in an admittedly unsatisfactory state.[10] Elsewhere, as I since found, there was a convention of agreeing to believe that it was no problem. My article (written in a somewhat light-hearted style) was innocently remarking that the Emperor had no clothes.

After this, I worked out, rather clumsily, a number of points that became clearer with the publication of Sraffa's *Production of Commodities by Means of Commodities*. In particular, I constructed what later became known as a pseudo-production function. I interpreted the neoclassical conception of 'a given state of technical knowledge' as a 'book of blueprints' showing a variety of techniques for producing a whole flow of net output in a particular economy, each with the stock of physical inputs that its technique requires. The value of any stock, in general, varies with the rate of profit. There is nothing surprising in this; costs are made up of two parts, a wages bill and an interest bill (the rate of interest, in perfect tranquillity, being equal to the rate of profit) and these vary inversely to each other – a higher rate of profit corresponding to a lower level of cost per unit of labour. Thus the cost of capital goods relatively to a unit of net output is higher or lower, with a higher rate of profit, according to whether the capital to labour ratio is higher or lower in investment good industries than in final output. Only in the special case where the ratio of capital to labour is the same in all industries do labour-value prices rule, so that the value of a given physical stock of capital is independent of the rate of profit. This should always have been obvious, but since it cut the ground from under the feet of the theory

---

[9] Introduction to 2nd edition of *CEP*, Vol. II.
[10] See below p. 77 note 3.

that the rate of interest measures the 'marginal product of capital', it was not acceptable.

Professor Samuelson had taken over 'marginal productivity' from J. B. Clark and he maintained that, though 'capital' is not really made of putty that can be squeezed into various forms without loss of its substance, yet it is *like* putty in the relevant respect. He evidently took this on faith and had not given it much thought.

In 1961 I was invited to take a couple of seminars at MIT. I chose the subject: The Use and Abuse of the Production Function. During the first session, I asked Samuelson: When you define the marginal product of labour, what do you keep constant? For a moment, he was quite disconcerted, and then started off on some baffling rigmarole. I cut in: Paul, I asked you a simple question, can't you give me a simple answer? He replied that he would have to think it over. This scene was long remembered by the students at MIT who witnessed it.

Samuelson turned the joke against himself. He put round a paper next day as follows: Thursday at 4.40, Mrs. Robinson asks the question. Professor Samuelson: Well I mean to say, the Kings of England were William the First, and William the Second . . . Mrs. Robinson: Come, come sir, answer the question!

Friday 6.30 a.m. (implying a sleepless night) the answer is that either you keep all physical inputs constant or you keep the rate of interest constant.

This clue would have led him to the heart of the matter if he had followed it up, but he was deflected by the notion of a book of blueprints and produced his own pseudo-production function. In setting up the assumptions, he stumbled upon the conditions for labour-value prices, so that his diagram *looks* like a production function on which a technique that offers a higher output per unit of labour always requires a higher value of capital.

When the great 're-switching' debate broke out, Samuelson had to admit that, in the general case, a pseudo-production function may have any shape and that, at some points, the technique with the higher output per man may show a *lower* value of capital per man.

It was fun to tease Samuleson, but this debate took attention away from the main issue. A pseudo-production function is an imaginary comparison of stocks of physical capital each already in being; each must be supposed to have been produced by investment in the past and to be now kept intact because the future is expected to be like the past. When the future is expected to be different from the past, say because the current rate of profit has altered, it would not be possible to change the stock of capital except by a long process of investment and dis-investment.

After years of argument, the neo-neoclassics still refuse to understand the difference between a comparison of timeless equilibrium positions and the effects to be expected from a change taking place at a particular moment.

These controversies are described (naturally, from my point of view) in 'Capital theory up-to-date' (10) (1970) and in 'The meaning of capital' (11), written a few years later.

Though the 'Cambridge critics' were never answered, mainstream teaching, till today, seems to go on in the same old way.

I was delighted to find in a dictionary the word mumpsimus, which means stubborn persistence in an error after it has been exposed.

4

PRICES

In the pre-Keynesian doctrine there was a sharp distinction between the analysis of the general price level, which was treated in terms of money, and the theory of value which dealt with relative prices of particular commodities, determined by supply and demand. This dichotomy was broken down in the *General Theory*, which treats money prices of commodities and of investment goods as being governed by their costs of production in money terms.

As my education passed from Marshall to Keynes, I was never subjected to the now prevalent dominance of general equilibrium and the theory of the allocation of scarce means between alternative uses. When I was a student, Walrasian doctrines were in vogue at the London School of Economics and it was customary there to mock at the logical inconsistency in Marshall's method of treating markets for commodities 'one at a time', but the logical flaw in their own system was still more crippling. How can the market allocate resources between various uses when all endowments of means of production are already given in physical form? An equilibrium position could exist today only if all parties concerned had made investments in the past in the light of correct expectations about what today was going to be like in all relevant respects. The conception of a world of correct foresight, whether absolute or contingent, is a plaything for mathematicians without application. Moreover, the concept of equilibrium cannot be used to discuss the *effects* of *change*. It can only deal with *comparisons* of imagined *differences*. This point is elaborated in the paper on 'History versus Equilibrium' (12).

Pigou's marginal costs and my imperfect competition were no improvement, in this respect, on Walrasian tastes and endowments. The problem of the behaviour of prices in historic time remained to be solved.

Kalecki distinguished between two different areas of price formation. For many types of primary commodities a market is formed by dealers and there the operation of something like Marshallian supply and demand rules, though it by no means tends to establish equilibrium. For manufactures, the producer sets prices in advance and demand determines how much he sells. Here prices are formed by adding a gross margin to prime costs. Kalecki took over from imperfect competition the notion that the level of margins is governed by the *degree of monopoly* in the markets for various commodities. This has been much discussed, amended and submitted to empirical investigation.

We now have a more or less satisfactory theory of prices in a short-period situation, with given plant embodying technology, given money wage rates and given expectations. And we have an analysis of long-period normal prices corresponding to a uniform rate of profit on capital. But all important and interesting questions lie in the gap between the two.

I could never understand the claim that the free play of market forces establishes an optimum pattern of prices, but discussions with Polish and Soviet economists made me realize that there are very great merits in a system of prices for consumer goods in which flows of demand for particular commodities are in line with available supplies. Distribution according to queuing power is no more just and much more wasteful than distribution according to purchasing power, and it moreover invites corruption.

This question, among others, is raised in 'The philosophy of prices'. (14)

In 1957 a group of visiting economists were kindly entertained at the Academy of Sciences in Moscow. When it was my turn to put a question, I asked how the labour theory of value applies in agriculture. Khrushchev's reforms had recently raised prices for the products of the collective farms. I picked up a lump of sugar, and asked: 'Has the labour value of this increased?' At first, the answer was evasive: 'A lump of sugar is not an agricultural commodity. It is highly processed.' 'Very well. Take the labour value of raw sugar on the farm.' 'That is a very difficult question.'

I was asked to write a piece on this problem for *Voprosi Ekonomiki*, but when I sent in my 'Philosophy of prices' it was not accepted for publication.[11]

[11] *Introduction* to CEP, Vol. II.

I had no better success when I gave some lectures on these lines at Manchester to an audience of well trained neoclassics who could not make head or tail of what I was saying.

I wrote in 1974:

> In the western world, the decade of the 1950s was a time of prosperity, when high employment, rising consumption and a continuously expanding economy were being taken for granted.
>
> A revival was going on, particularly in USA, of pre-Keynesian theory — the defence of *laisser-faire* — while, in practice, more or less Keynesian methods of control were being followed to preserve near-stability. The equilibrium theory was not immediately laughed out of court because the results that it predicted were being established by quite other means.[12]

By that date the return of a serious slump had thrown everything into question. But even now, general equilibrium is still being taught as the main basis of the theory of prices.

5

TRADE AND EXCHANGE RATES

Reconsideration of the orthodox theory of international trade began even before the Keynesian revolution, for the prevailing doctrine was based on the concept of each country's trade being normally balanced in a regime of fixed exchange rates and free trade.

In 1925, sterling was returned to the gold standard at the pre-1914 exchange rate with the dollar when relative costs and prices had obviously become higher in Britain than in the United States. This was justified according to official opinion (formulated by Professor Pigou) on the ground that, under a resolute monetary policy, prices can quickly be brought into line with exchange rates.

Keynes pointed out, in *The Economic Consequences of Mr. Winston Churchill*, that a general fall in prices requires a fall in money-wage rates and predicted a period of industrial strife. True enough, in 1926 there was an abortive general strike.

Heavy unemployment, especially in export trades, failed to bring wages down sufficiently to restore the competitive position of British products. The economy continued to be depressed while the USA was enjoying the boom which broke in the autumn of 1929. There is a certain poetic justice in the fact that it was an attempt to save the exchange rate by cutting wages

[12] Ibid.

that finally forced sterling off gold; in 1931, heavy speculation against the pound became irresistible with the news that there had been a so-called mutiny in the Atlantic Fleet in protest against a reduction in pay and allowances for the British navy, along with other public services.

As soon as the gold par was abandoned, the public were much relieved, in spite of all the horror stories about inflation with which they had been dosed, and depreciation, along with some import protection, made a contribution to recovery from the worst of the slump in Britain. This dramatic episode did much to discredit orthodox belief in the advantages of a system of fixed exchange rates and free trade.

'Beggar-my-neighbour remedies for unemployment' (17) is one of the papers that I wrote in 1936 to draw riders from the *General Theory*. It was republished recently because it is once more painfully topical[13] but it is much dated. Because of the historical experience of 1931, faith in exchange depreciation as a reliable remedy for a deficit in the balance of payments was much stronger then than it is now.

'The new Mercantilism' (18), written in 1965, is more sophisticated, but it is still necessary to bear the date in mind, for the Bretton Woods system had in effect created a regime of fixed exchange rates which was still in force at that time under the hegemony of the American dollar.

Approaching the problems of international trade from this angle made the orthodox static equilibrium theory appear totally irrelevant.

Paul Samuelson visited Cambridge in 1947 with his factor-price-equalization theorem. I was baffled by it and tried to refute it, but I was caught in the mine-field of assumptions that make it tautological. With the dissolution of the neoclassical production function after 1953, the very concept of 'factor prices' came into question. 'The need for a reconsideration of the theory of international trade' (19) opens up the application of post-Keynesian theory in this sphere, but a lot of work remains to be done.

6

REFLECTIONS

The fifty years of work from which this selection is drawn has aimed to bring theoretical analysis nearer the actual problems of economic life instead of further away from them. For this reason, there are many contemporary reflections in all these papers, not only in those in the last group, which are specifically devoted to current historical situations.

Cambridge, December 1977   JOAN ROBINSON
[13] See *CEP*, Vol. IV, p. 175.

1

THE SECOND CRISIS OF ECONOMIC THEORY

THE title of this talk – the second crisis of economic theory, is related to the first crisis – the great slump of the 'thirties. It is the second crisis in our lifetime – there were others before. I should say rather in my lifetime. When I see this throng of superfluous economists – I am using that word, of course, in the Shakespearian sense – I am reminded how much the profession has grown since the 'thirties and how many more there are now to suffer from the second crisis than there were to be discredited in the first.

What was the state of orthodox opinion when the world was struck by the great slump? First of all, there was the famous Treasury View of 1929. Great Britain had been suffering from heavy unemployment while the United States was enjoying the long boom which culminated in the great bull market on Wall Street. The British situation had been exacerbated by what Keynes unkindly called *The Economic Consequences of Mr. Winston Churchill* – the return to gold at an overvalued exchange rate. In 1929 Lloyd George was campaigning for a policy of public works; Keynes, with Hubert Henderson, produced the pamphlet *Can Lloyd George Do It?* which first adumbrated the theory of the multiplier and of the relation of saving to investment. To answer Lloyd George, the Conservative government produced a White Paper in which various ministers stated the case against spending money in their respective departments on housing, schools, roads etc. The Chancellor of the Exchequer was Churchill; he could not bring himself a second time to defend deflation and sound finance. It was left to the officials to produce the argument for the Treasury. Their case was very simple. It was based on the idea that investment is governed by saving. If the government borrowed £100 million to spend on public works, there would be £100 million less for foreign investment. The surplus of exports would fall by a corresponding amount. There would be a transfer of employment but no change in the total. It is not fair to put much weight on this. The Treasury, after all, was required to say something and this was

---

Richard T. Ely Lecture, delivered to the American Economic Association meeting at New Orleans, 27 December 1971 with J. K. Galbraith in the Chair.

what they thought of to say. The fact that it appeared to be a respectable argument, however, certainly was a symptom of the state of opinion at that time.

In 1932, Professor (now Lord) Robbins published the famous essay in which he describes economics as the subject that deals with the allocation of scarce means between alternative uses. No doubt this was the expression of a long tradition but the date of publication was unlucky. By the time the book came out there were 3 million workers unemployed in Great Britain and the statistical measure of GNP in USA had recently fallen to half its former level. It was just a coincidence that the book appeared when means for any end at all had rarely been less scarce.

The main orthodox reaction to the slump was the argument that wages were too high. This could be backed up by statistical argument. In those old days, prices used to fall when there was a decline in demand, so that prices were lower relatively to money-wage rates than when employment was higher. In a style of argument nowadays familiar in another context, a correlation was exhibited as a cause. The theory that unemployment could be due only to wages being too high received solid support from the evidence.

In Chicago, Henry Simons maintained that there were two causes of the depression. One was the existence of trade unions which refused to allow wages to fall. The other was the existence of commercial banks. It must be observed that the trade unions support *money* wages while the theory required *real* wages to fall but no one at that time had ever discussed the influence of wages on prices. Prices were conceived to be something to do with money. It was because commercial banks were always allowing the quantity of money to expand and contract that Simons regarded them as the main source of the trouble.

While the controversy about public works was developing, Professor Robbins sent to Vienna for a member of the Austrian school to provide a counter-attraction to Keynes. I very well remember Hayek's visit to Cambridge on his way to the London School. He expounded his theory and covered a black-board with his triangles. The whole argument, as we could see later, consisted in confusing the current rate of investment with the total stock of capital goods, but we could not make it out at the time. The general tendency seemed to be to show that the slump was caused by consumption. R. F. Kahn, who was at that time involved in explaining that the multiplier guaranteed that saving equals investment, asked in a puzzled tone, 'Is it your view that if I went out tomorrow and bought a new overcoat, that would increase unemployment?' 'Yes,' said Hayek. 'But,' pointing to his triangles on the board, 'it would take a very long mathematical argument to explain why.'

This pitiful state of confusion was the first crisis of economic theory that I referred to.

To understand how disconcerting the slump was, it is necessary to recall the atmosphere of the times. For fifty years before 1914 the established economists of various schools had all been preaching one doctrine, with great self-confidence and pomposity, the doctrine of *laisser-faire*, the beneficial effects of the free play of market forces. In the English-speaking world, in particular, free trade and balanced budgets were all that was required of government policy. Economic equilibrium would always establish itself. These doctrines were still dominant in the 1920s.

The post-war atmosphere in 1919 was very different from that of 1945. Last time, the keynote was Never Again! All schemes of reconstruction and new policies were aimed at preventing a recurrence of the pre-war situation. In 1918 the mood was nostalgia. The world before 1914 appeared as normality to which all must desire to return. Of course this was an illusion. There is no such thing as a normal period of history. Normality is a fiction of economic text books. An economist sets up a model which is specified in such a way as to be in a normal state. He takes a lot of trouble to prove the *existence* of normality in his model. The fact that evidently the world does exist is claimed as a strong point for the model. But the world does not exist in a state of normality. If the world of the nineteenth century had been normal, 1914 would not have happened.

At the time, however, in the post-war scene, normality lay in the past. As far as the economists were concerned, they did not really know very much about that world. They knew what was in their books. In their books, a private enterprise economy tends to equilibrium and not only to equilibrium – to an optimum position. Trouble was often caused by politicians who were short-sighted and under the sway of particular interests. If only they would establish free trade, restore the gold standard, keep budgets balanced and leave the free play of the market forces to establish equilibrium, all would be for the best in the best of all possible worlds. Of course, there were footnotes making cautious reservations. Indeed, in the higher reaches of the profession there was something of the atmosphere of the augurs touching their noses behind the altar. Amongst themselves, they admitted it was not really like that. But their pupils took it all literally. They formed an official opinion deeply influenced by the conception of equilibrium which could be relied upon to establish itself provided that no one tried to interfere.

The doctrine that there is a natural tendency to maintain equilibrium with full employment could not survive the experience of the complete collapse of the market economy in the 'thirties.

Out of this crisis emerged what has become known as the Keynesian revolution. After the war, Keynes became orthodox in his turn. Unfortunately, the Keynesian orthodoxy, as it became established, left out the point. This is not the second crisis. This is still part of the first crisis.

Consider what was the point of the Keynesian revolution on the plane of theory and on the plane of policy. On the plane of theory, the main point of the *General Theory* was to break out of the cocoon of equilibrium and consider the nature of life lived in time – the difference between yesterday and tomorrow. Here and now, the past is irrevocable and the future is unknown.

This was too great a shock. Orthodoxy managed to wind it up in a cocoon again. Keynes had broken down the compartments of 'real' and 'monetary' theory. He showed how money is a necessary feature of an economy in which the future is uncertain and he showed what part monetary and financial institutions play in the functioning of the 'real' economy. Now the compartments have been restored in the division between 'micro' and 'macro' theory. Axel Leijonhufvud points out that an analysis of the harmony of an organism should be useful for dealing with the problems of its malfunctioning:

> Not so in economics. We use 'Walrasian' models for the first type of question, and 'macro-models' for the second; and we act as if this schizophrenic State of the Arts was something that we are willing to live with indefinitely. The theory of value and resource allocation deals with how economic activities are co-ordinated. Macro-theory deals with co-ordination failures – at least, that was the original problem. But the structure of the two types of models is so dissimilar that the price-theoretical content of 'Keynesian' macro-models is often difficult to distil.[1]

The price theory of Keynes' system (as opposed to a 'Keynesian' one) certainly cannot be fitted into Walras. Axel Leijonhufvud has made an heroic effort to show how a theory of unemployment could be derived from a Walrasian model – Walras without the auctioneer. But this in fact was not the basis of the argument. The peculiar mixture of Walras with Pigou – supply and demand for given resources with profit-maximizing firms of optimum size – which nowadays passes for 'micro theory' was first blended by John Hicks after the *General Theory* was published. Walras

---

[1] Two lectures on 'Keynes' Contribution to Economic Theory', *IEA Publications*.

leaves out the very point that Keynes was bringing in – historical time. I remember Keynes suggesting that Walras got his idea of crying prices from the Paris bourse where in his day deals were really made by shouting bids and offers. A stock market can operate so, for it is dealing with stocks. Anyone who tries to introduce a flow of production into Walras immediately falls into contradictions. Either the whole of future time is collapsed into today or else every individual has correct foresight about what everyone else will do, while they have correct foresight about what he will do, so that the argument runs into the problem of free will and predestination. This could not be of any use to Keynes. The very essence of his problem was uncertainty. He started from a Marshallian short period. Here we are today with whatever stock of capital equipment, training of labour and business organization that the past has produced; decisions are being taken today on the basis of expectations about the future. The Treasury View, that savings govern investment, is knocked out by the observation that investment is free to fluctuate under the influence of expectations so that income and employment are continually being pushed to the level at which overall *ex post* saving is equated to investment.

In the new macro-micro theory, this point is lost. By one simple device, the whole of Keynes' argument is put to sleep. Work out what saving *would be* at full employment in the present short-period situation, with the present distribution of wealth and the present hierarchy of rates of earnings for different occupations, and arrange to have enough investment to absorb the level of saving that this distribution of income brings about. Then hey presto! we are back in the world of equilibrium where saving governs investment and micro theory can slip into the old grooves again.

Keynes himself was not very much interested in the theory of value and distribution. Kalecki produced a more coherent version of the General Theory, which brought imperfect competition into the analysis and emphasized the influence of investment on the share of profits. Kalecki's version was in some ways more truly a *general* theory than Keynes'.

In the orthodox micro theory, having put Keynes to sleep, perfect competition and optimum firms come back and all the problems of the New Industrial State drop out of the argument. At this very time, when the great concentrations of power in the multinational corporations are bringing the age of national employment policy to an end, the text books are still illustrated by U-shaped curves showing the limitation on the size of firms in a perfectly competitive market.

This is all part of the first crisis that has by no means been resolved before the second crisis sets in.

Keynes' monetary theory has also been lost. His point was that in any given short-period situation, plans for investment are being made in the light of expectations of profit. The supply of finance has an influence on these plans – cheap money makes investment easier. In my opinion, Keynes rather exaggerated the influence of the rate of interest, but in any case it was always the rate of interest *relatively* to expected profits that had an influence. If the economy is always in equilibrium anyway, where is the room for expectations?

The strangest of all is to set up a model of a one-commodity world where there are no prices, saving governs investment, full employment is guaranteed by the real-wage rate, the difference between the future and the past is eliminated by making capital 'malleable' so that mistakes can always be undone and equilibrium is always guaranteed; then when every requirement for money as a medium of exchange, a store of value and an object of liquidity preference has been eliminated from the model, money is introduced to finance the national debt.

In the one-commodity world, of course, the distinction between real and money wages does not arise, and with 'malleable capital' the demand for labour depends on the level of wages. So Simons is proved right after all. By the one simple trick, time is abolished, Keynes is smothered, Kalecki is ignored and equilibrium theory is enthroned once more.

This is all part of the first crisis but it helps to prepare the setting for the second crisis.

What about the Keynesian revolution on the plane of policy? Certainly the 25 years after the end of the last war were very different from the 20 years after the first. The notion that it is the responsibility of a government to maintain a 'high and stable level of employment' in its national economy was a novelty. Perhaps its acceptance as orthodoxy was mainly due to the realization that unemployment did not occur in planned economies. Private enterprise had to vindicate itself before its own employees. A doctrine that promised to show how it could do so was very welcome.

Keynes was writing and arguing *against* the prevailing orthodoxy. He had to argue first and last that something could be done. He did not have an opportunity to describe the workings of an economy in which employment policy was an accepted feature of government. He did throw out the suggestion that he did not expect either monetary or fiscal instruments to be powerful enough to maintain stability; he believed that it would be necessary to have a general social control over investment. This has not been seen in any private enterprise economy. So-called Keynesian policy has been a series of expedients to deal with recessions when they occurred.

Kalecki had a much less optimistic view than Keynes of how it would work out. Unemployment could be overcome by government loan-expenditure. With very low unemployment, the 'captains of industry' find that discipline in the factories breaks down, and prices rise.

> In this situation a powerful block is likely to be formed between big business and the rentier interests, and they would probably find more than one economist to declare that the situation was manifestly unsound. The pressure of all these forces, and in particular of big business would most probably induce the Government to return to the orthodox policy of cutting down the budget deficit. A slump would follow.[2]

Then the next election looms up and pressure to relieve unemployment grows strong again. So, he predicted in 1943, after the war we shall have overcome the problems of the commercial trade cycle and we shall be living under the regime of a political trade cycle. Just now, in 1971, the political trade cycle seems to be taking a more violent turn than ever before.

The advocates of 'Keynesian' policies accepted only half of Keynes' diagnosis of the instability of capitalism. He described how the level of output is determined (in given technical conditions) by investment and consumption. He described how the level of prices is determined by the level of money-wage rates. It was sufficiently obvious that if continuous near-full employment was maintained without any change in traditional institutions and attitudes in industrial relations, there would be an irresistible pressure to inflation. I think that in the United States this element in Keynes was somehow swept under the carpet. It seems that the extraordinary vogue in recent years of an argument so unplausible as the Quantity Theory of Money was due to a refusal to accept the fact that the main influence on the general price level in money terms is the level of money-wage rates and the level of wage rates at any moment is more or less an historical accident, depending on conditions in the labour market over a long past. This was such a serious blow to notions of equilibrium and the rationality of a market economy that any theory was better, even a theory that consisted of nothing but a set of incantations.

In England the point was met by a new Treasury View that it would be desirable to maintain enough unemployment to keep prices stable. To make this policy acceptable it had to be argued that a 'small' amount of unemployment, say 3 per cent, would be enough. The famous Phillips

[2] 'Political aspects of full employment', *Political Quarterly*, 1943, reprinted in *Selected Essays on the Dynamics of the Capitalist Economy*, Cambridge, 1971.

curve was used to support this point of view. After a run of years with statistical unemployment between 1 and 2 per cent, 3 per cent is not regarded by the workers as just a little, especially as, of course, it is not evenly spread, so that some regions are running into 10 per cent and more. In any case the experimental demonstration of the Phillips curve has failed. Prices go on rising along with unemployment. Now suddenly and abruptly the second half of Keynes theory has been accepted and President Nixon decides to alter the rules of the game in industrial relations by decree.

This is a fresh upheaval in the private enterprise economy but so far as economic theory is concerned it is still an element in the first crisis – the breakdown of *laisser-faire* in face of the problem of effective demand.

The second crisis is quite different. The first crisis arose from the breakdown of a theory which could not account for the *level* of employment. The second crisis arises from a theory that cannot account for the *content* of employment.

Keynes was arguing against the dominant orthodoxy, which held that government expenditure could not increase employment. He had to prove, first of all, that it could. He had to show that an increase in investment will increase consumption – that more wages will be spent on more beer and boots whether the investment is useful or not. He had to show that the secondary increase in real income is quite independent of the object of the primary outlay. Pay men to dig holes in the ground and fill them up again if you cannot do anything else.

There was an enormous orthodox resistence to this idea. The whole weight of the argument had to be on this one obvious point.

The war was a sharp lesson in Keynesism. Orthodoxy could not stand up any longer. Governments accepted the responsibility to maintain a high and stable level of employment. Then the economists took over Keynes and erected the new orthodoxy. Once the point had been established, the question should have changed. Now that we all agree that government expenditure can maintain employment, we should argue about what the expenditure should be for. Keynes did not *want* anyone to dig holes and fill them. He indulged in a pleasant daydream of a world in which, when investment had been kept at the full employment level for thirty years or so, all needs for capital installations would have been met, property income would have been abolished, poverty would have disappeared and civilized life could begin.

But the economists took up the argument at the point where it had broken off before the war. When there is unemployment and low profits the government must spend on something or other – it does not matter what. As we know, for twenty-five years serious recessions were avoided by following this policy. The most convenient thing for a government to spend on is armaments. The military-industrial complex took charge. I do not think it plausible to suppose that the cold war and several hot wars were invented just to solve the employment problem. But certainly they have had that effect. The system had the support not only of the corporations who make profits under it and the workers who got jobs, but also of the economists who advocated government loan-expenditure as a prophylactic against stagnation. Whatever were the deeper forces leading into the hypertrophy of military power *after* the world war was over, certainly they could not have had such free play if the doctrine of sound finance had still been respected. It was the so-called Keynesians who persuaded successive Presidents that there is no harm in a budget deficit and left the military-industrial complex to take advantage of it. So it has come about that Keynes' pleasant daydream was turned into a nightmare of terror.

In spite of wastage and slaughter, there certainly was a great increase in economic wealth in twenty-five years without a slump. This was especially true in the countries which were initially not allowed to dissipate their resources on arms and could put all their investment into productive forms so that they are now threatening the overburdened US industry with 'unfair competition'. But even in the United States, certainly, wealth increased. Even in Great Britain, limping along playing at being a great power after the game was over, wealth increased. The socialist countries began to envy the consumer society. Capitalism with near-full employment was an impressive spectacle. But a growth in wealth is not at all the same thing as reducing poverty. A universal paean was raised in praise of *growth*. Growth was going to solve all problems. No need to bother about poverty. Growth will lift up the bottom and poverty will disappear without any need to pay attention to it. The economists, who should have known better, fell in with the same cry. Economists used to know (but they had evidently forgotten) that the decent acceptable standard of life, in any society, is somewhere about the average that that society provides. It is a law of nature that much more than half the population (for lower incomes are more numerous) is always living below the decent standard, whatever their absolute level of consumption may be.

That is not the only point. Not only is subjective poverty never overcome by growth, but absolute poverty is increased by it. Growth requires technical progress and technical progress alters the composition of the labour force, making more places for educated workers and fewer for uneducated, but opportunities to acquire qualifications are kept (with a few exceptions for exceptional talents) for those families who have them already. As growth goes on at the top more and more families are thrown out at the bottom. Absolute misery grows while wealth increases. The old slogan, 'poverty in the midst of plenty', takes on a new meaning.

Then consider the notorious problem of pollution. Here again the economists should have been forewarned. The distinction that Pigou made between private costs and social costs was presented by him as an exception to the benevolent rule of *laisser-faire*. A moment's thought shows that the exception is the rule and the rule is the exception. In what industry, in what line of business, are the true social costs of the activity registered in its accounts? Where is the pricing system that offers the consumer a fair choice between air to breath and motor cars to drive about in? The economists were the last to realize what is going on and when they did recognize it they managed to hush it up again. *Laisser-faire* and consumer's sovereignity were still absolute except for a few minor points discussed under the heading of 'externalities' that could easily be put right.

These problems arise in the economies that boast of their wealth. Perhaps they can afford the luxury of an economics profession that builds intricate theories in the air that have no contact with reality. But this luxury is too expensive for the so-called developing world where the doctrines of *laisser-faire* and the free play of market forces are exported along with armaments to keep them from looking for any way out of their infinitely more grievous situation.

The second crisis of theory is already far advanced. I do not regard the Keynesian revolution as a great intellectual triumph. On the contrary, it was a tragedy because it came so late. Hitler had already found how to cure unemployment before Keynes had finished explaining why it occurred. This time also the real situation is crowding upon us before we have begun to discuss our problems.

A sure sign of a crisis is the prevalence of cranks. It is characteristic of a crisis in theory that cranks get a hearing from the public which orthodoxy is failing to satisfy. In the 'thirties we had Major Douglas, and Social Credit – it can all be done with a fountain pen – and Warren and Pearson, who convinced President Roosevelt that raising the dollar price of gold would raise the price of everything else and bring the slump to an end. The cranks are to be preferred to the orthodox because they see that there is a problem.

Nowadays we have plenty of cranks taking up the problems that the economists overlook. Charles Reich proposes to turn America green with a spade and hoe. J. W. Forrester proves on a computer that humanity is bound to be wiped out either by poison or by famine within a hundred years. Our distinguished Chairman can hardly be classed with the cranks, considering the seat he occupies this year, but next year, perhaps, he will be relegated once more to the position outside the pale of those who commit *lese-majesty* against consumer's sovereignty. The cranks and critics flourish because the orthodox economists have neglected the great problems that everyone else feels to be urgent and menacing.

The whole trouble arises from just one simple omission; when Keynes became orthodox they forgot to change the question and discuss what employment should be for.

This primarily concerns the allocation of resources between products, but it is also bound up with the distribution of products between people. On the subject of distribution, of course, there is quite a lot in the orthodox text books, but is it not at all easy to make out what it means. Keynes did not need a theory of distribution for the long run, though he had a vague idea of a falling rate of profit in his daydream of future civilization. He was concerned mainly with the short period, here and now, when only expectations of future profits come into the argument. What is the orthodox theory of profits actually received? Many years ago I set out to write a little book on Marxian economics; when I had written a chapter on Marx's theory of profits, I thought I had to write a chapter on the orthodox theory for comparison, and blest if I could find one high or low. Ever since I have been inquiring and probing but I still cannot find out what it is. We have Marshall's theory that the rate of interest is the 'reward of waiting' but 'waiting' only means owning wealth. A man 'may have obtained the *de facto* possession of property by inheritance or by any other means, moral or immoral, legal or illegal. But if, having the power to consume that property in immediate gratifications, he chooses to put it in such a form as to afford him deferred gratifications, then any superiority there may be in deferred gratifications over those immediate ones is the reward of his waiting'. In short, a man who refrains from blowing his capital in orgies and feasts can continue to get interest on it. This seems to be perfectly correct, but as a theory of distribution it is only a circular argument. The passage I just quoted came from the first edition of Marshall's *Principles*. Later he muddled up 'waiting' with saving – that is refraining from consuming income, not refraining from dissipating capital. This idea seems to have been taken up in the modern orthodoxy. The rate of interest is accounted for by the discount of the future of owners of wealth. Household saving, of course, is mainly saving up to spend later, and Marshall himself admitted that it is likely to respond the wrong way. A higher rate of return means that *less* saving is necessary to get a given pension or whatever. But there may be some savers who have the psychology required by the text books and weigh a preference for present spending against an increment of income (interest, dividends and capital gains) to be had from an increment of wealth. But what then? Each individual goes on saving or dis-saving till the point where his individual subjective rate of discount is equal to the market rate of interest. There has to be a market rate of interest for him to compare his rate of discount to. But of course the whole thing is quite beside the point once we have accepted the Keynesian view that investment governs saving, not saving investment.

This concerns the broad division of national income between work and property or, as the British tax system describes it, between earned and unearned income. There is also the problem of the relative levels of different types of earned income. Here we have the famous marginal productivity theory. In perfect competition an employer is supposed to take on such a number of men that the *money* value of the marginal product *to him*, taking account of the price of his output and the cost of his plant, is equal to the money wage he has to pay. Then the *real* wage of each type of labour is supposed to measure its marginal product *to society*. The salary of a professor of economics measures his contribution to society and the wage of a garbage collector measures his contribution. Of course this is very comforting doctrine for professors of economics but I fear that once more the argument is circular. There is not any measure of marginal products except the wages themselves.

In short, we have not got a theory of distribution. We have nothing to say on the subject which above all others occupies the minds of the people whom economics is supposed to enlighten.

Here the second crisis links up with the first. The first crisis failed to be resolved because there was no solution to the problem of maintaining near-full employment without inflation. Experience of inflation has destroyed the conventions governing the acceptance of existing distribution. Everyone can see that his relative earnings depend on the bargaining power of the group that he belongs to. The professors become quite nervous when they are discussing the earnings of the garbage collectors. Now it is clear enough that income from property is not the reward of waiting but the reward of employing a good stock broker. On top of this a sudden freeze comes down. If it is successful it is to keep everyone in the position where he happened to be when the scramble for relative gains was brought to a halt and it will perpetuate the division of income between work and property that happened to exist when it set in. But it does not seem likely that it will be as successful as all that. Rather it will add a political element to the distribution of bargaining power. Perhaps this is going to create a crisis in the so called free-enterprise economy. I am not talking about that. I am talking about the evident bankruptcy of economic theory which for the second time has nothing to say on the questions that, to everyone except economists, appear to be most in need of an answer.

THE THEORY OF MONEY AND THE ANALYSIS OF OUTPUT

THE plain man has always found the Theory of Money a bewildering subject, but at the present time many academic economists are as much bewildered by it as the plain man. The reason for this state of affairs is that the Theory of Money has recently undergone a violent revolution. It has ceased to be the Theory of Money, and become the Analysis of Output.

The conclusions and methods of economic analysis are naturally much influenced by the technique of thought employed by the economists, and in almost every case where a divergence between 'schools of thought' is to be found in economics the difference between one 'school' and another arises from a difference in the mental tools which their members employ. Now the orthodox Theory of Money may be generally described as an attempt to apply the supply-and-demand tool to the analysis of the purchasing power of money. Just as, in the Theory of Value, the supply-and-demand mechanism is used to analyse the forces determining the value of a single commodity, so in the traditional Theory of Money the supply-and-demand mechanism, with some necessary modifications, is used to analyse the forces determining the value of money. The entity with which this analysis is mainly concerned is therefore the price level.

It has always been admitted that the chief justification for a study of the price level lies in the fact that changes in the price level may affect the volume of output, that is to say, they may affect the amount of employment and the wealth of the community. But until recently no economist appears to have considered the possibility of tackling this problem directly, and setting the supply-and-demand apparatus to work on the question in which he was really interested – the forces determining the volume of output.

The apparatus used to analyse the determination of the price level were tautological statements known as Quantity Equations. The 'Cambridge' equation was consciously designed to deal with the value of money in terms of supply and demand. In its simplest form the 'Cambridge' equation was as follows:

$$\pi = \frac{kR}{M}$$

where π is the purchasing power of money, R the real national income, k the proportion of real income held in the form of money (cash and bank balances), and M the quantity of money. kR then represents the demand for money in terms of real wealth, and M the supply of money. The equation leads naturally to the simple argument that the greater the supply of money (M), the smaller is its value (π), and the greater the demand for money (kR), the greater is its value.

The Fisher equation was not cast in so definitely supply-and-demand a form, but it was essentially of the same nature.

$MV = PT$ or $P = \frac{MV}{T}$, where P is the price level, M the quantity of money, V its velocity of circulation (V varies roughly inversely with k), and T the volume of transaction. MV represents the effective supply of money, and PT the amount of work that money is required to do. The price-level, P (which is roughly equivalent to $\frac{1}{\pi}$) is then regarded as the resultant of T, which without straining our terms too much may be regarded as the demand for money, and MV the supply of it. An increase in M or V is equivalent to an increase in the supply of money, and leads to a fall in its value, that is, to a rise in P; while an increase in T is equivalent to a rise in the demand for money, and leads to a rise in its value, that is, to a fall in P.

An imposing theoretical structure was built up on these simple tautologies. The exponents of the Theory of Money were never satisfied with their apparatus, and were always finding themselves led into paradoxical positions. The necessity to adapt the equations to the analysis of observed events led to greater and greater refinements and complications, but in essence the apparatus of thought remained the same.

The nature of the equations, the fact that they were tautologies, devoid of causal significance, was recognized by the experts. But in the hands of the inexpert they were very misleading. Any student of economics who was set the beginner's question – 'Describe the manner in which the price level is determined upon an island in which the currency consists of shell picked up on the beach', would glibly reply, 'The price level on this island is determined by the number of shells and their velocity of circulation', and nine times out of ten would omit to mention that it was equally true to say that the number of shells in circulation was determined by the price level. And economists who had ceased to be students were prone to say that the rise of prices in Germany in the great inflation was caused by the increase in the note issue and aggravated by the increase in the velocity of circulation due to the 'flight into real values' induced by the rise of prices.

It was in protest against this naïve view of the theory of money that Mr. Kahn set out the Quantity Equation for hairpins. Let P be the proportion of women with long hair, and T the total number of women. Let $\frac{1}{V}$ be the daily loss of hairpins by each woman with long hair, and M the daily output of hairpins. Then $M = \frac{PT}{V}$, and $MV = PT$. Now suppose that the Pope, regarding bobbed hair as contrary to good morals, wishes to increase the proportion of long-haired women in the population, and asks a student of economics what he had best do. The student sets out Mr. Kahn's equation, and explains it to the Pope. 'All you need do', he says, 'is to increase M, the daily output of hairpins (for instance, you might give a subsidy to the factories) and the number of long-haired women is bound to increase.' The Pope is not quite convinced. 'Or, of course,' the student adds, 'if you could persuade the long-haired women to be less careless, V would increase, and the effect would be the same as though the output of hairpins had increased.'

Now, the experts in the Theory of Money certainly avoided these crude errors, but when they recognized that their equations were tautologies without causal significance they were beset by an uneasy feeling that their theory only provided them with wisdom after the event. Anything that had happened could always be explained in terms of their truisms, but they were never very confident in predicting what would happen next. Moreover, their methods condemned them to discuss the price level, when what they had really at heart was the volume of employment.

Now, once Mr. Keynes has shown us how to crack the egg, it appears the most natural thing in the world to attack the interesting part of the problem directly, instead of through the devious route of the Quantity Theory of Money. If we are interested in the volume of output, why should we not try what progress can be made by thinking in terms of the demand for output as a whole, and its cost of production, just as we have been taught to think of the demand and cost of a single commodity? But though the altered line of approach appears, once it has been seen, to be the obvious one to adopt, the sudden change of angle has caused a great deal of bewilderment. The new analysis still masquerades under the name of the Theory of Money; Mr. Keynes published his book on the subject under the title of a

Treatise on Money. Moreover, Mr. Keynes, when he published the *Treatise*, had no very clear perception of the fact that the subject with which he was dealing was the Analysis of Output. This can be illustrated from several of the conceptions in the *Treatise*. For instance, consider the Widow's Cruse of profits.[1] Mr. Keynes' analysis may be summarized thus: When prices are in excess of costs, windfall profits are earned by entrepreneurs, and however much of these profits the entrepreneurs spend, the total of profits remains unchanged, since spending by one entrepreneur only serves to increase the windfall profits of others. This argument is valid upon the assumption that an increase in demand for consumption goods leads to no increase in their supply. Now, to assume that the supply of goods is perfectly inelastic is a natural simplification to make, at the first step in the argument, if we are primarily interested in the price-level, but to make such an assumption when we are primarily interested in the volume of output is to assume away the whole point of the argument.

A second example of Mr. Keynes' failure to realize the nature of the revolution that he was carrying through is to be found in the emphasis which he lays upon the relationship of the quantity of investment to the quantity of saving.[2] He points out that if savings exceed investment, consumption goods can only be sold at a loss. Their output will consequently decline until the real income of the population is reduced to such a low level that savings are perforce reduced to equality with investment.[3] But he completely overlooks the significance of this discovery, and throws it out in the most casual way without pausing to remark that he has proved that output may be in equilibrium at any number of different levels, and that while there is a natural tendency towards equilibrium between savings and investment (in a very long run), there is no natural tendency towards full employment of the factors of production. The mechanism of thought involved in the equations of saving and investment compels its exponent to talk only of short-period disequilibrium positions. And it was only with disequilibrium positions that Mr. Keynes was consciously concerned when he wrote the *Treatise*. He failed to notice that he had incidentally evolved a new theory of the long-period analysis of output.

Moreover, Mr. Keynes, like the exponents of the Quantity Theory of Money, was apt to fall into the hairpins fallacy, and attribute a causal significance to his tautologies. The price level will only be in equilibrium

[1] *Treatise on Money*, p. 139.
[2] Using 'saving' as it is defined in the *Treatise on Money*.
[3] Op. cit., p. 178.

when savings are equal to investment. Well and good. But suppose that over a certain range the supply of goods is perfectly elastic? Then, whatever happens, prices cannot rise or fall. Since Mr. Keynes' truisms must be true, a rise or fall in demand for goods, which will be met by an increase or decrease of output without any change in prices, must necessarily be accompanied by changes in savings and investment which keep the two in equality. When an increase in output is brought about by an increase in investment, if prices do not alter, the increase in output must bring about an increase in savings (as defined by Mr. Keynes) equal to the initial increase in investment, for Mr. Keynes' truisms must be true. Or, as Mr. Hawtrey[4] points out, in face of a very-short-period decline in demand, the supply of goods is perfectly elastic because shopkeepers do not immediately lower prices, but allow stocks to accumulate on their shelves. This also can be explained in terms of Mr. Keynes' equations. The demand for consumption goods falls off, say, because of an increase in savings. This leads to an accumulation of stocks, that is to say, an increase in investment, exactly equal to the increase in saving, and prices do not fall. But to say that prices do not fall *because* investment has increased is merely to argue that women bob their hair because the output of the hairpin factories has fallen off.

The case of a perfectly elastic supply of output as a whole presents an interesting analogy with the traditional Theory of Value. Marshall's analysis is described by him as showing how the price of a commodity is determined by utility and by cost of production. He himself shows that when cost of production is constant for all amounts of output, the price of a commodity will not be altered by a change in demand, but he complains that it is idle to argue that price is determined more by cost than by demand. This violent contradiction can be resolved by substituting the word 'output' for the word 'price'. It is true that the output of single commodities is determined by the interaction of supply and demand even when the price is uniquely determined by cost. It was this earlier misapprehension of the subject-matter of the so-called Theory of Value which misled the economists into supposing that the proper subject-matter of the so-called Theory of Money was the level of prices, and not the volume of output.

A further example of Mr. Keynes' initial failure to understand the significance of his new analysis is to be found in the emphasis which he lays upon profits as the 'mainspring of action' determining output. Here, again, there is an analogy with the traditional Theory of Value. When profits are more than normal in a certain industry, we are taught, new firms will enter the industry, and output will expand. Now it is sufficiently obvious that

[4] *Art of Central Banking*, p. 341.

entrepreneurs who are deciding whether to set up in a certain industry are not guided merely, or even mainly, by the level of profits being earned by existing firms. They will take a general view of the conditions in the market, and of future prospects, and make their choice accordingly. It is idle to say that the abnormal profits *cause* the new investment. At the same time, it is true that if the new entrepreneur decides to set up in the industry, then (if he expects that his cost will be about the same as those of existing firms) it must be the case that abnormal profits are being earned by the existing firms, for unless the price of the commodity is greater than their costs (including normal profits) it will not be worth while for additional entrepreneurs to enter the trade. Thus the abnormal profits are a symptom of a situation in which new investment in the industry will take place. But to speak of them as a cause of new investment is only legitimate as an artificial device adopted to simplify the exposition of what is happening. In the same way profits as defined by Mr. Keynes are a symptom of a situation in which output will tend to increase. Output tends to increase when the price of commodities exceeds their cost of production because, in that situation, it is profitable for entrepreneurs to increase their sales. To regard the profits as a direct cause of the increase in output is apt to be misleading, and since in long-period equilibrium there are no profits in Mr. Keynes' sense, a theory which regards profits as the mainspring of action is incapable of dealing with long-period analysis.

When Mr. Keynes himself overlooked the fact that he was writing the analysis of output, as these examples show, it is small wonder that the change in the Theory of Money should have caused bewilderment. But once it becomes clear what has happened the confusion disappears. The Theory of Money, relieved of its too-heavy task, can be confined to its proper sphere, and become indeed a theory of money, while the Analysis of Output can continue to develop an analysis of output.

3

OBSTACLES TO FULL EMPLOYMENT

VARIOUS definitions of 'full employment' have been used by English writers. Keynes originally used a definition in terms of Marshall's concept of 'disutility of labour'.[1] Beveridge says there is full employment when there are more unfilled vacancies than unemployed workers.[2] Others call full employment the level of employment at which money-wage rates begin to rise.

On all these definitions there may be large numbers of workers unemployed when 'full employment' is said to exist. It is preferable to take a simple-minded definition, and to say that there is 'full employment' when no one is unemployed.

There is a difficulty in giving a precise definition of 'available labour'. Hours of work may vary. The number of married women 'available' for employment may not be clear cut. But if we can take a rough working definition of 'available labour' then we may say that 'full employment' exists when all available labour is employed.

This is a state of affairs that can never be completely attained. In a changing world there are always bound to be, at any moment, some workers who have left one job and have not yet found another.

Technical changes and changes in tastes both at home and in foreign markets bring about shifts in demand between industries. Although seasonal unemployment could be very much reduced by dovetailing operations with different seasonal peaks, there is probably an irreducible minimum of seasonal unemployment in some districts. Changes in occupation for personal reasons will always be going on. So long as such shifts in employment are taking place, there is always likely to be some unemployment even when the general demand for labour is very high. Thus completely full employment can never be seen.

[1] *General Theory of Employment, Interest and Money*, p. 15.
[2] *Full Employment in a Free Society*, p. 18.

Nationaløkonomisk Tidsskrift, 1946. This paper is based on a lecture given to the Nationaløkonomisk Forening at Copenhagen on 6 December 1946.

Nor is completely full employment desirable. The attainment of full employment, in this absolute sense, would require strict controls, including direction of labour. To raise the average of employment from 86 per cent (the average for Great Britain, 1921–38) to, say, 95 per cent, would be compatible with a much greater amount of individual liberty than to raise it from 95 per cent to 98 per cent. To raise it from 95 per cent to 98 per cent (not momentarily – but on the average) would involve great sacrifices of liberty, and to raise it from 98 per cent to 100 per cent would involve complete conscription of labour.

No one regards 100 per cent employment as a desirable objective. 'Full employment policy' does not mean aiming at 100 per cent employment, but aiming at a continuous level of employment as near to 100 per cent as is practicable with the methods of control which are acceptable to the public. In what follows I shall use the phrase 'full employment' loosely, to mean 'as near full employment as is reasonable'.

This use of language, though not exact, is sufficiently clear for all practical purposes.

In England, we are now living under a regime where it is generally accepted that it is the duty of government to maintain full employment. This was accepted even before the Labour Government came into power. For us, this is a great revolution in ideas. During the great slump of the '30s it was the orthodox and official view that government action could not increase employment. In 1929, when Lloyd George was running an election campaign on the promise to abolish unemployment by means of government outlay on public works, the Treasury enunciated the doctrine that government outlay could not, in fact, increase the total level of investment.[3]

Looking back now, it seems almost incredible that such views should have been taken seriously. There are still in England many who are sceptical or unsympathetic about the new policy, but they have to use far more subtle and sophisticated arguments than the 'Treasury View' of 1929.

The change in official and orthodox ideas is of the greatest importance. But up to the present we are living in a fool's paradise. We have accepted a full employment policy, and we are in fact enjoying a high level of employment. There is some unemployment in certain areas, where reconversion to peace-time production is held up for want of buildings. Apart from this there is substantially 'full employment' in the sense of as high a level of employment as is reasonable to expect.

But this is largely a coincidence. It has little to do with the new policy,

[3] Command Paper, 3331.

because just now there would be full employment in any case. At the moment we are living in an inflationary situation – that is, there is an excess of demand over supply for labour as a whole. The acute shortage of houses, due to bombing and to the cessation of building during the war; the drive for exports, which is being conducted not in order to maintain employment, but in order to balance our trade; the great reduction in private stocks of clothes, furniture, and so forth combined with war-time savings ready to be spent on goods as soon as they become available; and the requirements of industry for reconversion to peace-time production – all these add up to an effective demand for labour in excess of supply.

The consequent tendency to inflation is kept in check by the methods evolved during the war. Heavy taxation, rationing, control of prices, a vague and unformulated, but nevertheless fairly successful wages policy, control of imports, licensing of private investment, propaganda for saving, in short, all war-time methods of checking inflation are still in force. These methods are fairly well understood by the Government, and accepted with more or less good-natured grumbling by the public.

If it were possible to keep up permanently a condition of near-inflation and run the machine on the brakes – that is, with controls to curb excessive demand – employment policy would be straightforward and compara-tively easy to manage.

The real test of the new policy will come when there is a fall in demand. How will it be met? The danger may come from within or from without. Let us first consider the internal danger. There may be a fall in the rate of private investment when the reconstruction boom comes to an end, but this is unlikely to be serious. Industrial investment, in equipping factories and so forth, has never been a very large part of all home investment. The main bulk of home investment is in building and civil engineering. If the Government can control the rate of building, the investment plans of nationalized industries, and the timing of large schemes, such as the electrification of rural districts, then it should be possible to plan for a steady level in the great bulk of investment. This in itself would help to steady private investment because it would go a long way towards stabilizing incomes, and therefore the general level of profits. Further, by consultation and persuasion, without overt control, the large firms can probably be induced to fit their investment plans into a national scheme. And a small uncontrolled fringe would probably not be very unstable.

The White Paper on Employment Policy[4] issued by the late Coalition Government was not based upon this point of view. It was based rather on

[4] Command Paper 6527.

the conception of 'counter-cyclical' government investment, that is, the idea that the Government should step in and increase its own investment when private investment falls off, and slow down its own investment when private investment increases. In my view, this policy is fundamentally wrong. It means giving private enterprise the first choice. When private firms choose to make investment they can. When they no longer want labour, the Government will use the labour for something or other. When private investment recovers, the Government must release labour again, so that it can be used for profitable investment. This whole point of view is subject to the gravest objection. Once we have accepted the idea that it is the business of the Government to see that labour is always employed, we must go on to admit that it is the business of the Government to see that labour is employed in the most useful possible way: that is to say, that schemes of investment should be directed to meet the needs of the community, and not to suit the whims and fancies of profit-seeking firms.

Indeed, it is impossible for the State to divest itself of responsibility for the direction of employment once it has accepted responsibility for the total amount of employment. There are many in England at present who advocate the use of 'global methods' designed to affect the total employment without exercising any discrimination over the allocation of labour between uses. But this is in fact impossible. Any policy, even if it is purely global in conception, will produce concrete results and have an influence upon the direction of employment. The decision not to interfere with private investment is itself a positive decision.

Thus the responsibility for deciding how the influence of the State upon the direction of employment is to be used cannot be escaped.

The problem of deciding what are the 'needs of society' and of adjudicating between conflicting needs is by no means simple. There is no one Platonic ideal of the 'best use of the nation's resources'. Conflicts of interest and conflicts of ideology are bound to persist. But somehow or other a democracy does decide what it wants. In England at present there is no doubt that the people want more than, in fact, can be done at all quickly. Housing – first in the sense of some kind of a roof over everyone's head, later in the sense of improving the disgraceful condition of our great cities and our backward rural districts. Re-equipment of industry – not for the sake of profit, but for the sake of meeting our desperate foreign trade position and for raising the general standard of production and therefore of consumption. Improvement of our education and our health services, which involves large investment in building and equipment as well as in training of personnel. Improvements in the efficiency and amenity of our transport system. Improvements in the amenity of the countryside (there are many cottages in England which are without gas or electricity and even without piped water) which are desirable both for their own sake and to check the drift away from agriculture, which is one of our serious economic problems. These and many other 'social needs' are agreed by the nation, in the vague and yet definite sense in which democracies do agree upon their needs.

The task of deciding between these needs, and reducing them to a scheme of priorities, must be the duty of the Government. The methods to be used are still in course of evolution, and no doubt they will work clumsily, and be the subject of much dispute and criticism. But a merely passive policy of compensating the vagaries of private enterprise would be the least hopeful of all possible methods of solving the problems involved.

The 'counter-cyclical' policy is subject to another objection. It is very unpractical. It is not at all easy to switch on and off schemes of investment at a moment's notice, or even at six months' notice. Besides, private and public investment are often closely bound up together. You cannot have factories built during the boom and wait for the next slump to make roads up to their gates. It is essential for a sane employment policy that investment should be planned as a whole and not merely stabilized by 'counter-cyclical' public works.

The second branch of the White Paper policy is to maintain consumption when investment falls off. When investment falls, incomes decline and there is 'secondary unemployment' due to the fact that consumers have less money to spend. The suggestion is that, at such a moment, the purchasing power of consumers should be increased, and the general level of demand for consumption goods kept up, so as to fend off the 'tertiary unemployment' which follows when consumer goods industries become less profitable, and investment in them in turn falls off.

The prejudice which still exists in the British Treasury (or which, at any rate, still existed when the White Paper was written) made it impossible to advocate remission of taxation and the deliberate creation of a budget deficit as a means of maintaining purchasing power. They did, however, suggest the creation of a deficit in the social insurance funds by reducing weekly contributions when demand threatens to fall. This would make rather a feeble contribution to solving the problem. Many more or less fanciful schemes for regulating purchasing power have been suggested by English economists. These seem often to be rather perverse. There is something repugnant to common sense in the idea of giving money to people to spend just in order to keep up the market for goods and make industry profitable. Ordinary people consider that they should be given money either because they deserve it, or because they need it, not just in order to make a market. It is necessary to provide at least the appearance of equity in releasing purchasing power even if the motive is to stabilize employment. The least arbitrary of these schemes is the device of 'deferred pay' invented by Lord Keynes as a measure of war-time finance. Part of the income tax paid is credited to the individual to be refunded at the decision of the Government. This provides a fund of purchasing power which people regard as their own money, which can be released when demand for consumer goods is threatening to fall.

This scheme was used, to a small extent, during the war, and the arrears of tax credited to the public are held up at present, to be released when the supply of consumer goods becomes adequate – that is to say, when normal demand no longer exceeds supply. The release of the credits would provide a stimulus to demand which could be regulated, in time and in amount, so as to give a salutary shock to the economy when a failure of demand is threatening. There is no reason why this system should not be permanent, so that there are always arrears of potential purchasing power in hand, to be released when required to maintain demand.

These methods can be used to prevent an internal failure of demand. But for Great Britain, and equally in Denmark, the main danger does not lie inside the country, but outside – that is, in a fall in demand for exports, whether due to a slump in the outside world or to a long-period change.

This would present a difficult situation even for a fully planned economy. It creates two problems – how to maintain employment and how to deal with the balance of payments.

If demand falls in export industries, work must be found for the labour released. If exports are highly specialized, this is by no means an easy matter. It is of little use just to increase purchasing power in general. Plans should be drawn up specifically for (a) buying up and using or storing products formerly exported, (b) turning labour to alternative products, or (c) arranging an alternative foreign outlet to replace the lost market. Such plans are not easy to work out satisfactorily, and although there is much talk in England now about employment policy, it may be doubted that plans on these lines are actually being prepared. If the world slump were to come soon there would be little difficulty, for the home market is starved of goods, and would eagerly absorb what is at present being exported. So far as miscellaneous consumer goods are concerned, actually the same goods could be sold at home. And where the same goods are not appropriate, alternative uses for labour could easily be found. For a country whose exports are primarily agricultural the difficulty would probably be greater, and alternative employment might be harder to arrange.

If the immediate problem of maintaining employment is solved by switching labour from the foreign to the home market, the further problem will arise of switching it back again when the foreign market recovers. This must require a fairly high degree of control over industry. For if we are to do without the brutal methods of a market economy – unemployment and bankruptcy – we must have other means of directing production.

The problem of maintaining employment when export demand falls off is complicated and difficult enough, but if it is solved a worse difficulty remains – the problem of the balance of payments.

The 'natural' remedy for a fall in exports, under *laisser-faire* conditions, is a fall in employment and in income, which reduces demand for imports also (though not necessarily to the same extent). But if employment is successfully maintained, then the demand for imports does not fall, and the balance of trade runs into a deficit. For a country with ample monetary reserves this would not matter. But for Great Britain it would present a very serious problem. Discussions are going on now as to means to help countries which do their duty to the world by maintaining their demand for imports in face of a slump elsewhere. Let us hope that some world agreement will be arrived at on these lines, for the provisions of the Bretton Woods fund only scratch the surface of the problem.

The main remedy for a trade deficit envisaged under Bretton Woods is exchange depreciation. But this is not a remedy appropriate to the disease. If the trouble is caused by a decline in total world demand, there is first of all very little reason to expect that depreciation would bring about a recovery of exports for a particular country. Depreciation works by reducing the *relative* price of the country's exports, and, in a general slump, there are probably very few commodities for which price-elasticity of demand is high. Moreover, even if it does do good from the point of view of the country in question, it can do so only at the expense of other countries, for it works by improving the competitive position of the depreciating country, and securing for it a larger share of the shrunken world trade, by reducing the share of its rival producers. No remedy is beneficial to the world as a whole that does not increase the total of world demand.

Behind this balance of trade problem again lies a further difficulty – the difficulty of distinguishing cyclical from long-period changes in foreign demand. The remedies required are quite different in the two cases. If demand for exports has fallen temporarily, the capacity of the export industries should be preserved with the utmost care, and any transfer of labour from them made with an eye to restoring it to them as soon as possible. Imports should be kept up as far as reserves permit. But if the change is permanent it is necessary as quickly as possible to reduce the productive capacity of the trade which has lost its market – to foster, if possible, alternative exports, and if that cannot be done, to set about cutting down imports. Thus a mis-diagnosis of the situation would lead to a totally wrong policy being pursued; the medicine for one disease is poison in another, and diagnosis will never be easy, since long-run and cyclical changes are often mixed up together.

At the present time, framing of policy is particularly difficult, for one great unanswerable question hangs over everything – what will the USA do in the coming slump? We can be pretty sure that history will not repeat itself, and economists planning now for the return of the 1930s would be like the generals who are accused in peace-time of planning to win the last war.

The most that one can say is, that we must prepare for a flexible policy and for an intelligent and quick response to events.

Flexibility requires control. It is a popular error that bureaucracy is less flexible than private enterprise. It may be so in detail, but when large-scale adaptations have to be made, central control is far more flexible. It may take two months to get an answer to a letter from a government department, but it takes twenty years for an industry under private enterprise to readjust itself to a fall in demand.

For this reason, full-employment policy requires a high degree of central control over the economic system. Just how much control remains to be seen. The problem of combining the necessary degree of control with the traditional methods of democracy is the dominating political problem of the present time.

If all these problems are successfully solved, certain difficulties arise from the very success of the full-employment policy.

For people who have a secure income in any case, full employment is a great nuisance. There are no domestic servants, the theatres are always full and the holiday resorts overcrowded. Goods are in short supply, not because less are produced, but because other people are consuming more. Shopkeepers become over-bearing instead of obsequious.

For managers in industry discipline is hard to preserve because workers are no longer frightened of losing their jobs.

Unpleasant tasks such as coal-mining cannot recruit labour on the old terms.

All these 'drawbacks' are, of course, the reverse side of the advantages of full employment for the mass of the people.

Finally, there is the problem of preserving the value of money. If the demand for labour is strong, money-wage rates tend to rise, and since the demand for commodities is also high, prices rise with costs. A successful employment policy, just because it is successful, entails a chronic danger of inflation.

Up till now, in England, the 'vicious spiral' has been kept within bounds, but we have no definite wages policy, nor are we likely to have one, for individual Trade Unions are jealous of their independence.

The danger of an all-round rise in wages could probably be dealt with by an over-all understanding with the Trade Unions, but the problem of relative wage changes is not easy to solve. There are many trades, of which mining is the chief example, where wages are obviously too low, whether we consider it from the human point of view of the disagreeableness and danger of the work, or from the economic point of view of the need to attract labour away from less onerous occupations. So long as unemployment was general, a completely irrational wage system could persist, but once there is full employment, wages must conform broadly to the text-book rule of equalizing the 'net advantages' of different occupations. The process of raising wages which are too low, involves raising the general level of wages (no one advocates lowering wages rates which are relatively high) and therefore is likely to involve a rise in the cost of living. Thus even right and necessary wage changes contain the threat of the 'vicious spiral'.

All this sounds pessimistic, but only because dangers and difficulties can be clearly foreseen. Whatever may happen, we are better off if our eyes are open, and nothing that can happen now can be so bad as the blind misery of the great slump.

THE CONCEPT OF HOARDING

THE term 'hoarding' is used in current literature in a number of distinct senses.

1. 'An increase in hoarding' may mean an increase in the desire to hold money as opposed to securities. This may occur (*a*) as a result of a change in sentiment, as is implied in the phrase 'hoarding due to decline in confidence' or 'to financial panic'. It may occur (*b*) as a result of an increase in the total of wealth, for as wealth increases the demand for money as 'a store of value' normally increases, though by less than the total increase in wealth. The demand for money may also increase (*c*) as a result of an increase in the requirements of the active circulation.

If the total quantity of money is kept constant, an increase in the actual amount of money held by the community as a whole cannot occur, but an increase in the desire to hold money brings about a rise in the rate of interest (a fall in security prices). If an individual owner of wealth desires to increase his holding of money, he is free to do so, either by selling out securities or by holding new savings in the form of money. His action then raises the rate of interest to the point at which other individuals are prepared to part with the money which he acquires.

The rise in the rate of interest leads, after a certain time has elapsed, to a decline in the rate of investment, and a fall in incomes and trade activity.

It is in this sense of the word, particularly sense (1*a*), that the substantial meaning of 'hoarding' agrees with the aura of associations that the word carries with it in literary use.

2. 'An increase in hoarding' may mean an increase in the actual amount of money held by the public. This can only come about if the quantity of money is increased. An increase in the quantity of money, other things equal, leads to a fall in the rate of interest, and, after a time, to an increase in investment, incomes and trade activity.

In this sense 'hoarding' does not come about from the initiative of the public, but is induced by the action of the banking system.

Economic Journal, June, 1938.

These two senses of hoarding are combined in the cases where an increased desire to hold money is met by an increase in the quantity of money, which prevents the rate of interest from rising, or an increase in the quantity of money is offset by an increase in the desire to hold money, which prevents the rate of interest from falling.

3. 'Hoards' may be used to mean not the total quantity of money, but the total *minus* the active circulation ('idle balances'). 'An increase in hoarding', when the total quantity of money is constant, is then brought about by a decline in incomes and trade activity, which releases money from the active circulation, and is another name for a fall in the average velocity of circulation of money.

A fall in the velocity of the active circulation (such as may be due to lengthening customary intervals of income payments) causes an increase in the demand for money, and, if the quantity of money is constant, the rate of interest will rise to the point at which the additional money required by the active circulation is drawn away from 'idle balances'. In this case 'an increase of hoarding' sense (1c) causes a 'decrease of hoarding' sense (3).

'An increase in hoarding' in sense (1) is a cause of a rise in the rate of interest, but 'an increase of hoarding' in sense (3) is associated with a fall in the rate of interest. This fall acts as a brake upon the decline in activity, but cannot be sufficient to restore incomes (and consequently the demand for money in the active circulation) to the former level.

In this sense 'hoarding' is an automatic consequence of a decline in incomes, no matter what the cause of the decline may be.

'An increase of hoarding' in sense (1a) may lead to an increase in sense (3), since an increase in the demand for money, by driving up the rate of interest, tends to bring about a decline in incomes, and consequently a release of money from the active circulation. Such a combination of sense (1a) with sense (3) probably provides the most reasonable interpretation of the complex of ideas connected with the word 'hoarding'.

4. 'Hoards' may be measured not in money, but in real terms. In this sense 'an increase in hoarding' means an increase in the real value of the total stock of money. It is an automatic consequence of a fall in prices, no matter what the cause of the fall may be.

'An increase in hoarding' in sense (3) need not be associated with an increase in sense (4) (though commonly both occur together), for a decline in activity and incomes may come about without a fall in prices, though it is unusual for it to do so.

5. Senses (3) and (4) are combined when by 'hoards' is meant the real

value of 'idle balances' – that is, the real value of the total quantity of money *minus* the real value of the active circulation.

It appears that an 'increase in hoarding' in sense (1) may be an independent causal factor acting upon trade activity, incomes and prices *via* the rate of interest, while 'an increase in hoarding' in sense (2), (3), (4) or (5) is a consequence of changes in banking policy, in activity, or in prices, which occur for other reasons.

6. An individual is sometimes said to 'hoard part of his income'. This is a portmanteau phrase containing the conception of saving as well as the conception of acquiring money. The individual in question is saving and using the increment of his wealth to acquire money. The amount of money which he holds is then increasing continuously through time. This sense of hoarding must be distinguished from sense (1*b*), for there 'an increase in hoarding' (demand for money) is the consequence of saving, while here the word 'hoarding' is used actually to *mean* 'saving'.

Terminological confusions about the meaning of the word 'hoarding', like the cognate confusions about the word 'saving', have formed a smoke-screen which conceals important points of substance.

It is sometimes suggested that the savings of individuals fail to 'get invested' in real capital because they somehow 'run to waste in hoards' or 'get held up in the banking system'. Such phrases may imply merely 'an increase in hoarding' in sense (1*b*). Investment is going on at a certain rate, individuals, taken one with another, are adding to their wealth at a rate equal to the rate of net investment, and they wish to hold a part of the increment of their wealth in the form of money. Thus the demand for money is rising gradually through time, and, if the quantity of money is constant, there is a gradually increasing upward pressure on the rate of interest. Here the significance of the desire of individuals to hold an increment of wealth in the form of money does not lie in any tendency for investment to fall short of savings, but in a tendency for the rate of interest to move up gradually through time, exercising an increasing dis-couragement to entrepreneurs carrying out investment in real capital.

More often these phrases have a tincture of 'hoarding' sense (6), and introduce tacitly an increase in thriftiness into the story. An increase in thriftiness, showing itself in a decline in the rate of spending for consumption, leads to an all-round decline in activity and incomes. Some individuals may now be saving at a greater rate than before, while other individuals, owing to the decline in their incomes, are saving correspondingly less. Now, if those whose rate of saving has increased have the same desire to hold money as those who are saving less, there is no net effect upon the demand for money, except a once-and-for-all decline due to the contraction of the active circulation ('decrease in hoarding' sense (1c) and 'increase in hoarding' sense (3)). If, however, it happens that those individuals who save have more than the average desire to hold money, then the demand for money will increase gradually through time, and there will be a gradual upward pressure on the rate of interest. In short, an increase in thriftiness which happens to be accompanied by 'an increase in hoarding' in sense (1) will have a greater effect in reducing activity than one which is not accompanied by 'hoarding'. But the decline in activity is mainly to be attributed to the increase in thriftiness, not to any 'increase in hoarding' which happens to accompany it.

Another idea is also concealed behind the terminological smoke-screen. It is sometimes suggested that an increase in bank credit is somehow 'added to the supply of investible funds', so that the demand for funds represented by the current rate of investment in real capital is met by the savings of the public *plus* newly-created money. It is impossible to add the *stock* of money to the *flow* of saving. These phrases therefore imply that with a given rate of investment there is a given *rate of increase* in the quantity of money. And this is a phenomenon which is never likely to occur in practice.[1] But, for the sake of argument, let us contrast an increase in investment financed by bank credit with one financed by the issue of securities to the public.

There are two points to be considered. First, an increase in the rate of investment leads, so long as the investment continues, to an increased demand for money, both for the active circulation and for 'finance' ('an increase in hoarding' sense (1c)). Where there is no increase in the quantity of money, and no falling off in the demand for money for other reasons, an increase in the rate of investment therefore promotes a rise in the rate of interest, which acts as a brake upon the increase in investment. If, however, the stock of money is increased each week by an amount equal to the increase in the weekly rate of investment, the once-and-for-all rise in the demand for money will be outbalanced after a certain time by the increase in its total stock, and a decline in the rate of interest will set in, giving a further stimulus to investment.

Second, when a certain amount of investment has been completed, there

---

[1] An increase in the quantity of money due to (*a*) goldmining and (*b*) a budget deficit financed by borrowing from the central bank is discussed by Mr. Keynes, *General Theory*, p. 200, and by me, *Introduction to the Theory of Employment*, Chapter X. We are here concerned with an increase in money due to the action of the banking system increasing its loans to entrepreneurs.

is an equal increment in the total of wealth owned by individuals, and consequently an increase in the demand for money ('hoarding' sense (1*b*)). If the investment has been financed by securities and the quantity of money is constant, there is then an upward pressure on the rate of interest. If it is financed by bank loans, then after a certain amount of investment has been completed the banks are left with an equivalent increase in both their assets (loans) and their liabilities (deposits), while the public are left with an equivalent increase in their wealth and in their bank deposits. The increase in demand for money generated by an increase in wealth ('hoarding' sense (1*b*)) is less than the increase in wealth. The supply of money has therefore increased more than the demand for it, and there is a tendency for the rate of interest to fall. The difference between the two methods of finance shows itself in the behaviour of the rate of interest, not in a difference in the behaviour of savings.

These two conceptions, 'savings lost in the banking system' and 'an inflationary supplement to saving', cancel each other. For, over any interval of time, the 'excess savings added to hoards' are represented by the increment of bank deposits held by individual savers, while the 'credits supplementing saving' are represented by the increased loans of the banks. Since the increase in deposits is necessarily equal to the increase in bank assets, the 'excess of saving over investment' is equal to the 'excess of investment over saving'. The two notions have only to be confronted with each other for both to disappear.

It appears that some readers of Mr. Keynes' *General Theory*, themselves believing that the 'waste of savings due to hoarding' and the 'inflationary supplement to savings' are of prime importance, find themselves at a loss to understand why there is no place for 'hoarding' and 'excess investment' in Mr. Keynes' terminology, and attribute their absence to wanton perversity in the definitions. They are unable to conceive that the disappearance of these conceptions (to them all-important) from the analysis can be due to anything but verbal jugglery. But the reason why these notions have no place in the *General Theory* is not because Mr. Keynes has concealed a vital factor under a mask of unnatural terminology, but because, in his view, 'hoarding', except in sense (1), which is covered by the conception of 'liquidity preference', has no causal force, while the notions of 'savings lying idle in the banks' and of 'banks' loans as a supplement to current saving' are purely mythical conceptions. Mr. Keynes' repeated protestations that he regards the complex of ideas connected with these two conceptions as simply an error, a confusion of thought, have failed to take effect, and his critics continue to complain of his definitions instead of denying (or accepting) the substance of his analysis. The issue involved is a substantial one, not a question of terminology.

Postscript

Professor Robertson's conception of hoarding does not fit in anywhere in the above classification, for he uses the word in a special sense: 'A man is said to be *hoarding* if he takes steps to raise the proportion which he finds to exist at the beginning of any day between his money stock and his disposable income'.[2] Thus *hoarding* is an act which takes place at a moment of time. It is clear that if a man whose income is running at a steady rate owns a hoard of money, he is not *hoarding* in this sense. If his income falls, but his hoard is kept intact, the ratio of his money stock to his income has risen, but he has taken no steps, and so done no act of *hoarding*.[3]

If national income falls, for whatever reason, and the quantity of money remains the same, it is clear that some individuals are likely, at some stage in the process of adjustment, to perform acts of *hoarding*, but there does not seem to be any simple relation between the *hoarding* which occurs and the rise in the ratio of money to income for the economy as a whole.

Nor is it possible, in Professor Robertson's language, to distinguish between an increase in the desire to hold money which has a causal influence in raising the rate of interest, and an increase which is a consequence of a fall in the rate of interest.

[2] *Essays in Monetary Theory*, p. 67.
[3] This may sound strange, but I am told by Professor Robertson that it is the correct reading of his definition.

5

THE RATE OF INTEREST

THE problem to be discussed is the determination of the rate of interest in a closed economy, working under *laisser-faire* in the sense that the authorities use no means to influence conditions except monetary policy.

The question is to some extent imaginary because in the days when *laisser-faire* ruled, an important influence on the rate of interest in any one country was the state of its balance of payments, and the objective of monetary policy was control of the foreign exchanges. When the break-up of the world capital market, and exchange control, have largely insulated interest rates in each country there is no longer *laisser-faire* in other respects. However, our problem is sufficiently complicated to justify drastic simplification.

INTRODUCTION

The most important influences upon interest rates – which account for, say, the difference between 30 per cent in an Indian village and 3 per cent in London – are social, legal and institutional. Side by side with the industrial revolution went great technical progress in the provision of credit and the reduction of lender's risk and great changes in social habits favourable to lending; and in the broad sweep of history these considerations are more significant than any others. But we are here concerned with an economy in which the most up-to-date credit facilities may be taken for granted and a capitalist system is fully developed.

First let us consider the influence upon interest rates of the 'fundamental phenomena of Productivity and Thrift'.[1] It is generally agreed that a fall in interest rates tends to stimulate investment and that a low rate of interest is more likely to discourage than to encourage saving. In any given situation, then, we may say that there is some value of the rate of interest so low as to

[1] Robertson, *Essays in Monetary Theory*, p. 25.

This essay, which originally appeared in *Econometrica*, was the title-piece of *The Rate of Interest and Other Essays*. The last section is here omitted.

lead to full employment (but at times this rate may be negative). The full-employment rate is strongly influenced by the 'real force' of thrift and, if not by the 'real force' of productivity, at least by beliefs about the future profitability of capital, which is related to it. In a *laisser-faire* competitive economy, with free wage-bargaining, if the full-employment rate were ever above the actual rate, inflation would set in through a rise of money-wage rates and the rate of interest would be driven up. The full-employment value of the rate of interest may therefore be regarded as, in a certain sense, a lower limit to the possible value of the rate of interest. If this limit always lies far below any value of the actual rate of interest ever experienced, it has little influence on the actual rate. But if from time to time the 'real forces' sweep the full-employment rate above the actual rate, and force the actual rate up (whether by causing inflation or by inducing the monetary authorities to raise the actual rate in order to avoid inflation), then clearly they do play a part in determining the course of the actual rate.

Moreover, an important influence upon the actual rate, at any moment, are expectations of the future course of interest rates, and expectations are strongly influenced by the historical experience of interest rates which the community has lived through. If the real forces play some part in shaping that historical experience, they have some influence upon the position of the rate of interest even when the full-employment rate, at the moment, is far below it. Thus, the real forces have a roundabout influence on the actual rate of interest, as well as upon the full-employment rate. There is then, after all, a Cheshire cat to grin at Professor Robertson,[2] but it often happens that the grin, cheerful or sour, remains after the circumstances which give rise to it in the past have completely vanished from the present scene.

THE STRUCTURE OF THE MARKET

Let us turn to the monetary forces acting on the rate of interest. Keynes' theory treated the rate of interest as determined by the demand and supply of money. This was a useful simplification in the pioneering days of the theory, but it was always obvious that there is no such thing as *the* rate of interest and that the demand and supply of every type of asset has just as much right to be considered as the demand and supply of money.

To develop a more refined theory, the notion of liquidity preference, measured by the reward required to induce owners of wealth to hold assets other than money, must be broken up into a number of aspects. Among the

[2] Op. cit., p. 25.

disadvantages of various kinds of assets compared to money we may distinguish:

1. Illiquidity in the narrow sense. Liquidity partly consists in the capacity of an asset to be realized in money. A limited and imperfect market, the cost and trouble of making a sale, and the time required to effect it, reduce the liquidity of an asset quite apart from variability in its price. Liquidity in the narrow sense depends upon the power to realize its value in cash, whatever the value may be at the moment. To avoid confusion with Keynes' language we will call this quality 'convenience' instead of 'liquidity'.

2. Uncertainty of future capital value, or capital-uncertainty for short, due not to any fear of failure by the borrower but to the possibility of changes in capital values owing to changes in the ruling rate of interest. (This is the main ingredient in Keynes' conception of liquidity preference. He regards the rate of interest primarily as a premium against the possible loss of capital if an asset has to be realized before its redemption date.)

3. Lender's risk; that is, the fear of partial or total failure of the borrower.

Further, when comparing long-term bonds with other paper assets we have to add one more factor:

4. Uncertainty as to the income that a sum of money now committed to the asset will yield in the future, or income-uncertainty for short.

These qualities make up the character, or, so to say, natural colour, of various types of assets. (The relationship of present to expected prices is a separate element in the complex of influences governing the demand for the various assets at any moment.)

A modern capital market represents a bewildering variety of assets, with these qualities in all sorts of combinations. To make our inquiry manageable we must draw a simplified and stylized picture of the market, selecting only a few sharply defined types of assets, say three months' bills, irredeemable bonds and ordinary shares.[3] We will further simplify by assuming that

[3] The distinction between shares and loans raises some legal and philosophical problems. At one point in the *General Theory*, Chapter 12, Keynes creates confusion by calling ordinary shares 'real assets', and describing a purchase of shares on the Stock Exchange as an act of investment. It seems both simpler and less unrealistic to go to the opposite extreme, treating shares as a type of paper asset like the rest and regarding their yield as one of the rates of interest. This is, in essence, the way that those in charge of real investment decisions probably most often look at the matter; to the managing director of a joint-stock company there is a great deal in common between a shareholder and a creditor.

The conception of yield also presents some complications. It may be calculated on the basis of earnings or of dividends, and on the basis of expected future returns or past realized

owners of wealth hold only money or paper assets, while real assets are owned by entrepreneurs who hold them against borrowed funds;[4] that money consists only of bank deposits, without distinction between current and deposit accounts; and that the quantity of money is rigidly determined by the basis of credit which the Central Bank chooses to provide, as in the ideal text-book picture of the British banking system.[5]

Bills we will assume to be perfectly 'good' in the sense that they are free of lender's risk, and they are so short-dated that capital-uncertainty is very small.[6] Bills then differ from money in little except their inferior 'convenience'. Our bonds, we may suppose, also are perfectly good, and no less 'convenient' than bills, in the sense that they can be readily marketed at any time (or pledged against a loan).

The difference between them arises from uncertainty. In a world where past experience has been that interest rates vary from time to time there is uncertainty about future interest rates, in the sense that, whatever an individual may believe about the most probable future course of interest rates, he does not hold his belief with perfect conviction. An owner of wealth who buys a bill today knows what his capital will be in three months' time, but he is uncertain what interest he will then be able to get by re-investing it.[7] If he buys a bond, he knows his income for as long as he likes to hold the bond, but he is uncertain about what his capital will be worth at

---

returns. We shall not enter into these difficulties in the present discussion, but in general we are concerned with prospective yield.

[4] An entrepreneur operating real capital which he owns is regarded as *pro tanto* an owner of wealth lending to himself. Cf. Modigliani, 'Liquidity Preference and the Theory of Interest' (*Econometrica*, January 1944), p. 30. Where a citizen lives in his own house, we may regard him as an owner of wealth lending to himself as an entrepreneur who sells to himself as a consumer.

When there is doubt about the future purchasing power of money, owners of wealth become entrepreneurs; that is to say, there is 'flight into real values'. The whole question of liquidity then takes on quite a different aspect, and money ceases to be the asset to which liquidity preference attaches. We shall not concern ourselves with this problem, but assume that we are discussing a community which has confidence in the future purchasing power of its money.

[5] The argument can easily be modified to fit the case where the supply of money has some elasticity and responds to changes in the rate of interest which the banks can earn.

[6] But see below, p. 43.

[7] It is uncertainty about the whole complex of interest rates that is relevant, not expectations about the bill rate only. Mr. Kalecki (*Studies in Economic Dynamics*, p. 37) takes as typical the case of a person comparing the result of 'holding one or the other type of security over a few years' – that is, choosing between buying a bond now and deciding now not to buy a bond for a few years, holding bills during that time. But usually an owner of wealth

any date in the future. Perfectly good bills thus offer negligible capital-uncertainty, but relatively high income-uncertainty, while perfectly good bonds offer perfect certainty of income, but relatively high capital-uncertainty.

Shares are subject to income-uncertainty of a special kind because of uncertainty about the future profits to be earned by the real assets to which they correspond. They are therefore subject to a double dose of capital-uncertainty, for their prices vary both with changes in profit-expectations and with changes in the rates of interest. Moreover, they are subject to lender's risk, in varying degrees, according to the standing and reputation of the firms which they represent.

These qualities of the various types of asset are differently evaluated by different individuals. Some (widows and orphans) set great store on income-certainty, and do not bother much about capital-uncertainty, as they do not intend to realize in any case. Financial institutions set great store on their balance sheets, and value capital-certainty very highly. Owners of wealth with a taste for speculation, or those who have such a large fortune that they can spread their risks widely, have a smaller aversion than either to uncertainty about any particular asset. The general pattern of interest rates depends upon the distribution of wealth between owners with different tastes, relatively to the supplies of the various kinds of assets.

Each type of asset is a potential alternative to every other; each has, so to speak, a common frontier with every other, and with money. Equilibrium in the market is attained when the interest rates are such that no wealth is moving across any frontier. Prices are then such that the market is content to hold just that quantity of each type of asset which is available at the moment.

The complex of demands and supplies is not static, but is moving slowly through time. Over any period there is an increment to total wealth from saving equal to the borrowing for investment (and budget deficits) that has taken place during the period. The total of wealth, representing a demand for paper assets, increases with the supply. But the supply of any particular type may alter relatively to the demand for it. For instance, a budget deficit, financed by selling bonds, will generate savings which the owners wish to put partly into money or shares. The supply of bonds is then increasing relatively to demand.

---

feels himself free to switch his capital from one asset to another at any time in the future if it seems good to him. Mr. Kaldor, 'Speculation and Economic Stability', *Review of Economic Studies*, October 1939, p. 13, uses a similar argument, which is subject to the same objection.

A borrower who is free to choose the kind of paper assets he creates will try to offer those which require the lowest interest, and this sets up a certain tendency for supply gradually to be adjusted to demand (though changes in business methods – the growth of self-financing, the decay of the trade bill – may alter supply in a way quite unrelated to changes in demand).

There is also a much more immediate way in which supply is adjusted to demand. Where there is a difference between interest rates there is a possible source of profit. If the short rate were found on the average to rule above the long, because of the dominance in the market of widows and orphans with a strong preference for bonds, and if this situation were expected to continue, financial houses could issue bonds, which would be taken up by the widows and orphans, and use the funds thus obtained to carry bills. They would undergo a risk, for if there were an unforeseen change, and the short rate fell permanently, they could only get out of the now unprofitable business by redeeming their bonds, which might meanwhile have risen in price. Thus, the long rate would still have to remain normally lower than the short rate.

In the reverse case (which is the usual one, at least in recent times) where preference for capital-certainty predominates in the market, so that the bond rate exceeds the bill rate, there is an income to be made by borrowing short and lending long. This is commonly done by taking a bank advance. Assuming the basis of credit to remain constant, the banks must sell other assets when they increase advances, and their assets are short-dated (in our simplified world they could only hold bills) so that the effect is the same as though dealers in credit issued bills in order to hold bonds. The risk involved in this operation is that there may be an unforeseen rise in the bill rate, so that the dealers have either to renew their loans at a higher cost or to sell out bonds whose price may have fallen. Thus, these operations require a margin between long- and short-term rates and, since there is not an unlimited amount of credit available to dealers, the margin they require will be larger the greater the amount of bonds that they are holding.

Investment trusts issue what are intended to be less speculative securities in order to carry more speculative ones.

Operations such as these to some extent smooth out the differences in demand for securities of different types and bring the various interest rates closer together.

CHANGES IN THE QUANTITY OF MONEY AND IN EXPECTATIONS

Preferences for various types of asset, relatively to the supplies of them, determine the general pattern of interest rates, and it is against this sort of background that day-to-day changes in interest rates occur. The pattern most commonly found in actual markets is such that normally the bill rate is lower than the bond rate, and the yields of shares higher.

Given the general background, there are two quite distinct types of influence which play upon the equilibrium pattern of rates. One is the state of expectations and the other is the supply of money. To discuss them separately we require to be able to assume one constant when the other varies. It is difficult to frame the assumption that expectations are given without sawing off the bough we are sitting on. It is easiest to discuss expectations if they are quite definite. Everything can then be reduced to arithmetic. But if we assume that owners of wealth have clear and unanimous expectations about the exact future course of the prices of assets, in which they believe with perfect confidence, then we have ruled out uncertainty and stepped into a world quite unlike the one we want to discuss. Moreover, we have landed ourselves in a logical impasse, for either the expectations will turn out to be correct, in which case there is no more to be said, or they will turn out mistaken, in which case perfect confidence cannot persist.

The whole subject of expectations bristles with psychological and philosophical difficulties,[8] and I can offer only a sketchy and superficial treatment of it. For the moment let us be content to assume that the bond rate is expected to move around the average level that has been experienced in the recent past, so that when it falls below that level it is expected to rise, some time or other, and when it rises above, to fall, but that everyone's view is hazy as to how long it will take to return to the average value and how far it will go meanwhile, so that there is great uncertainty about what its value will be at any particular date in the future. For simplicity of exposition we will suppose that we are examining the market at a moment when today's bond rate is equal to the average value. Further, we will assume that profits are expected to continue at the same level as in the recent past, so that the prices of shares are not expected to move except in response to changes in the rate of interest. Finally, we will neglect speculators operating on day-to-day changes in the price of assets.

Having thus tethered expectations, let us examine the effect upon the

[8] Cf. Shackle, *Expectation in Economics*, especially Chapter 7, and Fellner, *Monetary Policies and Full Employment*, pp. 152 *et seq.*

market of a change in the quantity of money. A change in the amount of
bank deposits is a special case of the kind of change in the stock of assets
relative to the total of wealth which we have already discussed.[9] The
essence of the matter is that when the Central Bank, say, increases the basis
of credit the member banks buy assets from the market to an amount which
restores the normal ratio of their cash reserves to other assets. They thus
reduce the amount of assets to be held by the market and so raise their prices.
To maintain our simplifying assumptions we will assume that the banks buy
only bills. The immediate consequence is a fall in the rate of interest on bills.
What effect does this have upon the bond rate?

The bond rate is bound to be affected, for even if all owners of wealth
have strong preferences, and are settled far from the frontier between bonds
and bills, so that it would need a very large change in values to shift them,
yet dealers in credit will react to small changes and so provide a
continuously sensitive frontier between bills and bonds. The profit to be
made by selling a bill and buying a bond is the difference in the interest on
them for three months *minus* the fall (or *plus* the rise) in the price of the bond
over three months. Dealing at today's prices, the difference in interest
which will be enjoyed is known, but the change in price of the bond is
unknown. A fall in the short rate increases the difference in interest rates,
and so raises the demand for bonds, but the consequent rise in the price of
bonds enhances the likelihood of a fall in their price in the future. If
expectations are clear and definite, only a very small fall in the long-term
rate of interest can occur. It needs a fall of only $\frac{1}{4}$ per cent in the price of
bonds over three months to wipe out the effect of a fall of 1 per cent in the
bill rate per annum, and a rise in today's price of bonds by $\frac{1}{4}$ per cent means
a fall in the bond rate of interest in the ratio 400:401.[10] Suppose, for
example, that there is a clear expectation that the bond rate will be back to
its average in three months' time; then today's rate cannot fall by more than
this ratio in response to each 1 per cent fall in the bill rate.[11] But if
expectations of what the bond rate will be in three months' time are vague
and dubious, the power of a rise in today's price of bonds to wipe out the
attraction of holding them is so much the weaker. Thus, the effect of a fall in
the short rate upon the long is greater, the greater the uncertainty in which
the market dwells.

[9] See p. 39.

[10] Cf. *General Theory*, p. 168.

[11] This relationship is quite sufficient to account for the observed sluggishness in the
movement of the long-term rate of interest in response to changes in the short rate. It is
unnecessary as well as unplausible to maintain that the long rate responds only to changes in
the *expected future* short rate. Cf. above, p. 38 note 7.

In the *Treatise on Money*, Keynes, so to speak, dramatized uncertainty as the existence of 'two views' leading to a 'bull-bear position'; that is, a dispersion of opinions, each confidently held.[12] The degree of uncertainty in the market as a whole then depends on the variety of opinion within it. The same effects follow where everyone is alike, but no one feels confident that his own best guess of what the future holds will turn out to be right. In any situation where there is inadequate evidence on which to base predictions, both elements will be present. Thus, a rise in today's price of bonds will induce some holders of bonds to sell before others, and will cause many holders to sell out to some extent. The greater the dispersion of opinion and the less confidently are opinions held, the greater the movement of bond prices in response to a given change in the quantity of money.

We have assumed that expectations of profit are constant. With lower interest rates the frontiers between bills and shares and bonds and shares are no longer in equilibrium at the old rate, and there is a sympathetic movement in the price of shares, governed by similar considerations to those which influence the movement of bond prices. Thus, an increase in the quantity of money lowers the whole complex of interest rates.

We may now look at the same situation the other way up and inquire what has happened to the increment of money which has been created. At any moment some money is in course of travelling round the active circulation – from income-earner to shopkeeper, from shopkeeper to producer, from producer to income-earner and so back again. Some is in the financial circuit, passing between buyers and sellers of paper assets. Some is lodged in what we may call a 'short hoard' either because its owner, who has recently made some savings, is shortly going to spend it in buying securities, or because its owner (who may be an entrepreneur) has some large-scale purchase of goods shortly to make. These short hoards may reasonably be classed as part of the active circulation. Some money is lodged, at any moment, in 'long hoards' because it has come into the hands of owners who choose to hold a part of their wealth in the form of money. Some is in 'bear hoards' whose owners are waiting for a fall in bond and share prices to go back into the market.

Some bears, and some owners of wealth with a high preference for capital-certainty, hold bills rather than money. But it is natural to assume that, in the main, money is preferred to bills for long hoards because dealing in bills is a specialized business, for which many owners of long hoards have

---

[12] In the *Treatise*, chapter 15, the two views refer to future share prices, but Keynes applies the same idea to views about the rate of interest (*General Theory*, pp. 169 and 173).

no inclination, and because it is not practicable in small sums. The advantage of money over bills for bear hoards is that it makes it possible to switch back into securities in less than three months, if that seems desirable, without the cost and the capital risk of switching into and out of bills.

Short hoards, long hoards and bear hoards correspond to convenience, precaution and speculation, mentioned by Keynes as motives for holding money.[13]

Now, the fall in interest rates which has occurred may slow down the active circulation somewhat. Money may idle a little longer in short hoards – the motive for economizing balances is less[14] – but this effect will be slight, for the velocity of active circulation is fixed by fairly rigid habits. Thus, when there is an increase in money relative to national income, most of the new money cannot find a lodgement unless long or bear hoards are increased.[15]

The yields of all paper assets have fallen, and this in itself may lead some owners of wealth to prefer money. But the main effect is that the rise in the price of bonds and shares has enhanced the fear of a fall in their value in the future, and so set a bearish movement on foot. Money, we have supposed, is usually preferred to bills for bear hoarding; if, however, some of the bears prefer bills, the bill rate is reduced all the more, and there is a further movement over the bill frontier into money.

Thus, the result of increasing the quantity of money is to lower the short rate and to pull the long rate below its expected value to the point where the combined effect of these two movements increases hoards by the amount of the increase in the quantity of money.[16] (If the fall in interest rates induces an increase in national income, of course, part of the new money is required for active circulation, and the interest rates will not fall so far.)

[13] *General Theory*, pp. 195–6. It is, of course, impossible to draw a hard and fast line between them. Convenience shades into precaution, and precaution would not give rise to a demand for money unless there was an element of speculation present. Cf. Fellner, op. cit., p. 147.

[14] Mr. Kalecki (op. cit., p. 32) suggests that it is only the short rate which is relevant here. But surely this is a mistake. If an individual (or a firm) decides to economize balances in order to enjoy interest he is just as likely to put the money into bonds as bills. See also Kaldor, loc. cit., p. 14.

[15] Mr. Kaldor seems to deny that hoarding ever occurs (op. cit., p. 13, note), but on closer examination his argument appears to be purely verbal, as he calls deposits money only if they are in active circulation.

[16] If the above is correct, it is misleading to say that the short rate is determined by demand and supply of money while the long rate is determined by the expected future short rate, for one of the main determinants of the demand for money is expectations about the course of the long rate itself.

A fall in national income relative to the stock of money (abstracting from a consequent change in expectations) has effects similar to the above. A reduction in the quantity of money or rise in national income has the converse effects.

To summarize: given the state of expectations, the long and short rates of interest both fall as the quantity of money increases relatively to national income. The fall in the short rate is steeper than the fall in the long,[17] so that the gap between the two increases with the quantity of money. The less the uncertainty (the more confident and unanimous the market that a departure of the rate of interest from its average value will quickly be reversed), the smaller is the response of the rates of interest to changes in the quantity of money, and the smaller is the gap between the two rates. In the limit, if the market confidently believes that it knows that from tomorrow the rate of interest will be at its past average value, the long and the short rate will be equal to that value today. (In this case liquidity preference in Keynes' sense is absolute.)

So far we have been discussing the situation at a moment of time, with given expectations, but time marches on. We have supposed that expectations of the future interest rates depend upon past experience. When the bond rate is below its past average, expectations tend to be revised as time goes by, and the demand for money tends gradually to fall, but this is a slow process, and before it has had time to produce any effect all sorts of changes occur. Thus, uncertainty is kept alive by the chances of history.

It has been objected against this theory that it leaves the rate of interest hanging by its own boot straps.[18] But there is no escape from the fact that the price today of any long-lived object with low carrying costs is strongly

---

[17] Unless uncertainty is so great that expectations about the future price of bonds have no influence at all upon the long rate.

[18] Both Mr. Hicks (*Value and Capital*, op. cit., p. 164) and Mr. Kaldor (p. 12) display a lively horror of boot straps, but it is not clear how they propose to escape from them. The view that the long rate can be determined solely from expectations about the short rate is untenable. It is true, in a world in which expectations are definite and unanimous, that when we know today's bond rate and today's bill rate, we can reckon what change in the price of bonds is expected over the life of the bills. Then, looking into a further future, we can assume that the bill rate then expected to rule is known, and that by then the expected price of bonds is expected to obtain. Then we can reckon the expected change in bond prices over the further future, and so on to Kingdom Come. Then the whole pattern of expectations could be described in terms of the expected short rates alone. But all this means is that rational expectations must be self-consistent. It certainly does not detach the rate of interest from dependence on its boot straps for, in such a world, the only reason for a difference between short and long rates is the expectation of a change in the long rate. Indeed, one might say that there the short rate is simply an expression of expectations about bond prices. Moreover, the

influenced by expectations about what its price will be in the future. If the
rate of interest is hanging by its boot straps, so is the price of Picasso's
paintings.

We have very little knowledge of the influences shaping expectations.
Past experience is no doubt the major element in expectations, but
experience, as far as one can judge, is compounded in the market with a
variety of theories and superstitions and the whole amalgam is played upon
from day to day by the influences (including the last bank chairman's
speech) which make up what Keynes called 'the state of the news'. Any
theory that is widely believed tends to verify itself, so that there is a large
element of 'thinking makes it so' in the determination of interest rates.[19]
This is all the more true when short-term speculation is prevalent.

A speculator has not the same attitude as an owner of wealth to liquidity,
income-uncertainty or capital-uncertainty. He is concerned with making
money by forestalling changes in prices from day to day by 'anticipating
what average opinion expects the average opinion to be'.[20] So long as the
great bulk of transactions is made by owners of wealth and dealers in credit,
the speculator has to guess how they will behave. The effect of speculation is
then to speed up the movement of today's prices towards expected future
prices. But, as soon as speculators become an important influence in the
market, their business is to speculate on each other's behaviour. The market
then becomes unstable, and falls into the condition described by Keynes
under that misleading chapter-heading, 'The State of Long-Term

---

conception of expectations without uncertainty plunges us into philosophical difficulties (see
above).

Professor Robertson (op. cit., p. 25) appears to hold (though he states positively only
what he does *not* hold) that the long rate is determined partly by the 'real forces' and partly
by beliefs about how the real forces are going to behave in the future. But, if so, with these
beliefs he has admitted a Trojan horse full of expectations and liquidity preference into the
citadel of the real forces.

In Mr. Kalecki's system expectations about the long rate, based on past experience, are a
separate determinant of today's rate, and the system here set out is broadly the same as his
(except for the point made above, p. 38, note 7) and owes a great deal to it.

My chief debt is to some pregnant hints to be found in Mr. Harrod's *Dynamic Economics*,
see especially p. 62.

[19] This gives the 'real forces' one more card of entry. If it is widely believed that, for
example, an increase in the rate of investment raises the rate of interest, then the appearance
of any symptom which is taken to indicate that investment is going to increase will have
a tendency to raise interest rates.

[20] *General Theory*, p. 156. In reality, of course, there can be no quite clear-cut
demarcation between speculators and owners of wealth who take a view about future prices,
and the two classes shade into each other at the edges.

Expectations'.[21] The operations of the speculators cast a thick fog over future prospects for the owners of wealth, increase uncertainty all round and so raise the general level of interest rates.

They also create a fog for the economist describing the capital market, which very much reduces the cogency of the above type of analysis, and totally deprives it of utility as a source of tips.

AN INCREASE IN THE RATE OF INVESTMENT

Abstracting from speculation (for if we do not, there is little to be said) we will now examine the effects of an increase in the rate of investment (say induced by an improvement in prospective profits) which increases national income but does not go far enough to hit full employment and create inflationary conditions. If the banking system follows the policy of meeting the needs of trade, interest rates are held constant. To make the story interesting we will assume that the quantity of money is not altered.

Investment plans must be made before any actual outlay takes place. If entrepreneurs proceed by issuing shares before they begin to place orders for new capital goods, and hold money in short hoards for the time being, there is an increase in demand for money relatively to the supply and an increase in supply of shares relatively to demand, and the interest rates rise before the actual investment begins.[22] It is more natural to suppose, however, that entrepreneurs take bank advances as required and retire them by the issue of shares after the investment has been under way for some time.

Possible cases offer an endless variety of patterns. To simplify, we will assume that investment remains steady at the new higher rate during the period that we are discussing, that all investment is financed in the same way, and that it is financed by taking overdrafts which are repaid by issuing securities at a certain interval after they have been drawn upon. With these assumptions, while the investment continues there is a certain volume of bank advances outstanding at any moment, and the supply of securities keeps pace with the addition to wealth due to saving, after an initial wobble, which may go either way according as the issue of securities begins before or after the pattern of saving has become adjusted to the new rate of investment.

We will abstract from the gradual effect of a rise in the proportions of shares to total wealth, and consider only the immediate influences upon interest rates coming from the change in the rate of investment.

[21] *General Theory*, Chapter 12.
[22] See Keynes, 'Alternative theories of the rate of interest', *Economic Journal*, June 1937.

Let us compare a date in Period II, when the multiplier has run its course and national income has settled at the level appropriate to the new higher rate of investment, with a date in Period I, when investment was being carried out at the old rate.

There is now a larger national income, and a larger demand for money in active circulation, including a swollen demand for short hoards, corresponding to the higher level at which saving is running.[23] Entre-preneurs have taken bank advances, and the banks sold out bills, so that the short rate has risen. Bond rates, as usual, have risen in sympathy.

The rise in interest rates puts a brake on the rise in demand for money by increasing the velocity of active circulation; at the same time it has drawn money out of bear and long hoards. The rates of interest have risen to the point where equilibrium is restored at the frontiers around money.

What has happened to shares? The same cause which induces the increase in investment – a rise in prospective profits – gives rise to better and more confident expectations of future dividends. For the time being, at least, the optimism which started investment off appears justified, for profits are in fact ruling higher while investment goes on. The price of shares has therefore risen at least sufficiently to keep yields at the level corresponding to the rate on bonds. (If we allow speculators out of the cage where we are keeping them assumed away, the price of shares may rise to any extent, and the normal relationship between bond and share yields may be reversed.) If this were all, share yields would move sympathetically with the bond rate; that is to say, they would be raised slightly by the increase in demand for money. But there is a further effect. With greater confidence in future profits, credit is improved and the risk attached to shares is felt to be reduced. Different shares will be differently affected. On the very 'good' ones, for which the risk premium is in any case small, the yield will have risen in sympathy with bonds; on others, particularly those whose firms are taking the biggest part in the industrial boom, it will have fallen. Lumping all shares together, their yield, on balance, is most likely to be reduced.

Our interest rates now stand thus, at a date in Period II compared to Period I: The short rate is higher. Bond rates are higher (but not by much) and share rates are likely to be lower.

The yield on existing paper assets has a strong influence on the cost of new borrowing. Concerns which borrow at near the gilt-edged rate will find borrowing a little dearer and may be inclined to defer investment plans

[23] Professor Fellner (op. cit., p. 149) suggests that hoards held by entrepreneurs fall as general confidence increases. If this effect were to predominate, the rates of interest would normally fall as investment increases.

(though it is more likely that in the general atmosphere of optimism, they will take the rise in their stride). Industrialists in the main find borrowing easier. The improved prospect of profit counts twice over — once in promoting investment at a given cost of borrowing and once in lowering the cost of borrowing.[24]

Keynes himself makes this point,[25] but the habit of thinking in terms of *the* rate of interest led him to overlook the fact that the most relevant interest rate is likely to be falling when investment is increasing, and to make the quite unnecessary concession to classical ideas that the movement in interest rates which accompanies a boom sets a drag upon the increase in investment.

AN INCREASE IN THRIFTINESS

We may now consider the much debated question of the effect of thriftiness on the rate of interest.[26] Our discussion of the 'real forces' implied that, in a very broad sense and a very long run, a high state of thriftiness relative to investment opportunities helps to keep interest rates low. In so far as it does so, accumulation of real capital may be greater than it would have been if interest rates had been higher, though not necessarily greater than it would have been if thriftiness had been less. In what follows we are not concerned with such long-run considerations, but with examining the impact of an increase in thriftiness upon interest rates in a very short and in a medium run.

Let us suppose that the thriftiness of our community has increased, which shows itself in the first instance in a reduction in the rate of outlay for consumption goods by some section of the public. We will first consider how the situation would develop *if* planned investment were unaffected, and then re-examine the influence of what has happened upon investment plans. It simplifies exposition if we postulate that the rate of planned investment is zero, but this means only that sentences such as 'the stock of capital is unchanged' are substituted for 'the stock of capital is the same as it would have been if this had not happened', and so forth. We must divide time up into periods, not necessarily of the same length. Period I is the time

[24] This argument has not much force in the case of a large established firm, for which there need not be any close connection between the timing of borrowing and of investment, but there is much investment which cannot be undertaken until finance for it has been secured.

[25] *General Theory*, p. 158.

[26] Cf. Robertson, op. cit., pp. 18 et seq.

before the change occurred. In Period II consumption is lower than in Period I by the amount of the designed increase of saving, but nothing else has had time to alter. Stocks have piled up in the shops. If we value the stocks at full retail prices, including the retailers' profit, we may say that national income is unchanged. At the end of Period II *ex-post* saving has occurred equal to the undesigned rise in stocks. In Period III (which is likely to be longer than II) retailers reduced purchases, the fall in national income works its way through the system, and there will be a secondary decline in consumption on top of the first. Stocks have to be reduced to the level appropriate to the new rate of consumption, so that there will be an extra fall in income and fall in employment while the redundant stocks of Period I and the undesigned accumulation of Period II are worked off. In Period IV disinvestment in stocks has come to an end, there is a recovery of employment relatively to Period III and we settle down to a new position of short-period equilibrium with a lower level of consumption appropriate to the now higher thriftiness and the unchanged rate of investment.

How have the rates of interest been behaving? Let us place ourselves at the point of time where Period II ends. We find members of the public with an increment of wealth compared to their position in Period I. There are a great many possible consequences in the financial sphere. Let us pick out two simple cases:

1. The savers are holding short hoards, equal to their increment of wealth, which they have not yet placed in securities.

2. They have already purchased bonds.

Retailers have acquired real assets to the value of the undesigned increase in stocks. Part of this value is represented by profits which they have failed to realize. According to the convention we have adopted of calling the national income constant, the missing profits must be regarded as savings which the retailers have, willy-nilly, invested in stocks. The rest of the value of stocks represents outgoings which they would normally have paid out of receipts, and for which they now require finance. This division of the value of the stocks into two parts complicates the argument. At first we will abstract from it by assuming that the retailers finance the whole value of the stocks in the same way. Methods of finance vary greatly according to the way business is conducted. Again we may pick out a few simple cases from amongst all the possibilities:

(*a*) The retailers have run down cash balances.

(*b*) They have taken bank advances.

(*c*) They have sold bonds which they were formerly holding.

Combining (1) with (*a*), cash released from retailers' balances matches the increase in cash held by savers, and nothing alters. Combining (2) with (c), the retailers sell bonds equivalent to those that the savers buy, and again nothing alters. Combining (1) with (c), the savers hoard money and the retailers sell bonds. The demand for money has increased, which raises interest rates in the converse of the manner described above. Besides this, the demand for bonds has fallen, which tends to increase the gap between long and short rates. Combining (2) with (a), the savers have bought bonds and the retailers have parted with money. The rates of interest fall, and the gap between them tends to narrow.

In case (b) the banks have made advances and, since the quantity of money is assumed constant, they have sold out bills. This raises the short rate of interest, and the long rate tends to rise in sympathy. If we combine this with case (1) (savers holding money), the increase in demand for money reinforces the rise in interest rates. If we combine it with (2) (savers holding bonds), the increase in demand for bonds tends to counteract it.

In so far as the various types of case occur together they tend to offset each others' effects upon the interest rates.

Slight differences are introduced if we take account of the retailers' missing profits. Suppose that their savings in Period I exceeded the missing profits, and that their personal expenditure is the same in Period II as in Period I; then, in the case which combines (1) and (a), the absorption of cash by savers is equal to the full value of the undesigned accumulation of stocks, while the release of cash by retailers which finances them is short of the full value by the amount of the missing profits. There is thus a net increase in demand for money, and the interest rates rise. And so on.

But the argument has grown tedious. Its upshot is that in Period II the effect upon interest rates is not likely to be large, and, in so far as there is an effect, it may go either way.

Let us now jump over the turbid eddies of Period III and place ourselves at a point of time some way along in Period IV, when things have settled down.

Still assuming, provisionally, that planned investment is unchanged at zero, we have a national income lower than that in Period I by the reduced consumption of the first group of savers *plus* the reduction brought about by the secondary decline in incomes and employment in accordance with the multiplier. A smaller amount of money is required in active circulation than in Period I. Bank advances have been paid off and (assuming a constant quantity of money) the short rate of interest is lower than in Period I. No net investment has taken place; therefore there has been zero *ex-post* saving over the period as a whole (neglecting the effect of disinvestment in stocks and working capital owing to the fall in the level of output), so that the total of outstanding assets and the total of privately owned wealth are unchanged. Abstracting from any change in expectations about the long rate of interest owing to the experiences of the transition period, there has been a fall in the bond rate, in sympathy with the short rate. The consumption trades are doing badly compared to Period I, and shares are likely to be adversely affected. On the very 'good' ones the yield may move in sympathy with the fall in bond and short rates, but many will suffer from a rise in riskiness, owing to poor prospects of profit in the consumption trades. Thus our picture is: a lower short rate in Period IV compared to I, a slightly lower bond and best share rate, and a higher yield of shares in general.

This pattern of interest rates does not look very encouraging to investment, and it seems that our provisional assumption of a constant rate of investment must be revised in the downward direction because of the surplus capacity and low profits in the consumption trades and the high cost of industrial borrowing.

6

KALECKI AND KEYNES

1

IT is difficult now to recapture the state of orthodox opinion in the capitalist world in the early years of the great depression.

There was heavy unemployment in England even before the world slump set in. In 1929 Lloyd George was campaigning for a programme of public works. In reply, British officials propounded the 'Treasury View' that if the Government borrowed, say, a hundred million pounds to set men to work on road building and so forth, foreign investment would be reduced by an equal sum and no overall increase in employment would occur.

In 1931 the British Labour Government was led to destruction through the belief that it was necessary to balance the budget in order to save the exchange value of sterling.

Academic opinion was serenely oblivious to the problems of reality. Professor Robbins, surrounded by unemployed labour and idle plant, defined economics as 'the science which studies human behaviour as a relation between ends and scarce means which have alternative uses'.[1]

According to accepted theory the price level was determined by the quantity of money. But the suggestion that the depression might therefore be relieved by increasing the quantity of money was confined to cranks. In the orthodox view it would create a dangerous inflation.

The Marxists abused the academics, but they shared their belief in the principles of sound finance.

In this fog Keynes was groping for a theory of employment. He had backed up Lloyd George with a rather vague and half-baked argument that an increase in investment would generate an increase in saving (so that borrowing in one form need not be subtracted from borrowing in another)[2] and a young pupil of his, R. F. Kahn, worked it out properly. During the

[1] *Essay on the Nature and Significance of Economic Science.* 1932.
[2] J. M. Keynes and H. D. Henderson, *Can Lloyd George Do It?*

sessions of the Macmillan Committee on currency and banking Keynes was
coming to the view that there was a fallacy in the accepted argument that a
cut in money wage rates would restore profitability to enterprise, by
lowering costs relatively to prices, because prices would come down more
or less in proportion. But in his great theoretical *Treatise* his mind was
working in a different plane, and it failed to produce a theory of
employment, though it contained the highly significant conception that an
increase of investment without (as we should now put it) a corresponding
increase in propensity to save raises profits, while an increase in propensity
to save without a corresponding increase in investment reduces them.

Over the continent, no doubt including Poland, the fog of orthodoxy
was even thicker than in England. Only in Sweden Wicksell's pupils were
puzzling out a new line. In *Monetary Equilibrium* published in Swedish in
1931, Gunnar Myrdal twitted Keynes upon his 'attractive Anglo-Saxon
kind of unnecessary originality', but he was not altogether clear of the fog
himself.

The *Treatise on Money* was passed for the last time to the printers in
September 1930, and Kahn's article appeared in the *Economic Journal* of June
1931, setting out the analysis of the multiplier – the relation of an increase in
employment in investment to the total increase in employment that it
generates – and showing how the rise in incomes that accompanies an
increase in investment brings about a rise in savings of an equal amount.

There followed a great bout of argument that churned over these ideas
for three years.

In 1933 I published a kind of interim report, which clears the ground for
the new theory but does not supply it.[3] It was not till the summer of 1934
that Keynes succeeded in getting his theory of money, his theory of wages
and Kahn's multiplier into a coherent system.

In January 1935 he wrote to Bernard Shaw: 'I believe myself to be
writing a book on economic theory which will largely revolutionize – not,
I suppose at once, but in the course of the next ten years – the way the world
thinks about economic problems.'[4]

The General Theory of Employment, Interest and Money was published in
January, 1936.

Meanwhile, without any contact either way, Michał Kalecki had found
the same solution.

His book, *Essays in the Theory of Business Cycles*, published in Polish in
1933, clearly states the principle of effective demand in mathematical form.

[3] See above, 'The theory of money and analysis of output'.
[4] R. F. Harrod, *Life of Keynes*, p. 462.

At the same time he was already exploring the implications of the analysis for the problem of a country's balance of trade, along the same lines that I followed in drawing riders from the *General Theory* in essays published in 1937.

The version of his theory set out in prose (published in 'Polska Gospodarcza', No. 43, X, 1935) could very well be used today as an introduction to the theory of employment.

He opens by attacking the orthodox theory at the most vital point – the view that unemployment could be reduced by cutting money wage rates. And he shows (a point that the Keynesians came to much later, and under his influence) that, if monopolistic influences prevent prices from falling when wage costs are lowered, the situation is still worse, because reduced purchasing power causes a fall in sales of consumption goods, so that higher profit margins do not result in higher profits.

Having demolished the case for the orthodox remedy for a depression, he shows how an increase of investment, coming about, for instance, as the result of a great new invention, would increase employment, and then points out that if a spontaneous increase in investment is possible, it must be possible also by deliberate government policy to carry out schemes of investment that would not otherwise be undertaken and so relieve unemployment and increase consumption as well.

Kalecki's statement of the theory avoids the problem of the equality of saving and investment, which plagued us so much, by relying simply on the fact that the equivalent of investment outlay is added to profits. He cuts through another passage where Keynes made heavy weather by taking it for granted that the rate of interest is a monetary phenomenon. When investment, income and saving increase, it is necessary for the supply of the medium of exchange to be increased also; otherwise the rate of interest would rise and a drag be set upon investment.

Kalecki did not approach the theory of employment through the multiplier, which makes his version in a way less rich than Keynes', though no less forceful. On the other hand, he went straight to a theory of the trade cycle, on which Keynes was very weak. In this essay there is a clear statement in a few lines of the capital-stock-adjustment mechanism which is now recognized as the basis for all modern trade-cycle models.

Michał Kalecki's claim to priority of publication is indisputable. With proper scholarly dignity (which, however, is unfortunately rather rare among scholars) he never mentioned this fact. And, indeed, except for the authors concerned, it is not particularly interesting to know who first got into print. The interesting thing is that two thinkers, from completely different political and intellectual starting points, should come to the same conclusion. For us in Cambridge it was a great comfort. Surrounded by blank misunderstanding, there were moments when we almost began to wonder if it was we who were mad or the others. In the serious sciences, original work is *discovery* – finding connections that were always there, waiting to be seen. That this could happen in economics was a reassurance that what we had discovered was really there.

I well remember my first meeting with Michał Kalecki – a strange visitor who was not only already familiar with our brand-new theories, but had even invented some of our private jokes. It gave me a kind of Pirandello feeling – was it he who was speaking or I? Reading his article of 1935 (now for the first time available in English)[5] gives me the same feeling. Several times, in those old days, I wrote that very article – though with less concentrated force – trying to explain Keynes' theory in simple words.

Kalecki had one great advantage over Keynes – he had never learned orthodox economics. The preface to the *General Theory* ends thus: 'The ideas which are here expressed so laboriously are extremely simple and should be obvious. The difficulty lies, not in the new ideas, but in escaping from the old ones, which ramify for those brought up as most of us have been, into every corner of our minds.'

Kalecki was not brought up so. The only economics he had studied was Marx. Keynes could never make head or tail of Marx. In the letter to Shaw, quoted above, he maintains that his new theory is going to cut the ground from under the feet of the Marxists. But starting from Marx would have saved him a lot of trouble. Kahn, at the 'circus' where we discussed the *Treatise* in 1931, explained the problem of saving and investment by imagining a cordon round the capital-good industries and then studying the trade between them and the consumption-good industries; he was struggling to rediscover Marx's schema. Kalecki began at that point.

2

In his *Essays in the Theory of Economic Fluctuations* published after he had been a little while in England, he filled in several gaps in Keynes' formulation of the theory of employment.

In Keynes' scheme, the concept of *marginal efficiency of capital* means that, at any moment, there is in existence a schedule of possible investment projects, listed in descending order of their prospective profitability (allowing for risk). The schedule is cut off at the point where the

---

[5] Reprinted in *Essays on the Dynamics of the Capitalist Economy*, Cambridge, 1971.

prospective rate of net profit is equal to the rate of interest to be paid for finance. This determines the total value of investment to be undertaken. Kalecki asked the pertinent question: If there are schemes which promise a rate of profit greater than the rate of interest, would not each individual enterprise be willing and anxious to carry out an indefinitely large amount of investment? It was no use to reply that a faster rate of investment would raise the cost of capital goods and so reduce the prospective rate of profit; for the rise in costs would come about as a result of actual investment, *ex post*, while the marginal efficiency of capital concerns investment plans *ex ante*.

Kalecki supplied an answer, first by making clear the separation between investment decisions and actual investment; and second, by introducing into the argument the obvious fact that no individual enterprise can command an indefinitely large amount of finance at a given rate of interest. He took risk over from the demand side (where it lies rather uneasily in Keynes' scheme) to the supply side, and postulated that the amount of finance that each individual enterprise will commit to investment is in an increasing function of the prospective rate of profit, depending upon the ratio of its borrowing to its own capital. Then, with any given distribution of capital amongst enterprises, there is a particular relation between the total amount of investment plans being drawn up at any moment and the level of prospective profits.

The second difficulty was that, though Keynes himself attached great importance to the idea that the present is always overweighted in forming a view about the future, he treated his schedule of prospective profits as though it was independent of the actual rate of investment. Kalecki shows how a higher level of investment this year than last, means a higher level of current profits, therefore a higher expected rate of profit, therefore enlarged investment plans, therefore a higher rate of investment next year.

A rise in the actual rate of investment cannot go on indefinitely. When the rate of investment ceases to rise, the level of current profit ceases to rise. But the amount of productive capacity competing for sales is steadily growing. The rate of profit is therefore declining, and so the boom will break. Thus prosperity can never last. 'The tragedy of investment is that it causes crisis because it is useful.' He ended the argument with the poignant phrase: 'Doubtless many people will consider this theory paradoxical. But it is not the theory which is paradoxical, but its subject – the capitalist economy.'

The third point at which Kalecki tightened up the slack in the *General Theory* was in connection with the relation of prices to wages rates. Keynes relied upon a rather vague sort of Marshallian concept of competition, with short-period diminishing returns, so that an increase in employment is accompanied by a fall in real wages for workers already employed. Kalecki elaborated his original insight into the relation of monopolistic price policy to employment with the analysis of imperfect competition (then in its heyday) to produce his famous short-period theory of distribution in which the share of wages in the value of output is determined by the degree of monopoly.

This formulation has been attacked as being merely circular, since the degree of monopoly is defined as the ratio of gross margins to the value of output, and so is identically equal (on the stated assumptions) to one minus the share of wages. The apparent circularity lies only in the way the argument is set out. When by degree monopoly we mean, not the *ex-post* level of gross margins, but the price policy of firms, then, in slumpy conditions, when all plants are working under capacity, it is clearly true to say that if firms pursue a competitive policy, cutting prices in an attempt to sell more, real-wage rates will be higher, and the utilization of existing plant greater, than if they pursue a monopolistic policy, maintaining or even raising gross margins.

These amendments have been incorporated into 'Keynesian' thought; few of the present generation of 'Keynesians' stop to inquire how much they owe to Kalecki and how much indeed to Keynes. All the same, as Michał Kalecki is the first to admit, the 'Keynesian Revolution' in Western academic economics is rightly so called. For without Keynes' wide sweep, his brilliant polemic, and, above all, his position within the orthodox citadel in which he was brought up, the walls of obscurantism would have taken much longer to breach.

3

The political interpretation of the new theory for Kalecki was very different from the 'moderately conservative' implications that Keynes saw in it.

Keynes was thoroughly disgusted with latter-day capitalism for moral and aesthetic reasons, but he was by no means a socialist. After proving that building pyramids or digging holes in the ground and filling them up again would maintain effective demand and so prevent a fall in useful production, he adds, 'It is not reasonable, however, that a sensible community should be content to remain dependent on such fortuitous and often wasteful mitigations when once we understand the influences upon which effective demand depends'. He believed, or at least he allowed himself to hope, that once the new theory was understood, capitalism would reform itself. If full employment could be maintained for a generation by useful investment (without much growth of population) poverty would melt away, and the rate of interest would fall so low that unearned income would cease to be a burden upon the economy. Only honest toil and imaginative speculation would be rewarded by society. (We have seen near-full employment maintained in the Western world since the war, not by useful investment, but, less harmlessly foolish than digging holes, by piling up armaments. Keynes' analysis has proved correct, but his pleasant day-dream has turned into a nightmare.)

Kalecki saw a less agreeable vision. In an article written during the War,[6] he predicted that now that the causes of the commercial trade cycle are understood, we shall have instead a political trade cycle. The Government will make a full-employment policy by means of a budget deficit. When full employment prevails, prices will be rising and the bargaining position of workers will be strong.

'In this situation a powerful block is likely to be formed between big business and *rentier* interests, and they would probably find more than one economist to declare that the situation was manifestly unsound.' A return to 'sound finance' will create unemployment again. But as the next election looms up, the Government returns to the vote-getting policy of full employment.

'The regime of the "political business cycle" would be an artificial restoration of the position as it existed in nineteenth-century capitalism. Full employment would be reached only at the top of the boom, but slumps would be relatively mild and short lived.' This is a remarkably exact prediction of life in the Western world since the war. (But now that even a Conservative Government in England admits the need for planning, we may be entering a new phase.)

4

After the war Michał Kalecki was mainly occupied with applications of theory to the diagnosis of current developments in the capitalist world, and to the problems of planning in the socialist world. But in the new wave of theory in Cambridge concerned with long-run growth his influence is still at work.

As well as the short-run theory of distribution connected with the

[6] 'Political aspects of full employment', *Political Quarterly*, October 1943.

'degree of monopoly' his *Essays* contained a long-run theory based on the principle that 'the workers spend what they get and the capitalists get what they spend'. From this is derived the conception that the rate of profit on capital is determined by the rate of accumulation and the propensity to save of capitalists. Kaldor has called this the Keynesian theory of distribution, since it is adumbrated in the *Treatise*, but, like the *General Theory* itself, it has a separate source in Kalecki.

7

MARX, MARSHALL AND KEYNES

THREE VIEWS OF CAPITALISM

THESE three names are associated with three attitudes towards the capitalist system. Marx represents revolutionary socialism, Marshall the complacent defence of capitalism and Keynes the disillusioned defence of capitalism. Marx seeks to understand the system in order to hasten its overthrow. Marshall seeks to make it acceptable by showing it in an agreeable light. Keynes seeks to find out what has gone wrong with it in order to devise means to save it from destroying itself.

To summarize in few words a whole complex structure of ideas is necessarily to falsify by over-simplification, but so long as we recognize the danger it may be legitimate to set out in a crude way the essential contrast between the economic theories which are the bases of these three points of view.

The central contention of Marx's scheme as we find it in Volume I of *Capital* is that, under capitalism, the real wages of the workers tend to be held permanently at a low level, while the capitalists receive as profit the excess of product over wages. The capitalists, he maintains, are not much interested in a luxurious standard of life for themselves. Under pressure of competition and the greed for more and more profit they invest the surplus in more and more capital, and they strive with each other each to raise the productivity of his own workers, so that the total product is ever increasing. Over the long run, the level of real wages is more likely to fall than to rise. The share of profits in total output grows ever greater as productivity increases and the rate of accumulation rises, until the inner contradictions of the system cause it to explode and a socialist revolution brings a new system into being.

Marshall's view of wages, profits and accumulation cannot be so clearly seen, partly because he concentrates attention on the details of relative prices, the fortunes of individual firms and supply and demand of particular

Lectures delivered at the Delhi School of Economics, 1955. Published by the School as Occasional Paper No. 9.

commodities, while leaving the main outline into which these details fit extremely hazy. And partly because his whole system is based upon an unresolved conflict. The hard core of logical analysis in the *Principles* is purely static – it applies to an economy in which accumulation has come to an end – while all the problems that he discusses are connected with an economy in which wealth is growing as time goes by. In his view there is a *normal rate of profit* which represents the *supply price of capital*, but it is never clear whether this is the supply price of a certain amount of capital – the rate of profit at which there is neither growth nor decline in the total stock of capital – or whether it is the supply price of a certain rate of accumulation of capital. Profit is the *reward of waiting* – that is, of refraining from present consumption in order to enjoy future wealth – but it is never clear whether *waiting* means maintaining a stock of capital by refraining from consuming it or whether it means saving and adding to capital. It seems to mean sometimes one, sometimes the other and sometimes both at once, though Marshall is uneasily aware that they are not the same thing. This haziness makes his system impossible to describe in a clear way. But he states definitely enough that *waiting* is a factor of production and that the *real costs* of production are made up of efforts and sacrifices – efforts of the workers and sacrifices of the capitalists. The efforts are rewarded by wages and the sacrifices by profits. Taking the spirit of the argument which applies to a growing economy rather than the strict logic which requires a static economy, the capitalists invest and accumulate because profit is sufficient to counterbalance a sacrifice of present consumption. This causes total wealth to grow; the workers share in the benefit because wages rise with productivity while the supply price of capital remains more or less constant.

Keynes draws a sharp distinction between the two aspects of accumulation: saving – that is, refraining from consumption – and investing – that is, increasing the stock of productive capital. Marx's capitalists automatically save because they want to invest, so as to acquire more means of production in order to employ more labour and gain more profit. Marshall's capitalists automatically invest because they want to save, that is, to own more wealth.

Keynes points out that in a developed capitalist economy the two sides of accumulation are not automatically connected. Saving means spending less on consumption and narrowing the market for commodities, so that it reduces the profitability of investment. Investment means employing labour to produce goods which are not available to be consumed and so increases demand relatively to supply. The two sides of the process of accumulation are not linked together in such a way as to keep them in harmony. On the contrary, the very nature of private enterprise causes them to have a chronic tendency to get out of gear. At some time the economy is trying to invest more than it can; the demand for labour for consumption and investment taken together exceeds the available supply and there is inflation. But this is rare apart from war-time. Normally the reverse situation prevails; investment is less than it easily could be and potential wealth is wasted in unemployment.

Each point of view bears the stamp of the period when it was conceived. Marx formed his ideas in the grim poverty of the forties. Marshall saw capitalism blossoming in peace and prosperity in the sixties. Keynes had to find an explanation for the morbid condition of 'poverty in the midst of plenty' in the period between the wars. But each has significance for other times, for in so far as each theory is valid it throws light upon essential characteristics of the capitalist system which have always been present in it and still have to be reckoned with.

Each, moreover, is bound up with a particular political attitude to the economic system which is highly relevant to the problems that confront us today.

Marx maintained that capitalism is bound to develop in such a way as to bring about its own destruction, and urged the workers to organize themselves to hasten its overthrow. Marshall argued that, in spite of some blemishes, it is a system which promotes the good of all. Keynes shows that it has deep-seated defects which, however, he believed are capable of being remedied. Marx is making propaganda against the system. Marshall is defending it and Keynes is criticizing in order to improve it.

Economic doctrines always come to us as propaganda. This is bound up with the very nature of the subject and to pretend that it is not so in the name of 'pure science' is a very unscientific refusal to accept the facts.

The element of propaganda is inherent in the subject because it is concerned with policy. It would be of no interest if it were not. If you want a subject that is worth pursuing for its intrinsic appeal without any view to consequences you would not be attending a lecture on economics. You would be, say, doing pure mathematics or studying the behaviour of birds.

The once orthodox *laisser-faire* theory evaded the issue by trying to show that there is no problem about choosing policies. Let everyone pursue his own self-interest and free competition will ensure the maximum benefit for everyone. This obviously cannot apply where any overall organization is necessary – the banking system, the railways, the national exchequer. But even where it is technically possible to run the system on a basis of catch-as-catch-can, there is an inconsistency at the very root of the argument. In pursuing self-interest individuals find that it assists them to combine and agree not to compete. Monopolies, trade unions, political parties, arise out of the very process of competition and prevent it from being effective as a mechanism for ensuring the general good. Pure untrammelled individualism is not a practicable system, and the coherence of an economy depends upon the acceptance of limitations upon it. There must be a code of rules of the game, whether established by law or agreed by common consent. No set of rules of the game can ensure a perfect harmony of interests between all the groups in society, and any set of rules will be defended by those whom it favours and attacked by those whom different rules would suit better.

Economic theory, in its scientific aspect, is concerned with showing how a particular set of rules of the game operates, but in doing so it cannot help but make them appear in a favourable or an unfavourable light to the people who are playing the game. Even if a writer can school himself to perfect detachment he is still making propaganda, for his readers have interested views. Take, for example, a piece of pure analytical argument such as that the operation of the gold standard secures stability of the exchanges provided that money-wage rates are flexible. This means that it will not function well where Trade Unions are strong and prevent wages from falling when the preservation of the exchange rate requires that they should. This is a purely scientific statement and there is not much room for disagreement about it regarded as a description of the way the system works. But to some readers it will appear as strong propaganda against the trade unions, to others as strong propaganda against the gold standard.

This element of propaganda enters into even the most severely technical details of the subject. It cannot fail to be present when the broad issue of the operation of the system as a whole is under discussion.

Each of our three economists is concerned with describing the rules of the capitalist game, and therefore with criticizing or defending them. Marx shows that the rules are unfavourable to the workers, and for that very reason will not be tolerated for long. Marshall argues that the rules are framed in such a way as to produce the greatest possible growth of wealth, and that all classes benefit from sharing in it. Keynes is showing that the rules need to be amended so as to ensure that wealth will continue to grow.

The description and the evaluation cannot be separated, and to pretend that we are not interested in the evaluation is mere self-deception.

Marx is quite clear about his purpose. He is on the side of the workers and he makes the case against capitalism in order to encourage the workers to overthrow it.

Marshall was not openly and clearly on one side or the other in the clash of interests between workers and capitalists. His case is rather that if everyone will accept the system and not make a fuss about it, all will benefit together.

> In regard to sectional interests. Nearly all of them are changing their character and becoming increasingly plastic: but the chief change is the assimilation of the training, and consequently the capacity, of the working classes generally to those of the well-to-do. . . .
> We are indeed approaching rapidly to conditions which have no close precedent in the past, but are perhaps really more natural than those which they are supplanting – conditions under which the relations between the various industrial strata of a civilized nation are being based on reason, rather than tradition. . . . It is becoming clear that this and every other Western country can now afford to make increased sacrifices of material wealth for the purpose of raising the quality of life throughout their whole populations.[1]

Keynes is against waste and stupidity and unnecessary poverty. He is not so much interested in who gets the benefit of increased production, as in making sure that it takes place. He regards a greater equality of income as desirable but his attitude is 'moderately conservative'[2] and he holds that if only capitalism could be made to function efficiently it would be better than any alternative.

The burden of Marx's propaganda is that capitalism is pernicious and should be destroyed; of Marshall's, that it is beneficial and should be preserved; of Keynes', that it could be made fairly tolerable if people had a little sense.

Each of the three is trying to justify a particular view of the system and so is making propaganda for it. But each has sufficient faith in his own view to believe that the truth will bear him out, and each is trying to make a genuinely scientific approach to economic problems. They cannot help being propagandists, but they are scientists as well. To learn from them we first have to see what it is that they are driving at. Then we can make use of them as scientists while reserving the right to have our own opinion on questions of politics.

---

[1] *Industry and Trade*, pp. 4–5.
[2] *General Theory*, p. 377.

Ideas and Ideology

We must admit that every economic doctrine that is not trivial formalism contains political judgments. But it is the greatest possible folly to choose the doctrines that we want to accept by their political content. It is folly to reject a piece of analysis because we do not agree with the political judgment of the economist who puts it forward. Unfortunately, this approach to economics is very prevalent. The orthodox school has been largely stultified by refusing to learn from Marx. Because they do not like his politics they attend to his economics only to point out some errors in it, hoping that by refuting him on some points they will make his political doctrines harmless.

Thus the discussion of Marx has been mainly confined to criticizing the Labour Theory of Value. The labour theory is an omnibus title used to cover a number of aspects of the Marxian doctrine. One element in it is the theory of what determines the relative prices of commodities in long-run equilibrium. The orthodox economists can easily show that the view that prices are proportional to labour-time required for production is not an adequate theory of relative prices. By concentrating upon this question they succeeded in carrying the argument into a sphere where they could score a number of superficial points against the Marxists. They were not in the least interested in trying to learn from Marx or in inquiring what the relevance of these points was to the main issue.

In this they were very much helped by the Marxists, who instead of replying to all the intricate arguments about the theory of prices: so what? allowed themselves to be drawn into a number of sophistries in an endeavour to defend Marx even when he was not defensible.

Under the dust of all this controversy about inessentials the most valuable parts of Marx's theory was lost to sight by both parties.

To take one instance, the schema for expanding reproduction provide a very simple and quite indispensable approach to the problem of saving and investment and the balance between production of capital goods and demand for consumer goods. It was rediscovered and made the basis for the treatment of Keynes' problem by Kalecki and reinvented by Harrod and Domar as the basis for the theory of long-run development. If Marx had been studied as a serious economist, instead of being treated on the one hand as an infallible oracle and on the other as a butt for cheap sarcasm, it would have saved us all a great deal of time.

The Marxists have been just as bad as the orthodox economists in refusing to learn from those whose political views they dislike. Feeling on the defensive, they regard it as a kind of treachery to admit any point made by Marx's critics, and insist upon defending him in every detail, so that they will not even concede to Marshall that the Labour Theory of Value is a crude account of the determination of relative prices which requires to be amended and elaborated in certain respects.

This inflexibility is particularly marked in their reaction to Keynes. Because they reject the idea that capitalism can be rescued from crises by economic measures carried out by governments they deny the logic of Keynes' argument. They point out that Keynes is subject to an illusion when he appeals to the State as though it were a benevolent impartial arbiter which can be relied upon to do the best for everyone if only it can be made to understand how to set about it. They maintain that the State is an organ of the capitalists and that therefore it is vain to look to it to carry out policies to prevent unemployment for the benefit of the workers.

There is much force in the first part of the argument but the second is a *non sequitur*. Capitalists do not like having crises. Unemployment is accompanied by losses. And nowadays they have a very strong reason to dislike unemployment itself, for it provides dangerous ammunition to their political enemies. In preventing unemployment the governments would be doing for them something that they want done but cannot do for themselves.

Marx in his day had a far more penetrating and subtle insight into the workings of the system than his modern followers. In discussing the legal limitation of the working day he showed how each individual capitalist had an interest in preventing legislation that would limit his power to exploit his workers. Yet collectively it favoured their interests, for excessive exploitation ruins the labour force on which they all depend. Thus, under the guise of resisting the demand for labour legislation put forward by the workers and the humanitarians, they allowed it to be carried out.

In the same way, while declaiming against Keynesian policies as an illegitimate interference with the proper functions of private enterprise, they in fact rely upon it to save them from themselves.

The foolishness of rejecting economic analysis because of the political doctrines with which it is associated is shown by the fact that, as it happens, the aspect of capitalism which each of the great economists illuminates provides the basis for political conclusions the opposite of his own.

The best defence of capitalism as an economic system can be made on the basis of Marx's analysis. This was realized by Schumpeter, and recently carried a stage further by his disciple Professor Galbraith.[3] They provide a

[3] *American Capitalism.*

tough, cynical and intelligent defence of the capitalist rules of the game which is far more effective than the soft, sophistical special pleading of the orthodox school.

Marx emphasizes the manner in which the capitalist rules of the game foster accumulation and technical progress. His capitalists are not interested in luxurious living. They exploit labour in order to accumulate, and they increase productivity in order to have a greater surplus to invest. 'The productiveness of labour is made to ripen as if in a hot-house.' They prevent the workers from receiving any share in the increased production, for if the workers consumed more there would be less accumulation and the growth of total wealth would be impeded.

This provides an account of the function of exploitation. It explains, incidentally, why in a socialist economy which is undertaking rapid development the standard of life rises at first very slowly, and why it is necessary, when private profit does not create a gap between wages and prices, for a gap to be created by taxation in order to provide the funds for accumulation.

When Keynes was describing the flourishing capitalism of the pre-1914 world, before he became preoccupied with the problem of unemployment, he set out an analysis which is essentially the same as that of Marx.

Europe was so organized socially and economically as to secure the maximum accumulation of capital. While there was some continuous improvement in the daily conditions of life of the mass of the population, Society was so framed as to throw a great part of the increased income into the control of the class least likely to consume it. The new rich of the nineteenth century were not brought up to large expenditures, and preferred the power which investment gave them to the pleasures of immediate consumption. In fact, it was precisely the *inequality* of the distribution of wealth which made possible those vast accumulations of fixed wealth and of capital improvements which distinguished that age from all others. Herein lay, in fact, the main justification of the Capitalist System. If the rich had spent their new wealth on their own enjoyments, the world would long ago have found such a régime intolerable. But like bees they saved and accumulated, not less to the advantage of the whole community because they themselves held narrower ends in prospect.

The immense accumulations of fixed capital which, to the great benefit of mankind, were built up during the half-century before the war, could never have come about in a Society where wealth was divided equitably. The railways of the world, which that age built as a monument to posterity, were, not less than the Pyramids of Egypt, the work of labour which was not free to consume in immediate enjoyment the full equivalent of its efforts.

. . . . . .

In writing thus I do not necessarily disparage the practices of that generation. In the unconscious recesses of its being Society knew what it was about. The cake was really very small in proportion to the appetites of consumption, and no one, if it were shared all round, would be much the better off by the cutting of it. Society was working not for the small pleasures of today but for the future security and improvement of the race – in fact for 'progress'.[4]

There is no disagreement here with Marx's analysis, though the purpose of the argument is to explain why capitalism survived rather than to show why it ought to be overthrown.

In order to make the case against capitalism it is necessary to turn to Marshall's argument. It is true that, in the main, profit is desired for the purpose of accumulation, but that is not the whole truth. Profit is also the basis for consumption by capitalists. They have to be 'rewarded for waiting' and they will not save, or even preserve wealth accumulated in the past, unless they are fattened up to a certain point by a high standard of life for themselves. For society to pay for saving by permitting a great inequality in consumption is a very wasteful and expensive method of getting the job done. It would be far more economical to dispossess the capitalists, put past accumulated wealth into the safekeeping of society where no one can get at it, to consume property 'in immediate gratification' at the expense of the future, and to decide the rate of accumulation to be carried out on a general view of the development of the economy as a whole rather than according to the whims of individuals.

Marshall's analysis can be used to show why socialism is necessary. According to Marshall's own argument, a greater real benefit is gained from a given income if it is equally distributed than if some individuals are enjoying such a luxurious standard of life that saving is no effort to them, while others are struggling to survive. If the object of production is to provide for the welfare of human beings it is very uneconomic to have the fruits of a given rate of production unequally distributed. But if incomes are equally distributed there would not be enough saving done to permit development. In order to be able to have a more economic distribution of

4 *Economic Consequences of the Peace*, pp. 18–21.

income it is necessary for saving to be collective, and if the saving is done collectively, capital must be owned collectively.

If the capitalists fully lived up to Marx's description and really invested the whole surplus there would be no need for socialism. It is the rentier aspect of profit, as a source of private wealth, which Marshall emphasizes, that makes the strongest case for socialism; and the entrepreneur aspect of profit as the source of accumulation, which Marx emphasizes, that makes the strongest case for capitalism.

Keynes' analysis also provides a case for the opposite political conclusions. He shows, first that there is a natural tendency for an advanced capitalist economy to run into chronic stagnation, with permanent unemployment, and that it is by its very nature highly unstable. He argues that some measure of interference with the pure private-enterprise system is necessary to keep it running efficiently. In particular, governments must undertake a sufficient amount of investment to make up for the failure of private capitalists to keep investment continuously at the desirable level. But so long as a large part of investment is left in private hands it is necessary that the interference must not lead to a state of affairs in which the private section invests less just because governments are investing more. A high rate of accumulation necessarily leads to a decline in the profitability of further investment. It follows that, to keep up the level of demand for labour, wasteful investment is more effective than useful investment. 'Two pyramids, two masses for the dead, are twice as good as one; but not so two railways from London to York.'[5]

> In so far as millionaires find their satisfaction in building mighty mansions to contain their bodies when alive and pyramids to shelter them after death, or, repenting of their sins, erect cathedrals and endow monasteries or foreign missions, the day when abundance of capital will interfere with abundance of output may be postponed. 'To dig holes in the ground', paid for out of savings, will increase, not only employment, but the real national dividend of useful goods and services.[6]

Keynes' own purpose was to illustrate the paradoxes of capitalism and to plead for a rational control over investment, but the effect of his argument is to explain why it is that modern capitalism flourishes when governments are making investments in armaments. Instead of being a ruinous burden on a highly developed economy, the apparent economic waste of armaments is

[5] *General Theory*, p. 131.
[6] Ibid., p. 220.

really a method of maintaining prosperity. It follows that if there were no need for armaments it would be necessary to make useful investments and so to encroach upon the power and independence of the capitalists. The capitalists therefore prefer a situation in which armaments do seem necessary. This cure, most of us would agree, is even worse than the disease, and on the basis of Keynes' reasoning it can be argued that capitalism will not save itself from the tendency to unemployment by any other means.

Marx's analysis of capitalism shows its strong points, although his purpose was to attack it. Marshall's argument inadvertently shows the wastefulness of capitalism, although he meant to recommend it. Keynes in showing the need for remedies to the defects of capitalism also shows how dangerous the remedies may be.

To learn from the economists regarded as scientists it is necessary to separate what is valid in their description of the system from the propaganda that they make, overtly or unconsciously, each for his own ideology. The best way to separate out scientific ideas from ideology is to stand the ideology on its head and see how the ideas look the other way up. If they disintegrate with the ideology, they have no validity of their own. If they still make sense as a description of reality, then there is something to be learned from them, whether we like the ideology or not.

THE GREAT CONTRADICTIONS

It is foolish to refuse to learn from the ideas of an economist whose ideology we dislike. It is equally unwise to rely upon the theories of one whose ideology we approve.

An economic theory at best is only an hypothesis. It does not tell us what is the case. It suggests a possible explanation of some phenomenon and it cannot be accepted as correct until it has been tested by an appeal to the facts. The business of the disciples of a great economist is not to propagate his doctrines but to test his hypotheses. If the facts turn out not to fit an hypothesis, the hypothesis must be rejected. It is of no use to choose an hypothesis by the colour of the economist who puts it forward and then to reject the facts that do not agree with it.

Marx's hypothesis, in the simple form of his theory that he worked out and published in Volume I of *Capital* is that, taking it by and large, with exceptions and qualifications, it is to be expected that under capitalism real wages will remain more or less constant. He has two grounds for this point of view. One is purely metaphysical. Everything exchanges at its value; that is, for the product of an amount of labour-time equal to that which is required to produce it.

> The value of labour-power is determined, as in the case of every other commodity, by the labour-time necessary for the production, and consequently also the reproduction, of this special article. So far as it has value, it represents no more than a definite quantity of the average labour of society incorporated in it.[7]

This is a metaphysical approach to the problem of the determination of wages. When we ask *why* do you believe that labour power exchanges for its value? he replies: Everything that is exchanged is exchanged for its value.

But he also has an analytical answer. The workers are weak and unorganized. Employers can make wages as low as they please subject to the technical necessity to keep the labour force in being. Thus wages are set at the conventional subsistence level. When an excess demand for labour due to rapid accumulation tends to drive them up, or when trade unions face the employers with bargaining power equal to their own and extort concessions from them, the system reacts in such a way as to bring wages down again. First, the mere fact that wages are higher means that there is less accumulation. When population is growing, a slowing up in accumulation causes the demand for labour to lag behind the supply. Secondly, to overcome a threatening scarcity of manpower, labour-saving inventions are made; output per head rises and a given amount of capital employs less labour. The consequent unemployment undermines the bargaining power of the workers. Thus the real-wage rate can never for long be maintained much above the level at which it was first established 'when the class of free labourers was formed'; that is, when capitalism first took over from peasant and artisan production.

Now, by and large, this hypothesis has failed to be verified. In fact, in the developed capitalist economies the level of wages has risen. The rise in productivity has been sufficient to permit both accumulation *and* a rise in the standard of life of the workers.

Lenin tried to explain this away, and latter-day Marxists have a stock answer which they always produce when challenged on this point. The rise in wages, they say, applies only to the imperialist countries. Profits have been maintained by colonial exploitation and the capitalists could therefore indulge the workers at home by allowing them higher wages. They are pampered 'palace slaves' sharing in the exploitation of the colonial workers.

This argument smacks of special pleading – an attempt to force the facts

[7] *Capital* (The Modern Library), p. 189.

to fit the hypothesis instead of reconsidering the hypothesis in the light of facts. The argument that the high rate of profit obtainable from exploiting low-wage labour in the colonies raises home wages does not seem very plausible. Capitalists expect to get more or less the same rate of profit wherever they invest; if profits abroad are high they do less investment at home. The demand for labour at home is therefore reduced, not increased, by the existence of cheap labour abroad.

There is no doubt that home labour in the imperialist countries has gained from colonial exploitation, but by a different mechanism. Low colonial wages have helped to make raw materials cheap and so have made the terms of trade favourable to the industrial nations. No doubt also some advantage to the workers spills over from the wealth of capitalists who have made fortunes abroad, through their taxable capacity, charity and the demand for services. But it would be absurd to suppose that more than a small fraction of the rise in the standard of life of the industrial workers, especially in America, can be accounted for in this way. Wages have risen because of the great technical productivity which has been fostered by capitalism and because the system operates in such a way as to keep the shares of wages in the growing total of production more or less constant.

The fact of rising real wages requires a very important modification of the central thesis of Marx's theory. It has turned out not to be the case that increasing misery drives the workers to rebellion. The capitalists have succeeded in buying them off by giving them a share in the product which capitalism brings into being. Moreover, the workers become saturated with capitalist ideology and look at life in terms of capitalist values. They have developed a state of mind in which they do not want the rules of the game to be altered. It is very noticeable today that Marxism flourishes best in countries where capitalism is least successful.

Marx himself became aware that this was going on during his own lifetime.

> The English proletarian movement in its old traditional Chartist form must perish completely before it can develop itself in a new form, capable of life. And yet one cannot foresee what this new form will look like. For the rest, it seems to me that [the new policy] is really bound up with the fact that the English proletariat is becoming more and more bourgeois, so that this most bourgeois of all nations is apparently aiming ultimately at the possession of a bourgeois aristocracy and a bourgeois proletariat as well as a bourgeoisie.[8]

[8] *Marx, Engels: Selected Correspondence* (Lawrence & Wishart), p. 115.

This is even more true of modern America than it was of England in the sixties.

Marx never succeeded in completing his great plan. The last two volumes of *Capital* are compilations from his notes, not fully worked out and to some extent confused and inconsistent. It has often been suggested that the reason why Marx was held up was because he could not find a way through the contradiction between his hypothesis and the facts around him.

The contradiction is much more striking today. It is now clear that the revolutionary transition to socialism does not come in the advanced capitalist nations, but in the most backward. It is easy enough to say, being wise after the event, that it is natural to expect 'the weakest link in the chain to break'. But there is much more in it than that. Current experience suggests that socialism is not a stage beyond capitalism but a substitute for it – a means by which the nations which did not share in the Industrial Revolution can imitate its technical achievements; a means to achieve rapid accumulation under a different set of rules of the game. This makes a drastic reconsideration of Marx's central hypothesis necessary. There is much to be learned from Marx's analysis of capitalism, but if we simply swallow it whole we are liable to be seriously misled.

On the question of the standard of life, Marshall's theory stands the test of experience better than Marx's. But Marshall's theory also contained a fatal flaw. The unemployment of the inter-war period revealed the crack in his system which Keynes penetrated in order to explode it.

Marshall, like Marx, failed to complete the great three-volume work that he projected.[9] Like Marx, he himself saw the weak spot in his own theory. His whole argument depends upon the beneficial effect of accumulation. But abstaining from present consumption in order to save is not the same thing as adding to the stock of capital. Marshall was aware of this flaw in his system, and anticipated Keynes' exposure of it.

> But though men have the power to purchase they may not choose to use it. For when confidence has been shaken by failures, capital cannot be got to start new companies or extend old ones. . . . Other trades, finding a poor market for their goods, produce less; they earn less, and therefore they buy less: the diminution of the demand for their wares makes them demand less of other trades. Thus commercial disorganization spreads: the disorganization of one trade throws others out of gear, and they react on it and increase its disorganization.

[9] He did, indeed, publish *Money, Credit and Commerce*, but it is a pale ghost of the third volume of the *Principles* which he orginally intended it to be.

The chief cause of the evil is a want of confidence. The greater part of it would be removed almost in an instant if confidence could return, touch all industries with her magic wand and make them continue their production and their demand for the wares of others. . . . But the revival of industry comes about through the gradual and often simultaneous growth of confidence among many various trades; it begins as soon as traders think that prices will not continue to fall: and with a revival of industry prices rise.[10]

Here is the germ of the theory to account for crises and chronic stagnation with which Keynes exploded Marshall. Perhaps Marshall, like Marx, was frustrated by seeing the contradiction in his theory without being able to see a way through it.

The inadequacy of Keynes' doctrine does not lie in an inconsistency in the theory but in its narrow range. Keynes is discussing the problem of unemployment in a developed economy where there is productive capacity already in existence and all that is needed is a profitable market for its potential product. He is trying to find a cure for the diseases that beset wealthy nations. His argument throws little direct light on the problems of a country which suffers from a lack of productive capacity or on the kind of unemployment (which Marx deals with) that arises from having too little capital to be able to offer work to all available labour. It is of no use to apply Keynes' prescriptions in situations which they do not suit. Where lack of productive capacity is the problem, merely generating demand only leads to inflation, and expenditure for its own sake – building pyramids instead of railways – is clearly not what the situation demands.

In short, no economic theory gives us ready-made answers. Any theory that we follow blindly will lead us astray. To make good use of an economic theory we must first sort out the relations of the propagandist and the scientific elements in it, then by checking with experience, see how far the scientific element appears convincing, and finally recombine it with our own political views. The purpose of studying economics is not to acquire a set of ready-made answers to economic questions, but to learn how to avoid being deceived by economists.

[10] *Principles*, pp. 710–11. (8th Edition, original.)

8

THE PRODUCTION FUNCTION AND THE THEORY OF CAPITAL

INTRODUCTION

THE dominance in neo-classical economic teaching of the concept of a production function, in which the relative prices of the factors of production are exhibited as a function of the ratio in which they are employed in a given state of technical knowledge, has had an enervating effect upon the development of the subject, for by concentrating upon the question of the proportions of factors it has distracted attention from the more difficult but more rewarding questions of the influences governing the supplies of the factors and of the causes and consequences of changes in technical knowledge.

Moreover, the production function has been a powerful instrument of miseducation. The student of economic theory is taught to write $O = f(L, C)$ where L is a quantity of labour, C a quantity of capital and O a rate of output of commodities.[1] He is instructed to assume all workers alike, and to measure L in man-hours of labour; he is told something about the index-number problem involved in choosing a unit of output; and then he is hurried on to the next question, in the hope that he will forget to ask in what units C is measured. Before ever he does ask, he has become a professor, and so sloppy habits of thought are handed on from one generation to the next.

The question is certainly not an easy one to answer. The capital in existence at any moment may be treated simply as 'part of the environment in which labour works'.[2] We then have a production function in terms of labour alone. This is the right procedure for the short period within which

[1] Throughout this essay we shall be abstracting from land as a factor of production, so we will not bother the student with it.

[2] Keynes, *General Theory*, p. 214.

Part of an article published in the *Review of Economic Studies*, 1953–4, Vol. XXI (2), No. 55. Excisions have entailed a few words of alteration in the original text.

the supply of concrete capital goods does not alter, but outside the short period it is a very weak line to take, for it means that we cannot distinguish a change in the stock of capital (which can be made over the long run by accumulation) from a change in the weather (an act of God).

We may look upon a stock of capital as the specific list of all the goods in existence at any moment (including work-in-progress in the pipe-lines of production). But this again is of no use outside the strict bounds of the short period, for any change in the ratio of capital to labour involves a reorganization of methods of production and requires a change in the shapes, sizes and specifications of many or all the goods appearing in the original list.[3]

As soon as we leave the short period, however, a host of difficulties appear. Should capital be valued according to its future earning power or its past costs?

When we know the future expected rate of output associated with a certain capital good, and expected future prices and costs, then, if we are given a rate of interest, we can value the capital good as a discounted stream of future profit which it will earn. But to do so, we have to begin by taking the rate of interest as given, whereas the main purpose of the production function is to show how wages and the rate of interest (regarded as the wages of capital) are determined by technical conditions and the factor ratio.

Are we then to value capital goods by their cost of production? Clearly money cost of production is neither here nor there unless we can specify the purchasing power of money, but we may cost the capital goods in terms of wage units; that is, in effect, to measure their cost in terms of a unit of standard labour.

To treat capital as a quantity of labour-time expended in the past is congenial to the production-function point of view, for it corresponds to the essential nature of capital regarded as a factor of production. Investment consists, in essence, in employing labour now in a way which will yield its fruits in the future while saving is making current products available for the workers to consume in the meantime; and the productiveness of capital consists in the fact that a unit of labour that was expended at a certain time in the past is more valuable today than a unit expended today, because its fruits are already ripe.

---

[3] In Professor Robertson's example, when a tenth man joins nine who are digging a hole, nine more expensive spades are turned into nine cheaper spades and a bucket to fetch beer. (*Economic Fragments*, p. 47.)

But here we encounter a fundamental difficulty which lies at the root of the whole problem of capital. A unit of labour is never expended in a pure form. All work is done with the assistance of goods of some kind or another. When Adam delved and Eve span there were evidently a spade and a spindle already in existence. The cost of capital includes the cost of capital goods, and since they must be constructed before they can be used, part of the cost of capital is interest over the period of time between the moment when work was done in constructing capital goods and the time when they are producing a stream of output. This is not just a consequence of capitalism, for equally in a socialist society a unit of labour, expended today, which will yield a product in five years' time, is not the same thing as a unit which will yield a product tomorrow.

Finally, even if it were possible to measure capital simply in terms of labour-time, we still should not have answered the question: Of what units is C composed? When we are discussing accumulation, it is natural to think of capital as measured in terms of product. The process of accumulation consists in refraining from consuming current output in order to add to the stock of wealth. But when we consider what addition to productive resources a given amount of accumulation makes, we must measure capital in labour units, for the addition to the stock of productive equipment made by adding an increment of capital depends upon how much work is done in constructing it, not upon the cost, in terms of final product, of an hour's labour. Thus, as we move from one point on a production function to another, measuring capital in terms of product, we have to know the product-wage rate in order to see the effect upon production of changing the ratio of capital to labour. Or if we measure in labour units, we have to know the product-wage in order to see how much accumulation would be required to produce a given increment of capital. But the wage rate alters with the ratio of the factors: one symbol, C, cannot stand both for a quantity of product and a quantity of labour-time.

All the same, the problem which the production function professes to analyse, although it has been too much puffed up by the attention paid to it, is a genuine problem. Today, in country Alpha, a length of roadway is being cleared by a few men with bulldozers; in Beta a road (of near enough the same quality) is being made by some hundreds of men with picks and ox-carts. In Gamma thousands of men are working with wooden shovels and little baskets to remove the soil. When all possible allowances have been made for differences in national character and climate, and for differences in the state of knowledge, it seems pretty clear that the main reason for this state of affairs is that capital in some sense is more plentiful in

Alpha than in Gamma. Looked at from the point of view of an individual capitalist, it would not pay to use Alpha methods in Gamma (even if unlimited finance were available) at the rate of interest which is ruling, and looked at from the point of view of society, it would need a prodigious effort of accumulation to raise all the labour available in Gamma even to the Beta level of technique. The problem is a real one. We cannot abandon the production function without an effort to rescue the element of common sense that has been entangled in it.

THE QUANTITY OF CAPITAL

'Capital' is not what capital is called, it is what its name is called. The capital goods in existence at a moment of time are all the goods in existence at that moment. It is not all the things in existence. It includes neither a rubbish heap nor Mont Blanc. The characteristic by which 'goods' are specified is that they have value; that is, purchasing power over each other. Thus, in country Alpha an empty petrol tin is not a 'good', whereas in Gamma, where old tins are a source of valuable industrial raw material, it is.

The list of goods is quite specific. It is so many actual particular objects, called blast furnaces, overcoats, etc., etc. Goods grouped under the same name differ from each other in the details of their physical specifications and these must not be overlooked. Differences in their ages are also important. A blast furnace twenty years old is not equivalent to a brand new one of the same specification in other respects, nor is an egg twenty days old equivalent to a brand new one. There is another relevant characteristic of the goods. An overcoat requires one body to wear it, and an egg one mouth to eat it. Without one body, or one mouth, they are useless, and two bodies or mouths (at a given moment of time) cannot share in using them. But a blast furnace can be used by a certain range of numbers of bodies to turn iron ore into iron. Therefore the description of a blast furnace includes an account of its rate of output as a function of the number of bodies operating it. (When long-period equilibrium prevails, the number of bodies actually working each piece of equipment is the number which is technically most appropriate to it.)

There is another aspect of the goods which is quite different. Of two overcoats, completely similar in all the above respects, one is on the body of Mrs. Jones, who is purring with inward delight at her fine appearance. Another is on the body of Mrs. Snooks, who is grizzling because, her husband's income being what it is, she is obliged to buy mass-produced clothes. In what follows we shall not discuss this aspect of goods at all. We take it that an overcoat (Mark IV) is an overcoat (Mark IV), and no nonsense.

Now, this enormous who's who of individual goods is not a thing that we can handle at all easily. To express it as a *quantity* of goods we have to evaluate the items of which it is composed. We can evaluate the goods in terms of the real cost of producing them – that is, the work and the formerly existing goods required to make them, or in terms of their value expressed in some unit of purchasing power; or we can evaluate them according to their productivity – that is, what the stock of goods will become in the future if work is done in conjunction with it.

In a position of equilibrium all three evaluations yield equivalent results; there is a quantity which can be translated from one number to another by changing the unit. This is the definition of equilibrium. It entails that there have been no events over the relevant period of past time which have disturbed the relation between the various valuations of a given stock of goods, and that the human beings in the situation are expecting the future to be just like the past – entirely devoid of such disturbing events. Then the rate of profit ruling today is the rate which was expected to rule today when the decision to invest in any capital good now extant was made, and the expected future receipts, capitalized at the current rate of profit, are equal to the cost of the capital goods which are expected to produce them.

When an unexpected event occurs, the three ways of evaluating the stock of goods part company and no amount of juggling with units will bring them together again.

We are accustomed to talk of the rate of profit on capital earned by a business as though profits and capital were both sums of money. Capital when it consists of as yet uninvested finance is a sum of money, and the net receipts of a business are sums of money. But the two never co-exist in time. While the capital is a sum of money, the profits are not yet being earned. When the profits (quasi-rents) are being earned, the capital has ceased to be money and become a plant. All sorts of things may happen which cause the value of the plant to diverge from its original cost. When an event has occurred, say a fall in prices, which was not foreseen when investment in the plant was made, how do we regard the capital represented by the plant?

The man of deeds, who has decisions to make, is considering how future prospects have altered. He is concerned with new finance or accrued amortization funds, which he must decide how to use. He cannot do anything about the plant (unless the situation is so desperate that he decides to scrap it). He is not particularly interested (except when he has to make out a case before a Royal Commission) in how the man of words, who is measuring capital, chooses to value the plant.[4]

The man of words has a wide choice of possible methods of evaluation, but none of them is very satisfactory. First, capital may be conceived of as consisting either in the cost or in the value of the plant. If cost is the measure, should money cost actually incurred be reckoned? It is only of historical interest, for the purchasing power of money has since changed. Is the money cost to be deflated? Then by what index? Or is capital to be measured at current replacement cost? The situation may be such that no one in his senses would build a plant like this one if he were to build now. Replacement cost may be purely academic. But even if the plant is, in fact, due to be replaced by a replica of itself at some future date, we still have to ask what proportion of the value of a brand new plant is represented by this elderly plant? And the answer to that question involves future earnings, not cost alone.

If the capital is to be measured by value, how do we decide what the present value of the plant is? The price at which it could be sold as an integral whole has not much significance, as the market for such transactions is narrow. To take its price on the Stock Exchange (if it is quoted) is to go before a tribunal whose credentials are dubious. If the capital-measurer makes his own judgment, he takes what he regards as likely to be the future earnings of the plant and discounts them at what he regards as the right rate of interest for the purpose, thus triumphantly showing that the most probable rate of profit on the capital invested in the plant is equal to the most appropriate rate of interest.

All these puzzles arise because there is a gap in time between investing money capital and receiving money profits, and in that gap events may occur which alter the value of money.

To abstract from uncertainty means to postulate that no such events occur, so that the *ex ante* expectations which govern the actions of the man of deeds are never out of gear with the *ex-post* experience which governs the pronouncements of the man of words, and to say that equilibrium obtains is to say that no such events have occurred for some time, or are thought liable to occur in the future.

The ambiguity of the conception of a quantity of capital is connected with a profound methodological error, which makes the major part of neo-classical doctrine spurious.

The neo-classical economist thinks of a position of equilibrium as a

[4]   'A man of words but not of deeds
            Is like a garden full of weeds.'
This is sadly true of the theory of capital.

position towards which an economy is tending to move as time goes by. But it is impossible for a system to *get into* a position of equilibrium, for the very nature of equilibrium is that the system is already in it, and has been in it for a certain length of past time.

Time is unlike space in two very striking respects. In space, bodies moving from A to B may pass bodies moving from B to A, but in time the strictest possible rule of one-way traffic is always in force. And in space the distance from A to B is of the same order of magnitude (whatever allowance you like to make for the Trade Winds) as the distance from B to A; but in time the distance from today to tomorrow is twenty-four hours, while the distance from today to yesterday is infinite, as the poets have often remarked. Therefore a space metaphor applied to time is a very tricky knife to handle, and the concept of equilibrium often cuts the arm that wields it.

When an event has occurred we are thrown back upon the who's who of goods in existence, and the 'quantity of capital' ceases to have any other meaning. Then only that part of the theory of value which treats of the short period, in which the physical stock of capital equipment is given, has any application.

LONG–PERIOD EQUILIBRIUM

One notion of equilibrium is that it is reached (with a constant labour force) when the stock of capital and the rate of profit are such that there is no motive for further accumulation. This is associated with the idea of an ultimate thorough-going stationary state,[5] in which the rate of profit is equal to the 'supply price of waiting'. In this situation an accidental increase in the stock of capital above the equilibrium quantity would depress the rate of profit below this supply price, and cause the additional capital to be consumed; while any reduction would raise the rate of profit, and cause the deficiency to be made good. Equilibrium prevails when the stock of capital is such that the rate of profit is equal to the supply price of that quantity of capital.

But this notion is a very treacherous one. Why should the supply price of waiting be assumed positive? In Adam Smith's forest there was no property in capital and no profit (the means of production, wild deer and beavers, were plentiful and unappropriated). But there might still be waiting and interest. Suppose that some hunters wish to consume more than their kill, and others wish to carry consuming power into the future. Then the latter could lend to the former today, out of today's catch, against a

[5] Pigou, *The Economics of Stationary States*.

promise of repayment in the future. The rate of interest (excess of repayment over original loan) would settle at the level which equated supply and demand for loans. Whether it was positive or negative would depend upon whether spendthrifts or prudent family men happened to predominate in the community. There is no *a priori* presumption in favour of a positive rate. Thus, the rate of interest cannot be accounted for as the 'cost of waiting'.

The reason why there is always a demand for loans at a positive rate of interest, in an economy where there is property in the means of production and means of production are scarce, is that finance expended now can be used to employ labour in productive processes which will yield a surplus in the future over costs of production. Interest is positive because profits are positive (though at the same time the cost and difficulty of obtaining finance play a part in keeping productive equipment scarce, and so contribute to maintaining the level of profits).

Where the 'supply price of waiting' is very low or negative, the ultimate stationary equilibrium cannot be reached until the rate of profit has fallen equally low, capital has ceased to be scarce and capitalism has ceased to be capitalism. Therefore this type of equilibrium is not worth discussing.

The other way of approaching the question is simply to postulate that the stock of capital in existence at any moment is the amount that has been accumulated up to date, and that the reason why it is not larger is that it takes time to grow. At any moment, on this view, there is a certain stock of capital in existence. If the rate of profit and the desire to own more wealth are such as to induce accumulation, the stock of capital is growing and, provided that labour is available or population growing, the system may be in process of expanding without any disturbance to the conditions of equilibrium. (If two snapshots were taken of the economy at two different dates, the stock of capital, the amount of employment and the rate of output would all be larger, in the second photograph, by a certain percentage, but there would be no other difference.) If the stock of capital is being kept constant over time, that is merely a special case in which the rate of accumulation happens to be zero. (The two snapshots would then be indistinguishable.)

In the internal structure of the economy conditions of long-period equilibrium may then be assumed to prevail. Each type of product sells at its normal long-run supply price. For any one type of commodity, profit, at the rate ruling in the system as a whole on the cost of capital equipment engaged in producing it, is part of the long-run supply price of the commodity, for no commodity will continue to be produced unless capital invested for the purpose of producing it yields at least the same rate of profit as the rest. (It is assumed that capitalists are free to move from one line of production to another.) Thus the 'costs of production' which determine supply price consist of wages and profits. In this context the notion of a quantity of capital presents no difficulty, for, to any one capitalist, capital is a quantity of value, or generalized purchasing power, and, in a given equilibrium situation, a unit of any commodity can be used as a measure of purchasing power.

Since the system is in equilibrium in all its parts, the ruling rate of profit is being obtained on capital which is being used to produce capital goods, and enters into their 'cost of production'. Profit on that part of the cost of capital represented by this profit is then a component of the 'cost of production' of final output. A capitalist who buys a machine ready made pays a price for it which includes profit to the capitalist who sells it. The profit a capitalist who has the machine built in his own workshops will expect to receive, from sales of the final output, includes profit on the interest (at a notional rate equal to the ruling rate of profit) on the cost of having the machine built reckoned over the period of construction. For when he builds the machine himself he has a longer waiting period between starting to invest and receiving the first profit. If he could not earn profit on the notional interest cost, he would prefer to make an investment where there was a shorter waiting period, so that he could receive actual profit earlier. The actual profit he could plough into investment; thus acquiring (over the same waiting period) the same quantity of capital as in the case where he builds the machine for himself. (He would also have the advantage that he could change his mind and consume the profit, whereas in the first case he is committed to the whole scheme of investment once he begins.) Thus, investments with a long gestation period will not be made unless they are expected to yield a profit on the element of capital cost represented by compound interest over the gestation period (if there were uncertainty, they would have to be expected to yield more, to compensate for the greater rigidity of the investment plan).

We need not go back to Adam to search for the first pure unit of labour that contributed to the construction of existing equipment. The capital goods in being today have mutually contributed to producing each other, and each is assumed to have received the appropriate amount of profit for doing so.

So much for the supply price of an item of new equipment. How are we to reckon the supply price of part-worn equipment? Investment in new equipment is not made unless its gross earnings (excess of output over wages bill in terms of output) are expected to be sufficient to amortize the investment over its working life, allowing for interest at the ruling rate on accrued amortization funds, as well as providing profit at the ruling rate. The supply price of an equipment which has been working for a certain time may be regarded as its initial cost accumulated up to date at compound interest, *minus* its gross earnings also accumulated from the dates at which they accrued up to the present, for this corresponds to the expectations which induced capitalists in the past to make the investment concened.

Since initial cost is incurred at the beginning, and earnings accrue over time, the element of interest on cost in the above calculation exceeds the element of interest on earnings. Thus when an equipment has yielded a quarter of its expected total earnings, its supply price, in this sense, is somewhat more than three-quarters of its initial cost; half-way through, somewhat more than half its initial cost, and so forth, the difference at any moment being larger the higher the rate of interest. Over its life the accumulated interest on its earnings, so to say, catches up upon the accumulated interest on its cost, so that at the end of its life it is fully paid off and its supply price (abstracting from scrap value) has fallen to zero.

The value of an equipment depends upon its expected future earnings. It may be regarded as future earnings discounted back to the present at a rate corresponding to the ruling rate of interest. In equilibrium conditions the supply price (in the above sense) and the value of an equipment are equal at all stages of its life.[6]

Equilibrium requires that the stock of items of equipment operated by all the capitalists producing a particular commodity is continuously being maintained. This entails that the age composition of the stock of equipment is such that the amortization funds provided by the stock as a whole are being continuously spent on replacements. When the stock of equipment is in balance there is no need to inquire whether a particular worker is occupied in producing final output or in replacing plant. The whole of a given labour force is producing a stream of final output and at the same time maintaining the stock of equipment for future production. Nor is it necessary to inquire what book-keeping methods are used in reckoning

---

[6] The equalization of the value of two annuities at any point of time entails their equalization at any other point of time. If the cost of a new machine is equal, at the moment when it is brand new, to the discounted value of its expected gross earnings, it follows that, at any later point of time, the accumulated value of the original cost and gross earnings up to date will, if expectations have been proved correct up to date and are unaffected for the future, be equal to the present value of the remaining gross earnings expected over the future. Cf. Wicksell, 'Real capital and interest', *Lectures* (English edition), Vol. I, p. 276.

amortization quotas. These affect the relations between individual capitalists, but cancel out for the group as a whole.

In equilibrium the age composition of the stock of equipment is stable, but the total stock may be in course of expanding. The average age of the plants making up a balanced stock of stable age composition varies with the length of life of individual plants. If the total stock is remaining constant over time, the average age is equal to half the length of life. If the stock has been growing, the proportion of younger plants is greater and average age is less than half the life span. (There is an exact analogy with the age composition of a stable population.)

The amount of capital embodied in a stock of equipment is the sum of the supply prices (reckoned as above) of the plants of which it is composed, and the ratio of the amount of capital to the sum of the costs of the plants when each was brand new is higher the greater the rate of interest.[7]

Equilibrium requires that the rate of profit ruling today was expected to be ruling today when investment in any plant now extant was made, and the expectation of future profits obtaining today was expected to obtain today. Thus the value of capital in existence today is equal to its supply price calculated in this manner. The heavy weight which this method of valuing

---

[7] The order of magnitude of the influence of the rate of interest is shown by the formula provided in the Mathematical Addendum by D. G. Champernowne and R. F. Kahn.* For this formula it is necessary to assume (a) that the total stock of capital is constant over time, (b) that earnings are at an even rate over the life of the plant. C is the capital value of an investment, K the initial outlay, r the rate of interest and T the period over which the asset earns. For values of rT less than 2 we use the approximation $C/K = \frac{1}{2}(1 + \frac{1}{6}rT)$.

On the basis, when the rate of interest is, for example, 6 per cent, a machine of ten years' life costing £100 when new must earn £13·3 per annum surplus over the current outlay on working it (including current repairs). The yield will then be 6 per cent on a capital value of £55.

A group of ten such machines of ages zero to nine years have a pattern of values, at any moment, which corresponds to the pattern over time of a single machine. It requires an annual outlay on renewals of £100 permanently to maintain the stock of machines. They represent a capital value of £550 and yield a return of £33 per annum.

If the rate of interest were 10 per cent, rT would be equal to 1 and the capital value (abstracting from a higher initial cost of machines due to the higher interest rate) would be £583; the earnings of each machine would then have to be £15·8 to yield the required rate of profit.

If the length of life of machines was twenty years, and the rate of interest 5 per cent, capital value would again be £583, and each machine would have to yield £7·9 per annum (£5 for amortization and £2·9 for interest); at 10 per cent, rT would be equal to 2; the capital value would then be £666, and each machine would have to yield £11·7 per annum.

---

* This appears as an appendix to my *Accumulation of Capital*.

capital puts upon the assumptions of equilibrium emphasizes the impossibility of valuing capital in an uncertain world. In a world where unexpected events occur which alter values, the points of view of the man of deeds, making investment decisions about the future, and of the man of words making observations about the past, are irreconcilable, and all we can do is botch up some conventional method of measuring capital that will satisfy neither of them.

WAGES AND PROFITS

The neo-classical system is based on the postulate that, in the long run, the rate of real wages tends to be such that all available labour is employed. In spite of the atrocities that have been committed in its name there is obviously a solid core of sense in this proposition. To return to our road builders, employment per unit of output is much higher in Gamma than in Alpha, and it seems obvious that this is connected with the fact that real wages there are much lower – that the plethora of labour keeps real wages down, and so helps to get itself employed. Let us try to see what this means.

The basic data of the system are: the labour force, the amount of capital and the state of technical knowledge, expressed as the hierarchy, ranged according to degrees of mechanization, of the possible techniques of production. In order to satisfy the neo-classical postulate of full employment, the given amount of capital must employ the given amount of labour.

At any given wage rate, the interplay of competition between capitalists, each seeking to maximize his own profits, is assumed to ensure that the technique will be chosen that maximizes the rate of profit. Thus, the technique is a function of the wage rate. The outfit of productive equipment in existence is determined by the technique and the total amount of capital. A given outfit of equipment offers a given amount of employment. Thus, we have the amount of employment as a function of the wage rate. We can then state the neo-classical postulate: the wage rate is assumed to be such that the technique of production is such that the given quantity of capital employs the given labour force. It is necessary to postulate that the amount of real wages (which is not the same thing as the wage bill but is governed by it) in relation to the cost of subsistence is at least sufficient to maintain the given labour force in being.

The condition that the given amount of capital employs the given amount of labour thus entails a particular rate of profit. But the value of the stock of concrete capital goods is affected by this rate of profit and the amount of 'capital' that we started with cannot be defined independently of it.

What becomes of the neo-classical doctrine if we read it the other way round: that the rate of profit tends to be such as to permit all the capital that comes into existence to be employed? Suppose that the wage rate has been established at a level which yields some conventional minimum real wage, and that, the technique having been chosen which maximizes the rate of profit, the quantity of capital in existence does not employ all available labour, so that there is a reserve of unemployment. Accumulation can then proceed with unchanging technique and constant rate of profit until all available labour is employed. If population is increasing at least as fast as capital is accumulating, full employment is never attained, and the expansion of the economy can continue indefinitely (we have postulated that there is no scarcity of land, including all non-produced means of production).

So far the argument is dismally simple. What are we supposed to imagine to happen when there is full employment in the long-period sense, that is, when there is sufficient plant in existence to employ all available labour? One line of argument is to suppose that the capitalists who are accumulating act in a blindly individualistic manner, so that a scramble for labour sets in; the money-wage rate is bid up, and prices rise in an indefinite spiral. (It is of no use to bring the financial mechanism into the argument, for if the supply of the medium of exchange is limited, the interest rate is driven up; but what the situation requires is a fall in the rate of interest, to encourage the use of more mechanized techniques.)

Or we may postulate that the capitalists, while fully competitive in selling, observe a convention against bidding for labour – each confines himself to employing a certain share of the constant labour force. Then anyone who wishes to increase the amount of capital that he operates shifts to a more mechanized technique. Those who first make the change may be supposed to compete for wider markets and so to reduce prices relatively to money wages. A higher degree of mechanization then becomes eligible, and the switch to more mechanized techniques proceeds at a sufficient rate to absorb new capital as it accrues. Alternatively, we might imagine that an excessive number of plants of the less mechanized type are actually built, and that their redundancy, relatively to labour to man them, reduces profit margins, so that the wage rate rises and induces mechanization. (Whichever line we follow the argument is necessarily highly artificial, for in reality the state of trade is the dominant influence on investment. The situation which promotes the mechanization of production is full employment and full order books, that is to say, a scarcity of labour relatively to effective demand, but the equilibrium assumptions do not permit us to say anything about effective demand.)

Somehow or other, accumulation may be conceived to push down the rate of profit, and raise the factor ratio.

But the very notion of accumulation proceeding under equilibrium conditions at changing factor ratios bristles with difficulties. The rate at which the factor ratio changes is not governed in any simple way by the pace at which accumulation goes on — it depends upon the form which technical innovations take and the movement of the overall level of real wages. Moreover, the effect of a given change in technique depends upon the speed at which it is made, relatively to the length of life of plant. If capital per man is rising rapidly some capitalists' plants appropriate to a variety of degrees of mechanization will be operating side by side.

Even if we can find a way through these complications, there remains the formidable problem of how to treat expectations when the rate of profit is altering. An unforeseen fall in the rate of profit ruptures the conditions of equilibrium. Capitalists who are operating on borrowed funds can no longer earn the interest they have contracted to pay, and those operating their own capital find themselves in possession of a type of plant that they would not have built if they had known what the rate of profit was going to be.

Thus, the assumptions of equilibrium become entangled in self-contradictions if they are applied to the problem of accumulation going on through time with a changing profit rate. To discuss accumulation we must look through the eyes of the man of deeds, taking decisions about the future, while to account for what has been accumulated we must look back over the accidents of past history. The two points of view meet only in the who's who of goods in existence today, which is never in an equilibrium relationship with the situation that obtains today.

In short, the comparison between equilibrium positions with different factor ratios cannot be used to analyse changes in the factor ratio taking place through time, and it is impossible to discuss changes (as opposed to differences) in neo-classical terms.

The production function, it seems, has a very limited relevance to actual problems, and after all these labours we can add little to the platitudes with which we began: in country Gamma, where the road builders use wooden shovels, if more capital had been accumulated in the past, relatively to labour available for employment, the level of real wages would probably have been higher and the technique of production more mechanized, and, given the amount of capital accumulated, the more mechanized the technique of production, the smaller the amount of employment would have been.

POSTSCRIPT

I have included here only the negative part of this article as the constructive parts are expanded in my book, *The Accumulation of Capital*. The trouble which I was trying to expose arose from burdening the concept of a production function with inappropriate tasks. The notion of a range of possible techniques, co-existing in time in the form of projects, amongst which choices are made by firms or investment planners when new productive capacity is being set up, has a genuine operational meaning (though it is very difficult to apply in the complicated situations that arise in reality). In that context, it is appropriate to measure the investible resources about to be committed in terms of value. The difficulties that present themselves arise out of the uncertainty of the future and can be imagined to disappear in conditions of perfect tranquillity.

When presented with the task of determining the distribution of the product of industry between labour and capital, the neo-classical production function comes to grief (even in the most perfect tranquillity) on the failure to distinguish between 'capital' in the sense of means of production with particular technical characteristics and 'capital' in the sense of a command over finance.

When presented with the task of analysing a process of accumulation, the production function comes to grief on the failure to distinguish between comparisons of equilibrium positions and movements from one to another.

The remarks about equilibrium on page 78 above seemed very queer to Sir Dennis Robertson,[8] and, indeed, they are not well worded. My point was this: a state of equilibrium is one in which each individual is satisfied that he could not do better for himself by changing his behaviour. Applied to long-lived capital equipment, this means that the stock in existence today is in all respects what it would have been if those concerned had known, at relevant dates in the past, what expectations about the future they would be holding today. But periods affected by different decisions overlap and the relevant past stretches back indefinitely. Thus, an economy can be following an equilibrium path today only if it has been following it for some time already. A thorough-going stationary state is a limiting case in which nothing changes except the date as the economy moves along its equilibrium path.

[8] *Lectures on Economic Principles*, Vol. I, p. 95.

9

PRE-KEYNESIAN THEORY AFTER KEYNES

THE orthodox theory which produced the doctrines that Keynes was attacking thirty years ago had never got itself clearly stated; he was obliged to construct a cockshy to knock down. Nowadays it is being used as a basis for models set out in mathematical terms and so has to present itself more coherently. The practitioners in this line, however, are apt to be rather shy of making clear which of their assumptions are necessary to their conclusions and which are merely used to exclude inessential complications.[1]

The essential features of the economic system which appear in the pre-Keynesian models are that accumulation is governed by the propensity to save of the economy as a whole and that the wage bargain is made in terms of product. With a given amount of 'capital', profit-maximizing entrepreneurs offer more employment the lower the wage; thus, provided that there is enough 'capital' in existence to offer full employment at a positive wage, competition among workers for jobs eliminates unemployment.

The 'capital' that comes into the argument may be taken, in a short-period sense, to be the stock of concrete means of production in existence. There is then a *utilization function* relating output to employment, which figures also in Keynes' theory. What 'a quantity of capital' means in a long-period sense, when its form can be adapted to take advantage of different factor prices, is an old puzzle. Professor Solow is unable to see the problem, and treats the long-period production function as being identical with the short-period utilization function; but most of the latter-day neo-classicals are aware of the difficulty and evade it by assuming that capital goods are

---

[1] Among innumerable works in the genre, I rely particularly upon the contributions of Professors Samuelson and Solow to the *Review of Economic Studies*, June 1962; J. E. Meade, *A Neo-classical Theory of Economic Growth*; B. S. Minhas, *An International Comparison of Factor Costs*; R. M. Solow, *Capital Theory and the Rate of Return*; and on Professor Solow's Marshall Lectures. I have also benefited very much from conversation with Dr. C. von Weizsacker, a rare neo-classical who has the candour to explain clearly what his assumptions are.

made out of a homogeneous physical substance. There has been a great deal of fuss about the question of 'measuring capital', but, as we shall see, the failure of the neo-classicals to give a plausible account of it is a symptom, rather than a cause, of the real difficulties in their position.

In what follows we outline a number of questions that are discussed in terms of the neo-classical theory, stressing the assumptions and leaving the practitioners in this art to fill in the elegant details.

THE PSEUDO PRODUCTION FUNCTION

There are a number of economies, completely independent of each other, which however have in common the composition of the output of consumer goods and the book of blue-prints setting out the physical specifications for all the known methods of producing them. The labour force in each economy is alike. It is convenient also to take the money-wage rate per man hour to be the same in each. Each is in stationary equilibrium, with zero net saving; the stock of means of production is such that no entrepreneur wishes to be using any other than those he has. The difference between the economies consists in a difference in the rate of interest (equal to the rate of profit on capital) at which zero net saving obtains.

To compare these economies there is no need to make any fanciful assumptions about the nature of capital goods or to resort to any tricks for measuring capital. In each economy there is a specific stock of means of production, a set of prices, and a level of the real wage. The value of the stock of capital can be reckoned in any convenient *numeraire*, such as a man-hour of labour or a basket of consumer goods.

As we move down the series, from higher to lower rates of profit, we may see first a group of economies identical in every physical respect, with lower money prices (since the money-wage rate is the same in each). The real-wage rate is higher as we descend the series, but the value of the stock of capital in terms of product may be either rising or falling, according as the relative prices of capital goods and consumption goods change with the change in factor prices.

Some way down the series we come to a corner where two techniques of production are equally profitable.[2] Here there is a group of economies each with the same rate of profit and real-wage rate, but with progressively

---

[2] In Professor Samuelson's version, the series is represented by a curve relating the rate of profit to the real-wage rate; the economies with the same physical capital lie on a straight line and those with the same rate of profit are at a corner. If the curve is drawn in terms of the real-capital/labour ratio, the lines appear as corners and the corners as lines.

higher output per head and value of capital, as the proportion of the more mechanized of the two techniques grows. At the point where only one technique is in use we enter another stretch with economies all alike except for rising real wages, and so on down.[3]

This exercise is useful for clearing up some fuzzy points in the old theory but it has no application to anything on earth. Two economies with different rates of profit must be divided either by time or space, and they will neither have the same book of blue-prints (including specifications about the climate and human nature) nor will either be in stationary equilibrium with its own rate of profit. The exercise cannot be used to provide hypotheses for interpreting real data.

THE TRAM LINE

Another traditional question concerns an economy with a given labour force, a given book of blue-prints, and a given propensity to save, accumulating capital subject to the conditions that full employment is always preserved and that the form which investment takes is decided in the light of correct foresight about profit opportunities.[4] The economy is following a determinate path at a determinate pace. At any moment, today's prices and the expectations held today about future prices have been foreseen, the capital goods in existence today are of the form that will maximize profits for their owners, the level of real wages is such that the stock of capital in existence is offering full employment, and the division of output between consumption goods and capital goods is consonant with the desire to save. Since foresight has always been correct, any investments made in the past that are no longer yielding profits have been amortized. The value of the stock of capital in existence today is the cumulated sum of all the net savings made in the past. As we look back down the path into the past, there may be some ups and downs but broadly the value of capital and the real-wage fall, the capital/output ratio falls and the rate of accumulation rises. Contrariwise as we look forward into the future.

Savings may be a simple proportion of the value of total net income, or

[3] Samuelson's trick of measuring each stock of capital in terms of its own product is of no use, because the physical composition of gross output and the pattern of prices are both different in each economy. He is in error in saying that the elasticity of his curve corresponds to the relative shares of wages and profits in the value of output. I am indebted to von Weizsacker for the mathematical demonstration of this.

[4] For this story to be told, the book of blue-prints must show methods of producing capital goods with a low capital/labour ratio. See H. Uzawa, 'On a two-sector model of economic growth', *Review of Economic Studies*, Vol. 29 (1961–2).

some more complicated function of it. The pattern of interest rates for various terms must correspond to the expected future rates of profit. We cannot therefore make use of the interest rate, in a Keynesian manner, to ensure that investment absorbs saving. It is necessary just to postulate that savings are invested.

To get out of this difficulty Professor Meade invented a world in which foresight is unnecessary. There capital goods are made of ectoplasm and can be remoulded into the profit-maximizing form from day to day. He then operates on the rate of investment through monetary policy. His is a pseudo-Keynesian model rather than a truly neo-classical one. The assumption of ectoplasm is not really anything to do with the problem of 'measuring capital'; it is a substitute for the assumption of correct foresight.

Both assumptions are out of this world, and the analysis has no application.

WALRASIAN ACCUMULATION

In another type of model, there is correct foresight about the future starting from today, but, in the past, what today would be like was not foreseen. There is, therefore, in existence today a job lot of means of production, including machines of various kinds, which are in no particular relation to the pattern of demand now obtaining.

Walrasian supply-and-demand prices are ruling. There is a wage rate, say in terms of bread, at which all labour is employed. To keep the argument simple we may assume a constant labour force from now on.

With the incomes now being enjoyed, there is a certain volume of saving, reckoned in terms of bread. Saving consists in buying machines and building up working capital to operate them. There is a book of blue-prints for machines of types not inferior to those already in existence. It seems to be necessary to postulate that the minimum size of machine is rather large in terms of employment offered and that the savings function is somewhat 'classical'[5] so that most workers do not save; otherwise the economy would quickly become an artisan system, with all producers self-employed, to which another kind of model would be more appropriate.

The whole amount of savings in any one year is devoted to buying the type of machine that offers the highest prospective rate of return. There is a notorious difficulty about introducing a rate of profit into the Walrasian general equilibrium system. Since the future is known, we can reckon the

[5] This term has been suggested by R. C. O. Matthews to describe the postulate that saving out of profits is much greater than out of wages.

quasi-rents that any machine purchased today will earn for its owner. The rate of return is the rate of discount that reduces the future quasi-rents to a sum equal to the present cost of the machine. But how are we to find the present cost, which includes interest on the value of the capital that entered into its production?

One way of circumventing this problem is to assume that some basic tools, that can be used to make machines, are produced by labour alone. But if workers can produce tools with their bare hands from free raw materials gathered in the jungles, they have no need to work for wages. The price at which they sell tools to the savers depends upon supply and demand; there is no reason why their earnings should not exceed the wage offered by machine-owning employers (or fall short of it when demand is low, if they prefer freedom to extra bread).

Another way round the problem is to postulate that there is some basic equipment, let us call it a park of machine-tools, that can reproduce itself as well as making other machines. Let us suppose that when the story opens the park is rather small, and that machine-tools promise a higher rate of return than any other kind of machine. The bread price of a new machine-tool is then the year's physical output from the existing park divided into the year's savings valued in terms of bread.

The future quasi-rents of a new machine-tool being known, we can find the rate of discount that makes its value equal to its price. This is the rate of return on investment. When we know the rate of return we can value the park of pre-existing machine-tools accordingly. The cost of a new machine-tool is then equated to its value by including in the cost a bill for interest, at a rate equal to the rate of return, on the value of the machine-tools needed to make it. This is only arithmetic. Essentially the value of a new machine-tool is a demand-and-supply price.

All the old machines in existence are valued by discounting their expected quasi-rents at a rate equal to the rate of return. The cost of production (including interest on the value of the machine-tools required to produce it) of each type is greater than its value.

By the time that the park of machine-tools has been enlarged, their future quasi-rents have been reduced (the largest, nearest, ones have passed into the past). At the same time, supply having increased, the current price of a new machine tool has fallen, unless saving has increased correspondingly. The rate of return, therefore, may not have fallen. But even if it has not, the cost of production of other machines has been reduced, for this cost includes interest on the value of the machine-tools that make them, which has now fallen. When the cost equals the value of a machine, it begins to be produced, Since there was full employment already, the bread-wage rate rises, as the stock of new machines grows, sufficiently to reduce the current quasi-rent of some old machines to zero, so that labour is released to man the new ones. Current and remaining future quasi-rents are consequently falling and sooner or later the rate of return falls. When it does, the value of old machines rises. More types of machines become eligible to be produced.

Now there are two sectors in the economy. It is still true that the price level of the output of the machine industry as a whole is such as to equate the value of its physical output to the rate of saving, but within it all the machines being produced have values equal to their costs; each commodity produced by them is selling at a normal price, in Marshall's sense, which yields the appropriate amount of profit on their values. The calculation of normal prices is extremely complicated because of the expected future fall in the rate of return, but they are in principle quite unambiguous.

Meanwhile old machines whose value is still lower than their cost of production continue to operate. The New sector gradually grows and absorbs labour until the Old sector dwindles away to nothing. The Old Machines were not necessarily inferior in the strict sense, but they had been produced in proportions inappropriate to the situations that they lived to meet. Some may survive until their cost and value become equal, in which case they are absorbed into the New sector.

When all types of machines are being produced (or at least being maintained) all values are equal to costs and normal prices obtain throughout the economy.

The economy is approaching the position that it would have been in if perfect foresight had prevailed in the past. In due course it reaches the tram line, or rather comes close to it. Some scars from its actual history will always remain. It could now look back down the tram line into an imaginary past through which it could have approached its present position, with normal prices ruling all the time.[6]

Bensusan Butt[7] has worked out a story somewhat on these lines as a basis for the analysis of the process by which capitalism swallows up an artisan

---

[6] This story explains why it was necessary to postulate that the book of blue-prints specifying the course of the tram line must show a relatively low capital/labour ratio for the production of capital goods. If the output of machine-tools per machine tool is very low compared to other machines (measuring machines in units of employment offered) then by the time that the tram line is reached, the park of machine-tools is excessive to requirements and must shrink. If saving refuses to become sufficiently negative, machine-tools become valueless. Can this be reconciled with correct foresight?

[7] *On Economic Growth.*

economy. It does not seem to have much to contribute to the kind of problem with which the latter-day neo-classicals purport to be concerned.

TECHNICAL PROGRESS

In the old theory, technical progress was considered only in the form of a sudden shock which shifted the economy from one equilibrium to another. Harrod introduced the idea of technical progress going on continuously at steady rate. This conception, which was easily worked into the long-period Keynesian theory, has been taken up also by the neo-classicals. Here the notion of capital goods consisting of a homogeneous substance that retains its physical identity while its productivity changes is not only absurd but a great nuisance. When the economy is rolling along through time with both a constant rate of profit on capital and a constant share of profit in the value of output, the real wage rate is rising at the same rate as output per man, the capital/output ratio in terms of product is constant and the capital/labour ratio in terms of wage units is constant. There is no sense in distinguishing 'labour augmenting' from 'capital augmenting' progress. 'Embodied' and 'disembodied' progress may be mixed in various proportions. The technical nature of the technical progress tells us whether it is possible for both conditions to be fulfilled simultaneously. When a constant rate of profit entails a rising share, the progress has a capital-using bias; when it entails a falling share, a capital-saving bias. That is all that we need on this level of argument. Paddling about in the ectoplasm does not help us to say whether the rate of profit *will* remain constant; still less can it help in an inquiry into actual technical change and the kind of bias likely to be found in reality.

The assumption that saving governs accumulation is rather awkward in this connection. With a constant labour force and continuous technical progress, there is a certain sense in which saving has ceased to be necessary. As Harrod pointed out when he opened the question, if money-wage rates are constant and the rise of real wages comes about by prices falling, no net saving in money terms occurs. The reinvestment of amortization funds keeps output expanding and capital gains in terms of product drop into the laps of the heirs of those who saved when the stock of capital was being built up. If money-wage rates rise so as to keep prices constant, the money value of net saving is the same thing as the rise in the value of capital that is taking place.

To get over this difficulty, the assumption is sometimes changed to make gross saving a function of gross output. This looks rather like a concession to the Keynesian point of view, since gross saving must be under the control of firms rather than households, but the argument proceeds on the basis of the ratio of gross investment to gross income being somehow governed by the propensity to consume of the economy as a whole.

The model is set up as follows. Technical progress takes the form of an improvement in the design of machines, so that output per man employed in producing consumption goods (commodities for short) is higher on a machine of a later than of an earlier vintage. Machines once produced do not change (they are not made of ectoplasm) and each continues to be used until its product yields no surplus over the wage bill for the team of men operating it.

At any moment there are in existence batches of machines of various vintages. The real-wage is such as to secure full employment. The oldest machine in use is that whose product just covers its wage bill.

Now we draw up a short-period production-possibility schedule at full employment, for commodities and machines. At any product mix, the price ratio must be such as to make the two groups of products equally profitable at the margin. Thus we can draw up a schedule of the value in terms of commodities of gross output at various levels of gross investment. That level of gross investment is chosen whose value corresponds to the gross saving appropriate to the corresponding gross income. When this gross investment has borne fruit, some superior machines have been added to the stock. Unless the labour force has grown sufficiently, the real-wage rate must be raised to get hands to man them. These are drawn from the oldest machines, which were barely worth using at the former wage rate. Thus full employment is continuously maintained, whatever the investment ratio may happen to be.

In this model also there is no room for an independent inducement to invest based on expected profits and the rate of interest. If, at one round, an unusually large improvement were made, so that gross profits jumped up, it would not affect investment except in so far as the greater-than-usual increase in gross product led to a greater-than-usual increase in the volume of gross savings at the next round.

The model has been wrenched away from Harrod's purpose of discussing the relation between the warranted and the natural rate of growth; it is useless for dealing with his problem – the failure of effective demand to expand fast enough to permit a modern industrial economy to realize its full potential productivity.

The Neo-neo-classical Theorem

Combining the analysis of continuous growth at full employment with the pseudo production function, we can compare economies, each with the same rate of growth, with different rates of profit. It can be shown that the optimum position obtains when the rate of profit is equal to the rate of growth, which entails that consumption is equal to the wage bill. An economy in which there is consumption from unearned income in excess of saving out of earned income has a lower total consumption, at each phase of technical development, than the attainable level.

Marginal Products

The neo-classicals attach great importance to the principle of marginal productivity and (in spite of Marshall's warning)[8] seek to find in it an explanation of the distribution of the product of industry between wages and profits.

The marginal principle is essentially micro-economic. It comes into play when someone is maximizing something. In a short-period situation, with given means of production in existence, if we postulate conditions of absolutely perfect competition and assume that all employers are maximizing short-period profits, then marginal cost for each product is equal to its price. Another way of stating this relationship is to say that (when there is a perfectly elastic supply of labour at the ruling wage rate to each employer) the marginal net product of labour is everywhere equal to the wage. When interest on working capital and user cost of machinery can be neglected, and there is complete vertical integration, so as to eliminate raw materials, etc., the marginal net product of labour is equal to the value of the marginal physical product. The value of the marginal physical product when all available labour is employed with the given stock of means of production is what determines the real wage rate in the foregoing tales.

When the stock of means of production in existence can be represented as a quantity of ectoplasm, we can then say, appealing to Euler's theorem, that the rent per unit of ectoplasm is equal to the marginal product of the given quantity of ectoplasm when it is fully utilized. This does not seem to add anything of interest to the argument.

In a long-period context the marginal principle comes in to the choice of technique, from the available blue-prints, at the moment when an

[8] *Principles*, p. 518.

investment is being made. It is assumed that an individual entrepreneur, with confident expectations of future prices and costs, chooses the amount of employment to be offered by his investment in such a way as to maximize the return on it. Along the tram line the choice is excessively complicated because of the changing pattern of prices and wages that durable equipment will live through. This can be fudged by representing the degree of mechanization of technique as the ectoplasm/labour ratio.

In equilibrium with a constant expected rate of profit, no such fudge is necessary. But then the individual entrepreneur finds himself either in an economy on a flat in the pseudo production function, where only one technique is eligible, or at a corner where two techniques are equally profitable. In the first case there is nothing for the marginal principle to bite on. In the second, the additional investment required to raise the output of a given team of workers by equipping them for the more rather than the less mechanized technique is exactly rewarded, at the ruling rate of profit, by the additional output. The marginal return on investment to the individual is identically the same thing as the rate of profit. The marginal net productivity of labour is equal to the wage when the difference between the marginal gross product of an extra man employed and the wage is equal to the margin needed to pay interest at the ruling rate on the extra capital required to employ him.

We are merely chasing our tails round the implications of the assumption that the entrepreneur acts so as to maximize profits in the situation in which he finds himself.

But the main concern of the neo-classicals is to prove that the rate of profit is governed by the marginal productivity of investment from the point of view of society.

The marginal productivity of investment can be expressed as the rate of discount that reduces the additional flow of future output (valued in terms of bread) due to the investment to equality with the bread-cost of the machines concerned and the additional working capital required. When we take for granted a path that an economy is following, whether along the tram line of accumulation with a falling rate of return, or in a state of steady growth with a constant rate of profit, we can discuss the effect of a small *extra* bit of saving which is allowed to be re-absorbed later so that the economy returns to the path it would have been on anyway. It can then be shown that the rate of discount measuring the marginal productivity of the extra investment is equal to the rate of profit ruling at the moment when it is made.[9]

[9] Solow, op. cit., Lecture II.

It is hard to see why the neo-classicals derive pleasure from this theorem, for clearly something or other is determining the rate of profit, and whatever the rate of profit is, the marginal productivity of investment in this special sense is equal to it.

However that may be, it is more natural to consider the productivity of the investment that is being done on the path itself. Consider the investment due to the saving of, say, one year and calculate its marginal productivity. The rate of return at the end of the year is lower than at the beginning, compared to what it would have been if the investment had not been made, because of the rise in the real-wage rate that it induces. The marginal productivity of investment from the point of view of society includes the addition to wages of the team of workers operating the additional installation, which is not part of the profit that the investment will earn. This phenomenon was known to Wicksell[10] but it seems to have been dropped from the canon in modern times.

The crowning absurdity in this line of argument is the attempt to isolate the marginal productivity of education, as though labour and 'capital' retain their technical characteristics unaffected by education, so that all three can be treated as independent 'factors' whose products can be summed up according to the rules of Euler's theorem. This analysis is directed to the very worthy purpose of showing that education is a good thing; but surely that point could be made without such a large sacrifice of logic?

So What?

Certainly Keynes would have been saved a lot of trouble if he had found the target he wanted to shoot at so clearly displayed. But what is the purpose of re-erecting it today?

The object is not overtly ideological. Fairly radical conclusions can be drawn from the analysis, such as that the distribution of dividends is harmful to society. The elaborate mathematical formulations that have accompanied it find their sphere of application mainly in the problems of investment planning.

As for its use in analysing current events, we could hardly have believed, if we had not seen it in cold print, that anyone would ever suppose that a production function in terms of labour and ectoplasm would provide a useful hypothesis for interpreting statistical data. Even on its own ground it turns out to be otiose, for both in comparisons between nations and in time series, we commonly find a more or less uniform rate of profit on capital

[10] *Value Capital and Rent*, p. 137.

going with widely different real-wage rates. That is to say, each observation is on a different production function. When we find the share of profit as well as the rate of profit the same in the various observations, we can say, if we like, that evidently the elasticity of the production function is the same at each point, but we have not any clue as to what the elasticity is, or, indeed, whether there ever was a production function to have an elasticity.

Presumably, no one would deny that there is more hope of understanding what is going on in the world when we recognize that the wage bargain is made in terms of money; that the level of prices is influenced by effective demand and the degree of imperfection of competition; that accumulation is controlled by the policy of firms and governments, not by the propensity to consume of private citizens, and that today is an ever moving break in time between an irrevocable past and an uncertain future.

To understand is not easy, but at least we could try.

10

CAPITAL THEORY UP-TO-DATE

THE lectures which Professor Solow gave in Holland (published in 1963)[1] opened with the remark: Everybody except Joan Robinson agrees about capital theory. He did not say what it was that they agreed, and a few years later the 'reswitching' controversy brought some important differences of opinion to light. Now, fortunately, we have a clear exposition of what Professor Solow must have meant. Professor Ferguson, in *The Neoclassical Theory of Production and Distribution*, asserts that belief in neoclassical theory is a matter of faith. 'I personally have the faith' he declares, so that we can learn from him what it is that the neo-neoclassicals believe neoclassical theory to be. But first let us trace the history of the 'reswitching' affair.

1

RESWITCHING

In the course of investigating the meaning of a production function for output as a whole, I set up what Professor Solow later correctly described as a pseudo-production function, showing the possible positions of equilibrium, corresponding to various values of the rate of profit, in an imagined 'given state of technical knowledge'. The analysis showed that there is no meaning to be given to a 'quantity of capital' apart from the rate of profit, so that the contention that the 'marginal product of capital' determines the rate of profit is meaningless. (In the present argument 'land' as a separate factor of production is not taken into account.) Incidentally, I found that over certain ranges of the pseudo-production function the technique that becomes eligible at a higher rate of profit (with a correspondingly lower real-wage rate) may be less labour-intensive (that is, may have a higher output per man employed) than that chosen at a higher

---

[1] Robert M. Solow, *Capital Theory and the Rate of Return* (Amsterdam, 1963).

A review of C. E. Ferguson, *The Neoclassical Theory of Production and Distribution* (London and New York, 1969). Canadian Journal of Economics–Revue canadienne d'Economique, III, No. 2 May–mai 1970.

wage rate, contrary to the rule of a 'well-behaved production function' in which a lower wage rate is always associated with a more labour-intensive technique. (I attributed this discovery to Ruth Cohen – a private joke.)

I had picked up the clue from Piero Sraffa's Introduction to Ricardo's *Principles* and my analysis (errors and omissions excepted) was a preview of his. When his own treatment of the subject was finally published in *Production of Commodities by Means of Commodities* (in 1960) the 'Ruth Cohen case' (which I had treated as a *curiosum*) was seen to have great prominence; the striking proposition was established that it is perfectly normal (within the accepted assumptions) for the same technique to be eligible at several discrete rates of profit. It was from this that the soubriquet 'reswitching of techniques' was derived. (The difference between my treatment and Sraffa's was accidental. I put the main emphasis on differences in the amount of 'labour embodied' in the equipment appropriate to different techniques while Sraffa illustrates his point with a case in which two commodities require the same labour applied in different time-patterns. The backward switch, from a lower to a higher output per head with lower wages, is connected with the inter-relations of the time-patterns of the techniques; his examples gave more scope for it than mine.)

The neo-neoclassicals took no notice; they went on as usual drawing production functions in terms of 'capital' and labour and disseminating the marginal productivity theory of distribution. In 1961 I encountered Professor Samuelson on his home ground; in the course of an argument I happened to ask him: When you define the marginal product of labour, what do you keep constant? He seemed disconcerted, as though none of his pupils had ever asked that question, but next day he gave a clear answer. Either the physical inputs other than labour are kept constant, or the rate of profit on capital is kept constant.

I found this satisfactory, for it destroys the doctrine that wages are regulated by marginal productivity. In a short-period case, where equipment is given, at full-capacity operation the marginal physical product of labour is indeterminate. When nine men with nine spades are digging a hole, to add a tenth man could increase output only to the extent that nine dig better if they have a rest from time to time.[2] On the other hand, to subtract the ninth man would reduce output by more or less the average amount. The wage must lie somewhere between the average value of output per head and zero, so that marginal product is much greater or much less than the wage according as equipment is being worked below or above its designed capacity.

[2] See D. H. Robertson, 'Wage grumbles', 1930, republished in *Economic Fragments*.

In conditions of imperfect competition, under-capacity operation of plant is normal (except in an acute seller's market) and, in industry as a whole, it seems that, on average, wages are usually about half of value added. The marginal product of labour, in the short-period sense, is therefore generally about twice the wage.[3]

In long-period equilibrium, with a constant rate of profit, the stock of equipment and the amount of employment have been adjusted to each other. When competition prevails in the long-period sense of free entry to all markets, so that a uniform rate of profit tends to be established throughout the economy, the wage is equivalent to what Marshall called the marginal *net* product of labour – that is the value of average output per head *minus* a gross profit sufficient to pay for replacement and net profit at the going rate on the value of capital per man employed, when all inputs are reckoned at the prices appropriate to the given rate of profit. The wage is determined by technical conditions and the rate of profit, as at a particular point on a pseudo-production function. The question then comes up, what determines the rate of profit?

But this was going too far. Professor Samuelson retreated behind what he called a surrogate production function.[4] It was a special case (as Piero Garegnani promptly pointed out[5]) of a pseudo-production function with labour-value prices. When, for any one technique, the capital to labour ratio and the time-pattern of inputs are uniform throughout all the processes of production, prices are proportional to labour-time. The value of capital in terms of product, for that technique, is then independent of the rate of profit. When each technique in the 'given state of knowledge' has this character and the time-patterns are all alike, the order of techniques in terms of output per head is the same as the order in terms of value of capital per man for each technique at the rate of profit that makes that technique eligible; a higher output per man is associated with a higher wage and lower rate of profit. When a pseudo-production function of this type is set out as a relationship between 'capital' and output, it looks just like a well-behaved production function.

Professor Samuelson believed that in this he had provided for the 'neo-classical parables' of J. B. Clark 'which pretend there is a single thing called

---

[3] Cf. A. M. Okum, *Potential GNP. Its Measurements and Significance*, Cowles Foundation Paper 189.

[4] Parable and realism in capital theory: the surrogate production function', *Review of Economic Studies*, 29 (June 1962), 193–206.

[5] Ibid., 202n.

"capital" that can be put into a single production function and along with labour will produce total output.'[6]

At first the neo-neoclassicals were happy to accept his parable. (This was the period of Professor Solow's lectures and of the first draft of Professor Ferguson's book, in which, he tells us, he relied upon the surrogate production function to protect him from what he calls Cambridge Criticism.) For some years they remained cooped up in this position, repelling all attacks with blank misunderstanding. Then, growing bold, they descended to the plains and tried to prove Sraffa wrong.

This rash enterprise was not successful; Professor Samuelson very handsomely admitted that he had been mistaken.[7] But he mistook his mistake. The trouble was not merely that he had ignored Garegnani's warning and treated labour-value prices as the general case. The real mistake was to suppose that a pseudo-production function, which relates the rate of profit to the value of capital at the prices corresponding to that rate of profit, provides the 'neoclassical parable'. Neo-classical 'capital' is a physical quantity which is independent of prices.

2

CAPITAL

The neo-neoclassicals' concept of capital is derived from Walras, but they have transformed it into something quite different. In a Walrasian market, when dealing begins, there are particular supplies of factors already in existence each measured in physical terms – man-hours, acres, tons, pints, and yards. In the neo-neoclassical concept of capital all the man-made factors are boiled into one, which we may call *leets* in honour of Professor Meade's *steel*.[8] But leets, though all made of one physical substance, is endowed with the capacity to embody various techniques of production – different ratios of leets to labour – and a change of technique can be made simply by squeezing up or spreading out leets, instantaneously and without cost. A higher output per man requires a larger amount of leets per man employed. In Walrasian competitive equilibrium there can never be increasing returns from one factor applied to a given quantity of another. This rule is observed by leets. There is a well-behaved production function in leets and labour for each kind of output, including leets. Moreover, leets

---

[6] Ibid., 194.

[7] 'A summing up' in 'Paradoxes of capital theory: a symposium', *Quarterly Journal of Economics*, 80 (November 1966), 568–83.

[8] J. E. Meade, *A Neoclassical Theory of Economic Growth* (London, 1961).

CAPITAL THEORY UP-TO-DATE 107

can absorb technical progress, without losing its physical identity, again instantaneously and without cost. Then to simplify still further, output is also taken to be made of leets; the whole Walrasian system is reduced to a 'one-commodity world'.

This is the conception in which Professor Ferguson has reaffirmed his faith.

Many economists, nowadays, who are interested in practical questions, are impatient of doctrinal disputes. What does it matter, they are inclined to say, let him have his leets, what harm does it do? But the harm that the neo-neoclassicals have done is, precisely, to block off economic theory from any discussion of practical questions.

When equipment is made of leets, there is no distinction between long and short-period problems. The answer to Dennis Robertson's question is simply fudged. Nine spades are a lump of leets; when the tenth man turns up it is squeezed out to provide him with a share of equipment nine-tenths of what each man had before.

There is no such thing as a degree of utilization of given equipment rising or falling with the level of effective demand. (Professor Solow pretends that his production functions are drawn in terms of concrete capital goods, but the fact that the short-period utilization function is identical with the long-period pseudo-production function gives him away.)

There is no room for imperfect competition. There is no possibility of disappointed expectations – indeed, there is no difference between the past and the future, for the past can always be undone and readjusted to a change in the present situation.

There is no problem of unemployment. The wage bargain is made in terms of product and there is perfect competition both between workers for jobs and between employers for hands. Unemployed workers would bid down wages and the pre-existing quantity of leets would be spread out to accommodate them. The neo-neoclassicals have reconstructed the vague doctrines of the neo-classicals from which was derived the dogma which Keynes had to attack in the great slump of the 'thirties, that unemployment can be caused only by wages being too high.

In long-period analysis, the neo-neoclassics are prone to confuse a comparison of positions of equilibrium (as in a pseudo-production function) with a 'Wicksell process' of accumulation without technical progress. 'A given state of technical knowledge' consists simply of a production function in terms of leets and labour. Accumulation consists of adding some leets to the pre-existing stock and squeezing it into a new quantity per man employed. This entails raising the wage rate and reducing the return per ton of leets. Thus a process of raising the capital to labour ratio means creeping along the production function, moving step by step from lower to higher ratios of leets to labour. (It is notable that when Professor Samuelson conceded defeat in the 'reswitching' controversy, he did so in this form. He seemed to suppose that if the process of accumulation hit a backward switch, where a lower rate of profit is associated with a lower value of capital per man, the economy would suddenly find itself able to consume part of its capital without reducing its productive capacity.)

This brings into play the other aspect of pre-Keynesian theory. Saving consists in a decision not to consume a part of the current output and this causes investment to make a corresponding addition to the stock of 'capital'. The neo-neoclassicals have succeeded in tying themselves up again in habits of thought from which Keynes had had 'a long struggle to escape'. (However, when it comes to offering advice on questions of national policy many of them propound quite simple-minded Keynesian views.)[9]

3

WAGES AND PROFITS

The main function of the concept of leets is to provide a theory of the distribution of the product of industry between wages and profits.

At any moment, with a given quantity in existence of leets regarded as capital equipment, the wage in terms of leets regarded as product is at the level compatible with full employment of the available labour force. Then, with a few extra assumptions, such as that there is no charge for interest on the part of working capital which represents the wage fund, it is shown that the wage is equal to the marginal product of the available labour force, that is, the amount of product per week that would be lost if one less man were employed and the stock of leets squeezed up appropriately. If the wage were less than this, competition for hands would drive it up. If it was greater, less men would be employed and competition for jobs would drive it down. The wage being equal to the marginal product of labour, it is shown by Euler's theorem that the product minus the wage is the marginal product of a ton of leets multiplied by the quantity of leets in existence.

Now, capital in the world we live in has two aspects. It consists of the stocks of equipment and materials which (with education and training) permit workers to produce marketable goods and it consists of the

[9] Cf. R. M. Solow, *The Nature and Sources of Unemployment in the United States* (Wicksell Lectures, 1964).

command over finance which permits employers to organize the production of goods which they can sell at a profit. In the 'one-commodity world' the price a a ton of leets-capital in terms of leets-output is unity. The two aspects of capital are fused. A ton of leets is both a piece of equipment and a sum of purchasing power. Then the return to a unit of leets, leets over leets, is the rate of profit on capital. Thus labour and capital each receive a 'reward' equal to their marginal productivity. As J. B. Clark himself put it: 'What a social class gets is, under natural law, what it contributes to the general output of industry.'[10]

Here, indeed, we find the origin of the concept of leets. First came the dogma that the rate of profit that the owners of capital enjoy is equal to the productivity of capital equipment, and that saving continues to cause capital to accumulate so long as its marginal product exceeds the rate of interest which represents the 'discount of the future' in the minds of its owners. Then the question is asked, what is this 'capital' that has a marginal product? Leets had to be invented to give an answer to that question.

Of course, all this is not intended to be taken literally. Even Professor Ferguson admits that capital equipment actually consists of a variety of hard objects that cannot be squeezed up or pressed out, without cost, to accommodate less or more workers. Leets is only a parable, as Professor Samuelson claimed. But as soon as they give it up, their argument comes unstuck.

Professor Ferguson, for instance, incorporates a 'vintage model' in his system. The vintage model is taken over from Harrod's conception of an economy realizing the 'natural' rate of growth given by technical progress.

Gross investment, in each period, is embodied in equipment for the latest, most superior technique. The conditions for equilibrium growth are that technical progress should be raising output per head at a steady rate and that it should be neutral in Harrod's sense, so that a constant rate of profit on capital is compatible with a constant capital to output ratio and constant relative shares of wages and profits in net output. A constant share of gross investment in total output then produces growth of output per head at a steady rate.

On any one equilibrium path, the rate of profit on capital is constant through time, but there may be different paths (with the same sequence of technical innovations) with different rates of profit. Thus there is a kind of pseudo-production function relating the rate of profit to the value of capital in terms of product and the share of gross investment in output.

[10] J. B. Clark, 'Distribution as determined by a law of rent', *Quarterly Journal of Economics*, 5 (April 1891), 313.

The level of wages in terms of product rises in step with output per head (this follows from the condition that the rate of profit and the share of wages in output are constant) and the equipment for each technique is scrapped when the wage absorbs its whole output so that its quasi-rent is reduced to zero. A higher share of profit entails a wider gap between the wage rate and output per head with the latest, best, technique. Thus it entails a longer service life of equipment, therefore a higher proportion of older, more inferior, techniques in use at any moment, and lower average output per head. There is then a presumption that the pseudo-production function relating the rate of profit to the capital to output ratio will be well-behaved (a lower output per man being associated with a lower value of capital per man) though there still might be some 'Cambridge' tricks in it. But what determines the rate of profit?

Professor Ferguson follows Professor Solow's argument that a very small *extra* investment over and above that required by the equilibrium path yields a return equal to the rate of profit. That is true, whatever the rate of profit may be. And he shows that the marginal product of labour in the short-period sense is equal to the wage; the 'last man' is employed in the equipment that is just about to be scrapped. This is true because, for a given pseudo-production function, both the wage relative to output per head with the latest technique and the age of the least productive equipment are determined together by the rate of profit. Evidently they are so used to thinking in terms of leets (for whatever he may say, Professor Solow's capital is made of leets) that they forget that, when capital is embodied in specific equipment, the short-period marginal physical product of labour is not the same thing as the value of the net product allowing for profit at a particular rate. They describe the competitive equilibrium position corresponding to a given rate of profit without offering any explanation of what the rate of profit is.

There have been three types of theory of the distribution of the product of industry between wages and profits. In classical theory (of which von Neumann provides the most systematic account) the real wage per man is a technical datum; the rate of profit on capital emerges as a residual. In Marx, the rate of exploitation (the ratio of net profit to wages) is the result of the balance of forces in the class struggle. For Marshall, there is a normal rate of profit and the real wage emerges as a residual; an extension of Keynes' General Theory into the long period finds a clue to the level of normal profits in the rate of accumulation and the excess of consumption out of profits over saving out of wages.

When the neo-neoclassicals reconstituted orthodoxy after the

Keynesian revolution they eschewed all these and went to Walras, who does not have a theory of profits at all.

4

ECONOMETRICS

The strangest part of the whole affair is that many neo-neoclassicals seek to identify leets-capital with the dollar value of capital as it appears in statistics. Professor Ferguson concludes his account of 'reswitching' thus: 'The question that confronts us is not whether the Cambridge Criticism is theoretically valid. It is. Rather the question is an empirical or econometric one: is there sufficient substitutability within the system to establish neoclassical results?'[11] And he states in the Preface: 'Until the econometricians have the answer for us, placing reliance upon neoclassical economic theory is a matter of faith.' Statisticians, though with a very coarse mesh, can catch evidence of the capital to output ratio in terms of dollar values, and the shares of wages and profits in value added, over a particular period in a particular economy, and so they can offer an estimate of the *ex-post* overall rate of profit being realized. They cannot say what expectations of profit were in the minds of the managers of firms, or whether alternative schemes were on the drawing boards of engineers, when the investment decisions were taken that brought a particular stock of capital equipment into existence. Still less can they say what decisions would have been taken if present and expected prices and wage rates had been different from what they were. Professor Ferguson expects too much.

Consider a run of figures for a prosperous period of development in a modern industrial economy which conform more or less (as they often seem to do) to what Kaldor calls the 'stylized facts'. The capital to output ratio and the wage and profit shares are fairly constant over time, while the dollar value of output per man employed and the dollar value of capital per man have a strong upward trend. This would lend itself to interpretation as an approximation to the story of accumulation on a Harrod path, as in the vintage model, with neutral technical progress and a fairly steady overall average rate of profit (fluctuations in effective demand being smoothed out).

This will not do for the neo-neoclassicals. They want to separate out increases in the quantity of 'capital' from the effects of technical progress. To find this distinction, they puzzle themselves with their leets. Leets can absorb technical progress without any investment being required. An

[11] *The Neoclassical Theory of Production and Distribution*, p. 266.

'invention' raises the output per head of a set of workers equipped with a given quantity of leets. But output also consists of leets, so that if the share of saving in income is constant, leets per man employed begin to rise as a result of the invention. Is this to be attributed to accumulation or to the invention? To attribute the growth of leets per man to saving, it would be necessary to define as saving, refraining from consuming so much of additional leets as to keep leets per man constant.[12]

In any case, the statistics are in dollars, not in tons of leets. Whether technical progress is embodied in new types of equipment or affected by a rearrangement of existing equipment or comes from 'learning by doing' by workers without any change in equipment at all, the figures would be the same. The difference would appear only in the amount of gross investment required to keep the economy growing.

Output of capital equipment must be reckoned not in tons of any metal or in lists of items (a bus is a bus and a lathe is a lathe) but in terms of productive capacity. Overall, wages in terms of product are rising in step with output per head, and the rate of profit is constant. The capital to output ratio, overall, does not change much, either way. For embodied technical progress, therefore, the cost per unit of productive capacity is rising at the same rate as output per head.

Equally, the value of equipment absorbing disembodied progress (if there is such a thing) would rise at the same rate. Profit per man employed rises with output per head (since the real wage rises at the same rate) and no depreciation is required. Capitalize the profits at a rate of interest equal to the overall rate of profit and the value of the equipment rises at the same rate as output per head.

Professor Jorgenson uses just this procedure to account for the rise in the value of capital shown in his statistics but then he attributes its growth entirely to accumulation and maintains that no technical progress has occurred in US industry since 1945.[13] More often a set of statistics is used to draw up a production function in terms of 'capital' and labour and to separate the growth of the value of output per head into the part due to the increase in the quantity of 'capital' and the 'residual' due to technical progress. This required the statisticians to find out from the record of what actually happened, what the growth of output *would have been* if the value of capital had grown as much as it did without any technical progress having

[12] Cf. T. K. Rymes, 'Professor Read and the measurement of total factor productivity', *Canadian Journal of Economics* (May 1968).

[13] D. W. Jorgenson and Z. Griliches, 'The explanation of productivity change', *Review of Economic Studies*, 34 (July 1967), 249–83.

taken place. (It must have needed an even tougher hide to survive Phelps Brown's article on 'The Meaning of the Fitted Cobb–Douglas Function'[14] than to ward off Cambridge Criticism of the marginal productivity theory of distribution.)

No doubt Professor Ferguson's restatement of 'capital' theory will be used to train new generations of students to erect elegant-seeming arguments in terms which they cannot define and will confirm econometricians in the search for answers to unaskable questions. Criticism can have no effect. As he himself says, it is a matter of faith.

[14] *Quarterly Journal of Economics*, 71 (November 1957), 546–60.

11

THE MEANING OF CAPITAL

THE controversies over so-called capital theory arose out of the search for a model appropriate to a modern western economy, which would allow for an analysis of accumulation and of the distribution of the net product of industry between wages and profits.

1

The old orthodoxy, which relied heavily on Say's Law and a natural tendency to the establishment of equilibrium with full employment, had been discredited in the depression of the 1930s. Keynes had cleared the way for a new approach. He broke down the old dichotomy between *Principles* and *Money*, treating the financial system as part of the general functioning of the economy. He observed that, because prediction of the future is necessarily uncertain, behaviour affecting economic life (or private life, for that matter) cannot be governed by strictly rational calculations of the outcome. He pointed out that accumulation depends upon decision about investment taken by business firms and governments, not by decisions about saving taken by households, and he drew a clear distinction (which was confused in the old orthodoxy) between interest, as the price that a businessman pays for the use of finance to be committed to an investment, and profit, which is the return that he hopes to get on it. He pointed out that wage rates are settled in terms of money and the level of real wages depends upon the operation of the economy as a whole. All this cleared the ground for a model appropriate to modern capitalism, but Keynes' own construction was confined to dealing with short-period analysis.

In a short-period situation, here and now, the organization of industry, stocks of equipment, the training of the labour force and the habits of consumers are already settled. These elements in the situation are changing very slowly and for practical purposes may be taken as constant. The model is designed to deal with the causes and consequences of the changes in

Draft of the article which appeared in French in *Revue d'Economie Politique*, March 1977.

THE MEANING OF CAPITAL

employment of labour and utilization of given physical resources which occur with swings of effective demand.

The stock of means of production ('capital goods') in existence at a moment of time can be represented by a who's who of particular items. The value of the stock is not a very precise concept. Businesses reckon book value in terms of the accounting conventions that they choose to follow. The stock exchange value of a corporation depends upon the market's estimate of future profits and on the level of interest rates. Market expectations are notoriously unstable and interest rates are influenced by monetary policy or, in any one financial centre, by events in others.

Since the value of capital is not a precise concept, the *rate* of profit is not precise. This did not matter for Keynes. He needed to consider only the flow of actual gross profits today and the expected return in the future on finance invested today. Finance to be invested is a definite sum of money, with whatever purchasing power it has today over labour time and physical inputs, but the expected return is far from definite; it is based upon extrapolation of past experience, guesswork or convention, coloured by the subjective mood, 'animal spirits', in which investment plans are being drawn up.

This was sufficient for short-period analysis, but once Keynes' theory was accepted, long-run accumulation became the centre of interest; it was therefore necessary to come to grips with concepts of the quantity of capital and the rate of profit in the economy as a whole.

2

The 'mainstream teaching' being developed, particularly in the United States, seemed to be based upon three distinct types of model, often mixed up together.

In the first, the economy is represented by a grand co-operative without private property. Society saves, and society enjoys the benefit of the increased income which accumulation provides. To make sense of Frank Ramsey's elegant formula for the optimum rate of saving, it is necessary to suppose that output consists of some kind of homogeneous substance that can be consumed or used as means of production. Saving, that is, the excess of output over consumption, is added to stock and increases future production. The growth of output with the growth of stock is subject to diminishing returns, and so is the growth of utility for society as a whole with the growth of consumption.

The second type of model is based on the general equilibrium of Walras.

Here there is a stock of specific means of production, often called 'machines'. To overcome the problem of amortisation, machines are sometimes assumed to be indefinitely durable or, alternatively, subject to 'radio-active decay' so that their value at any moment is independent of their age. From one point of view this is similar to the short-period concept of a stock of equipment in existence at a moment of time, but from another point of view it is quite different. There is no utilization function, showing how output varies with employment. Labour and machines are fully utilized in equilibrium and the machines can be used, in different combinations, to make a great variety of alternative outputs, exhibited on a 'production-possibility surface'. The main emphasis of the analysis is on exchange. Production consists of hiring various inputs and combining them in various proportions. When the market is in equilibrium, the rentals of the various inputs required for each output absorb its value and there is no profit. This concept of equilibrium requires an exact definition of the number of workers in the economy (natives and immigrants?) and the hours of work per week and per year corresponding to 'full employment'.

The third type of model was derived from Marshall, vulgarized by J. B. Clark.[1] Here 'capital' is a factor of production, along with land and labour. The returns to factors are governed by their marginal productivities. 'Capital' is embodied in 'machines'; the marginal productivity of 'machines' governs the interest received by rentiers. There is a separate item for profits, which is the return to 'enterprise' or the 'co-ordinating function', that is, the management of business.

The concept of 'capital' as something distinct from physical means of production is connected with business experience. A new business sets out with a sum of money, whether owned by the proprietors or borrowed at interest. The money is invested in means of production and work in progress. So long as the business is successful, the value of the original investment is kept intact. It may be augmented by further investment financed out of profits or by further borrowing. A part of gross profit is treated as an amortisation fund. With the passage of time, the original form of the investment may cease to be the most profitable and the first stock of means of production is replaced by another, embodying a different technique or aimed at a different market. Thus the initial finance (so long as the business is successful) continues to exist as a sum of value being continuously embodied in different forms of productive capacity. But finance arises out of relationships within an economy. How can finance be treated as a factor of production?

[1] See *The Distribution of Wealth. A Theory of Wages, Interest and Profits*, 1899.

J. B. Clark blithely treated 'capital' as a quantity of something which could be embodied in various kinds of 'capital goods' and changed from one embodiment to another, but he did not try to explain what this quantity consisted of. Marshall at one moment pronounced that the factors of production should be regarded as land, labour and waiting.[2] Waiting means owning a stock of wealth. Thus the stock of capital is represented by the sum of the value of all assets owned by the individuals and institutions that the economy comprises. But Marshall was well aware that the value of assets is influenced by the level of the rate of interest and he admitted that it is impossible to derive the rate of interest from the value of capital without arguing in a circle. Wicksell was troubled by the same problem. Just before the eruption of the Keynesian revolution, Dennis Robertson posed the question of the meaning of a quantity of capital in terms of his story of ten men with nine spades.[3]

Apparently unaware that this problem had never been solved, the mainstream economists were drawing production functions of the form $O=f(K, L)$, the quantity of output is a function of the quantity of inputs of labour and 'capital'. Moreover, they were using this formula to interpret statistics of the performance of industry, and treating the actual levels of wages and profits as the marginal products of labour and capital. In an article published in 1953, I revived the old question and asked whether K, the quantity of capital, was supposed to be a sum of money or a list of 'machines'.

One answer was that a production function can be drawn up in terms of specified inputs, and that the value of 'capital' is an unnecessary concept. But these inputs, seemingly, were not produced by profit-seeking investment. They may have fallen from heaven, like Marshall's meteoric stones; there is no means of discussing how further accumulation will take place.

The more usual answer was to set up a model in which physical products are as like as possible to money. Ouput consists of a single homogeneous, divisible commodity, say, butter, which is both consumable and can be turned into a stock of means of production. The stock is 'malleable'; a stock of butter which has been used for one type of production can be withdrawn and moulded into another form without cost and without change in quantity. (This model is not quite the same as Frank Ramsey's co-operative, because the income of 'society' is divided between wages and profits.)

[2] *Principles*, first edition (1890), p. 614 n. 1. In later editions the same concept is overlaid with various complications.
[3] 'Wage grumbles', *Economic Fragments*.

The butter model made it possible to revive all the propositions of pre-Keynesian orthodoxy. Say's Law prevails; saving governs accumulations; uncertainty disappears, for one investment can be turned instantaneously into another when circumstances change. Interest paid to rentiers is identified with profits accruing to firms. There is a well-behaved production function in labour and the stock of butter; when the ratio of the stock to the labour force is rising as accumulation goes on, the butter wage rises and the rate of butter profit on butter capital falls. Most remarkable of all, technical progress raises the productivity of the stock of butter without cost and without changing its quantity. (At first there was a mistake in the argument here that was put right by Professor Rymes.)[4]

This model was described as a parable. A parable, in the usual sense, is a story drawn from everyday life intended to explain a mystery; in this case it is the mystery which is expected to explain everyday life.

In order to interpret a time-series of statistics, the stock of butter in the model was identified with the book value of physical assets of firms comprised by US industry. As the relative shares of wages and profits in value added were fairly constant in the period studied, it was possible to go through the motions of fitting a Cobb-Douglas production function to the figures. But it was found that the ratio of the value of capital to value of output was fairly constant through time, thus (with a constant share of profit) the *ex-post* overall rate of profit on capital must have been constant over the period, while the average real-wage rate rose in step with the rise of output per head. On a production function representing the 'state of technical knowledge', rising real wages entail a falling rate of profit. Evidently, the statistics, at each point of observation were drawn from a different state of technology. The figures might be interpreted to show that technical progress over a period had been roughly neutral; they could not exhibit a production function, or marginal productivities, 'in a given state of technical knowledge', as the mainstream theory required.

There was some argument about the problem of 'measuring capital' but there was no answer to the old problem that, if the total stock of capital is a sum of value, it already presupposes the overall rate of profit, whereas if it is a list of 'machines' there is no unit in which it can be reckoned as a quantity.

For some purposes, for instance a comparison between the industries in various countries, a very rough measure of the physical capital to labour ratio could be used, say horse power per man employed. But then it will not generally be found that where this ratio is highest, the rate of profit on capital is lowest.

[4] See *On Concepts of Capital and Technical Change*, Cambridge University Press, 1971.

The famous Leontief paradox was a result of this confusion. Because physical capital per man (by any measure) was highest in the United States, it was supposed that 'capital' there should be the cheapest factor of production and that therefore US exports should be more 'capital intensive' than imports. Leontief's calculation showed that the value of capital per man was on the average less in the export industries. This seems to indicate that, while US industry (at that time) was generally superior to its rivals in productivity, the superiority was most marked in the industries producing productive equipment. Why should this be considered a paradox?

The lack of an acceptable definition of a 'quantity of capital' was masked by the manner in which main-line teaching was (and still is) divided into two mutually exclusive departments. Micro theory was based on a mixture of the Walrasian model, in which there is an endowment of ready-made inputs (meteoric stones) with zero profits in equilibrium, and the Pigovian model in which each firm can borrow as much finance as it chooses at a given rate of interest and 'equilibrium firms' have earnings such that net profits exactly cover the interest bill. Macro theory was concerned with Keynes and the slump. Thus there was no place in the syllabus for a discussion of the mode of operation of a modern capitalist economy considered as a whole. 'Capital theory' was regarded as an esoteric doctrine which had no application to any question of general interest.

3

The discussion which I had tried to revive in 1953 took a new turn with the publication of Piero Sraffa's *Production of Commodities by Means of Commodities* in 1960.

In Sraffa's model, the treatment of physical capital, though highly simplified, is less fanciful than either meteoric stones or a stock of butter. We are presented with, so to speak, a snapshot of a process of production going on in a particular industrial economy. A particular labour force is producing a particular flow of output by means of a particular technique, specified in a system of equations. The technique dictates what physical inputs, in what proportions, are required for labour to produce the output, over what period of time. Stocks of inputs are continuously reproduced as they are used up (long-lived equipment is treated in a separate model which however, can be fitted into the same argument). The net output of any period is the excess of the product over stocks of inputs existing at the beginning of the period. Thus output consists of a list of quantities of particular commodities, independent of prices. Now, everything in physical terms remaining the same, the share of wages in net output is run through every value from unity to zero. Corresponding to each value of the share of wages is a set of prices (in any numeraire) for all outputs and inputs, and a uniform rate of profit on the value of the stocks of inputs at these prices.

These calculations must be regarded purely as an intellectual experiment. In reality neither the real-wage rate nor the rate of profit could be zero, and it is unnatural to suppose that the composition of output would be the same with widely different levels of real wages. In an actual economy of which a snapshot is taken, some particular pattern of prices is ruling. The 'changes' of the share of wages in the argument are not actual historical events, only calculations by the observing economist.

Sraffa was not trying to construct a model for positive analysis, though the concept of a technique of production as an input-output table in physical terms is certainly very useful. His own purpose was purely negative – to provide a prelude to the critique of economic theory.

The theory that Sraffa was preparing to criticize was the Marshallian orthodoxy that prevailed when he began to work on these ideas in the 1920s; but objections to his argument have been drawn mainly from the general equilibrium doctrines prevalent today. One objection is that he 'leaves out demand'. This objection does not stand. If we people his model with firms and households then, when a particular rate of profit obtains, firms are carrying out gross investment in order to earn profits from sales and households are purchasing goods at prices that yield the ruling rate of profit. The pattern of demand is evidently appropriate to the flow of production along with the distribution of income, and the flow of production is appropriate to the pattern of demand.

Another objection is that a Sraffa system is only a special case of general equilibrium with 'fixed coefficients', that is, with only one possible combination of inputs. This betrays a basic difference between two conceptions of the process of production. In the general equilibrium model, the story begins with an arbitrary stock of ready-made inputs which can be combined in various ways to produce a variety of different outputs. In Sraffa's model, the stock of inputs in existence today was the result of investments made in the past in order to produce today's output with the technique which is in use today. Which concept is the less inappropriate to an industrial economy?

Sraffa did in fact introduce a variety of techniques into his model. Where several techniques are known, it is assumed that, given the prevailing share of wages in net output, the technique has been chosen which maximizes profits when prices are such as to make the rate of profit uniform throughout the economy. Making quite orthodox assumptions about the character of technology, Sraffa showed that the same technique may be eligible at widely different rates of profit. It was this which alerted the mainstream economists to the fact that their orthodoxy was being questioned.

4

The furore about 'reswitching' raged around the conception of a pseudo-production function. There is supposed to be a book of blueprints specifying all possible techniques for producing a flow of net output of a given composition with a given labour force. Each technique is a Sraffa system of equations requiring a specific stock of inputs, which are continually reproduced as they are used up, and involving a particular time-pattern in the process of production. The techniques are listed in order of net output per unit of labour. Corresponding to each share of wages in net output is a profit-maximizing technique. Inferior techniques are eliminated, so that each technique in the book is eligible at at least one rate of profit. Each point represents an economy on a steady-state growth path. The stock of means of production in existence at that point has been produced in the light of expectations of profit which are turning out to be correct 'today' and are therefore renewed for the future. Since expectations are held with perfect confidence, we may suppose that the ruling rate of interest is equal to the rate of profit, but it is the rate of profit, determined by technical conditions and the share of wages in net output, that governs the rate of interest, not vice versa. (But here Piero Sraffa himself does not agree with my intepretation of his model.) In an uncertain world, of course, positive (or even zero) net investment will not take place unless interest rates are appreciably lower than expected profits.

Between each pair of techniques is a switch point at which the ratio of the two values of capital is equal to the ratio of the flows of profit per annum, so that the rate of profit is the same for both.

Contrasting this construction with the well-behaved production function in the butter economy, we see, first of all, that the production function is continuously differentiable, for the smallest difference in the stock of butter per man employed entails a difference in output per man, while the pseudo-production function may have wide gaps between switch points, over which the same output per head is associated with a falling rate of profit and rising share of wages. Moreover, however dense the pages of the book of blueprints, there must always be a discontinuity in engineering terms between one technique and the next. On both constructions a higher share of wages is associated with a lower rate of profit; the most fundamental rule of the production function is that a larger stock of butter per man is associated with higher output, whereas on the pseudo-production function there is no presumption that a technique giving higher output per man requires a higher value of capital at the rate of profit at which it is eligible. And even when two techniques are compared at the same rate of profit, it is not necessarily the case, on the pseudo-production function, that a lower rate of profit is associated with a higher value of capital per man and a higher output per head. In short, a more labour-intensive technique may be eligible at a lower rate of profit than another which provides a higher output per man.

This was the point that caused all the trouble. A pseudo-production function may contain backward switch points at which a technique with a higher output per head than the next is eligible at a higher rate of profit. This may be associated with 'reswitching', since at the lowest rate of profit the eligible technique must be one with a high output per head.

The reason for these differences between the two constructions is obvious. The well-behaved production function conflates the concept of the value of capital with a stock of physical means of production while the pseudo-production function distinguishes between the physical means of production required for a particular technique and its value at various rates of profit.

After some hesitation, Professor Samuelson accepted the logic of the pseudo-production function. In the *Summing Up* of the debate ten years ago,[5] he even referred to 'a general blueprint technology model of Joan Robinson and MIT type' but his interpretation of it was (and still is) very different from mine. He recognized that each point on a pseudo function is supposed to represent an economy in a steady state, in which inputs are being reproduced in unchanged physical form, and yet he supposed that saving could raise an economy from one point to the position at another. He envisages a process of accumulation creeping up the pseudo-production function from lower to higher shares of wages, and higher to lower rates of profit. But an increase in gross investment above the rate required to maintain a steady state would entail an enlargement of investment industries (which would have to shrink again when a new steady state was reached). The former pattern of prices would be upset. Inputs appropriate to one technique would have to be scrapped and replaced by those appropriate to another. And how are we to imagine that the prospect

[5] 'Paradoxes in capital theory', *Quarterly Journal of Economics*, November 1966, p. 578.

of a lower rate of profit in the future induces these changes to be made?

A steady state implies that everyone concerned holds perfectly confident expectations that the future will continue to reproduce the past. If those expectations fail to be fulfilled, the economy is thrown into short-period disequilibrium and analysis has to be conducted in Keynesian terms.

This is nothing to do with 'reswitching'. Professor Samuelson's first reaction to Sraffa had been to construct a special case of a pseudo-production function (the 'surrogate production function')[6] in which, at each point, labour-value prices rule, so that the cost of the stock of means of production, for each economy, is independent of the rate of profit. A higher value of capital is then always associated with a higher net output per head. On such a pseudo-production function, backward switch points cannot occur. But, like the general case, it can be used only for comparisons of supposed steady-state economies, not for analysing a process of accumulation changing the value of capital per man.

A similar difficulty arises in arguing from Walrasian general equilibrium: At a point on the production-possibility surface at which supply and demand are in equilibrium for each commodity, buyers and sellers evidently expect the same prices which obtain today to be ruling next week. A change in demand ruptures the equilibrium, disappoints expectations – some for the better and some for the worse – and requires investment in one kind of stock and disinvestment in others. Here also, further developments can be analysed only in Keynesian terms.

The notion that conditions of demand allocate scarce means between alternative uses might apply to the case of an independent peasant deciding what crops to grow to feed his family, but in modern industry the greater part of resources, at any moment, are committed, in fixed equipment, to a narrow range of uses. The question of allocation concerns new investment, but both the level and form of investment are decided, for the most part, from political motives (armaments, hospitals) and from judgments of their own interests by the great corporations. It can hardly be identified with the beneficient operations of a hidden hand in a perfectly competitive market.

The exposition both of general equilibrium and of long-run accumulation seems generally to be conducted by drawing a two-dimensional diagram on a blackboard and then introducing historical events into it. A change cannot be depicted on the plane surface of the blackboard. Changes occur in time, and as soon as a point moves off the

---

[6] 'Parable and realism in capital theory: the surrogate production function', *Review of Economic Studies*, 1962, XXIX, 193–206.

blackboard into the third dimension of time, it is no longer bound by the relationships shown in the diagram.

It seems as though, all this while, mainstream teaching has been inculcating defective methodology.

5

Since the mainstream flows awry, we must return to the source. The classical economists did not treat society as a co-operative and they did not treat capital as a quantity of homogeneous stuff. For them, finance was the means of organizing labour and physical inputs to produce outputs, and gross profit was derived from the excess of physical output over the physical wage bill. Keynes condemned Ricardo for his neglect of short-period instability but, as Luigi Pasinetti says: 'Keynes' theory of effective demand, which has remained so impervious to reconciliation with marginal economic theory, raises almost no problem when directly inserted into the earlier discussions of the Classical economists.'[7]

This is still more true of Michał Kalecki's version of the theory of employment, which grew out of the Marxian schema of expanded reproduction and which related imperfect competition to the Marxian concept of exploitation.

Pasinetti continues:

> Similarly . . . the post-Keynesian theories of economic growth and income distribution, which have required so many artificial assumptions in the efforts to reconcile them with marginal productivity theory, encounter almost no difficulty when directly grafted on to Classical economic dynamics.[8]

The pseudo-production function was a very useful piece of scaffolding but it is not to be incorporated in the construction of a dynamic theory. Obviously, two stocks of inputs appropriate to two different techniques cannot co-exist in time and space. There is no book of ready-drawn blueprints appropriate to different rates of interest. As accumulation goes on, technology evolves, and no technique is blueprinted before it is about to be used. Moreover, no stock of means of production in real life is ever perfectly adjusted to the expectations of profit being entertained when it is in use. The pseudo-production function was not a model for the analysis of

[7] *Growth and Income Distribution*, Cambridge University Press (1974), p. ix.
[8] Ibid.

capitalism but a device to smoke out the contradictions in mainstream teaching.

The controversy has been a great waste of mental energy, for

> He who is convinced against his will
> Is of the same opinion still.

It is high time to abandon the mainstream and take to the turbulent waters of truly dynamic analysis.

12

HISTORY VERSUS EQUILIBRIUM

KEYNES regarded the triumph of Adam Smith over the Mercantilists and of Ricardo over Malthus as a victory of dogmatism over good sense, and he could not make head or tail of Marx; yet the conceptions of the *General Theory* have much more in common with the classical school of the first half of the nineteenth century than with the neoclassical doctrines in which Keynes himself was brought up.

The main preoccupation of the classical economists was with an historical process of accumulation in a capitalist economy and its relation to the distribution of the product of industry between the classes of society while the neo-classicals concentrated upon conditions of equilibirium in a stationary state.

When Keynes summed up what he felt to be the main difference between his theory and that from which he had had 'a long struggle to escape', he pointed to the admission into his argument of the very obvious fact that expectations about the future are necessarily uncertain. The uncertainty that surrounds expectations of the outcome of a plan of investment, of the course of technical progress, of the behaviour of future prices, not to mention the effects of natural and political cataclysms, cannot be reduced to a 'calculated risk' by applying the theorems of mathematical probability. Keynes described equilibrium theory as 'a pretty, polite technique' 'which tries to deal with the present by abstracting from the fact that we know very little about the future'.[1]

As soon as the uncertainty of the expectations that guide economic behaviour is admitted, equilibrium drops out of the argument and history takes its place. The post-Keynesian theory reaches back to clasp the hands of Ricardo and Marx, skipping over the sixty years of dominance of neoclassical doctrines from 1870 to the great slump. This accounts for the paradox that post-Keynesian analysis derives equally from two such apparently incompatible sources as Piero Sraffa's interpretation of Ricardo and Michał Kalecki's interpretation of the theory of employment.

[1] 'The general theory of employment', *Quarterly Journal of Economics*, February 1937 reprinted in *Collected Writings of John Maynard Keynes*, Vol. XIV.

First published in the series 'Thames Papers in Political Economy'.

1

Equilibrium has been defined in these terms: 'Prices and input-output combinations are said to be equilibrium prices and input-output combinations if, when they rule, no economic agent has any inducement to change his method of production, and no input is in excess demand.'[2]

This entails that everyone knows exactly and in full detail what consequences would follow any action that he may take. (Indeed, the condition for reaching equilibrium is often stated to be 'perfect foresight'.) It rules out the holding of stock or money balances for contingencies, and it rules out any plans, say, for business investment or household saving, with consequences spread over future time in which circumstances are liable to change.

There is another curious feature of the concept. Equilibrium is described as 'the end of an economic process'; the story is usually told of a group of individuals each with an 'endowment' of ready-made goods or of productive capacity of some specific kind. By trading and retrading in a market, each ends up with a selection of goods that he prefers to those that he started with. If we intepret this as an historical process, it implies that, in the period of past time leading to 'today', equilibrium was not established. Why are the conditions that led to a non-equilibrium position 'today' not going to be present in the future?

Furthermore, the concept of 'stability', based on a mechanical analogy, is inappropriate in economic analysis. For mechanical movements in space, there is no distinction between approaching equilibrium from an arbitrary initial position and a perturbation due to displacement from an equilibrium that has long been established. In economic life, in which decisions are guided by expectations about the future, these two types of movement are totally different.

Some theorists, even among those who reject general equilibrium as useless, praise its logical elegance and completeness. A system of simultaneous equations need not specify any date nor does its solution involve history. But if any proposition drawn from it is applied to an economy inhabited by human beings, it immediately becomes self-contradictory. Human life does not exist outside history and no one has correct foresight of his own future behaviour, let alone of the behaviour of all the other individuals which will impinge upon his. I do not think that it is right to praise the logical èlegance of a system which becomes self-

[2] F. H. Hahn, *The Share of Wages in the National Income*, Weidenfeld and Nicolson, London, 1972.

contradictory when it is applied to the question that it was designed to answer.

The specification of a self-reproducing or self-expanding system such as that of Sraffa or von Neumann exists in logical time, not in history. Any point on it entails its past just as completely as it entails its future. To confront it with a question such as: 'What would happen if demand changed? is nonsensical. A different composition of output requires a different set of equations. We could work out alternative von Neumann rays for different compositions of the real wage, comparing say, a diet of potatoes with wheat, postulating the same spectrum of technical knowledge, and see which path yields the higher rate of profit. But even this is a somewhat idle exercise, for the path an economy follows necessarily influences its technology. An economy that has developed the technology for growing potatoes does not have the same spectrum of technical knowledge as one which only grows wheat. In a Walrasian model, the stock of inputs in existence at any moment is quite arbitrary – perhaps it dropped from the sky, like Marshall's meteoric stones. But for Sraffa or von Neumann the inputs available today were produced by labour and inputs in the proportions required, with the technology in use, to produce tomorrow's output.

If we construct the equations for a single self-reproducing system and then confront it with an unforeseen change, an event taking place at a particular date, we cannot say anything at all before we have introduced a whole fresh system specifying how the economy behaves in short-period disequilibrium.

The most obvious application of post-Keynesian analysis (the behaviour of an economy in conditions of uncertainty) is to Keynes' own problems – investment decisions, the determination of the pattern and level of interest rates, and the evolution of the general price level – but it is equally necessary to apply it to so-called micro economics and the behaviour of markets.

2

In a Walrasian economy there are a number of individuals each with his endowment, and his tastes and his technical expertise. Tastes, incomes and technical conditions determine the price and the volume of each output; from these are derived the hire prices or 'rentals' for the services of inputs; from the rental of his input the quantity that he owns is derived the income of each individual. There must be sufficient substitutability between commodities and versatility of inputs to ensure that there is a position of equilibrium in which each individual has at least a subsistence income. (Anyone who did not, died long ago.)

The weakest link in the circle of simultaneous equations is that which connects prices to incomes. We do not seem to be able to say anything about it except in the form of a census. Mr. Jones owns x tons of input type 'A' so that at the equilibrium rental p_a (per ton per week) his weekly income is xp_a. Mr. Smith provides 40 hours of work type 'B' so that his weekly income is w_b, and so forth. The approach in terms of a census blurs the distinction between income from work and income from property and leaves no room for the classical problem of the 'distribution of the produce of the earth between the classes of the community'.

Nevertheless, supporters of the Walrasian system often maintain that it provides a link between demand and distribution that is missing from Sraffa's model.

To deploy this argument, Professor Harry Johnson provides a highly reduced form of general equilibrium.[3] The economy produces only two commodities; resources consist of a number of perfectly similar versatile workers and a particular lump of 'putty-capital' that is, a homogeneous physical input that can be squeezed (without cost) into any form required by technology; there is a well-behaved production function in putty and labour time for each commodity. In the context of accumulation, 'putty' is a way of getting rid of differences between the future and the past; putty investment, once made, can be undone and squeezed into another form while still representing the same 'quantity of capital'. But in the context of a static model, it might be defended as a way of representing the indefinite substitutability between physical inputs which is characteristic of the general equilibrium system.

Professor Johnson's assumptions provide the essential characteristics of the Walrasian system, while making it more perspicuous.

First, it brings out clearly the conditions for so-called instability in general equilibrium. For instance, where putty owners have a strong preference for the more putty-intensive commodity, a higher price of that commodity in terms of the other, which yields a larger income to putty owners, must be associated with a higher demand for the commodity, and so a higher demand for putty, whereas the rule of substitution requires that a higher price of putty is associated with a lower demand for it.

In such a case, as Professor Johnson shows, there may be several widely

[3] H. G. Johnson, *The Two Sector Model of General Equilibrium*, Allen and Unwin, London, 1971.

separated price ratios yielding potential positions of equilibrium. (This is analogous to 'reswitching' on a pseudo-production function.) In a 'well-behaved case' there is one equilibrium position corresponding to one set of equations.

Secondly, it is clear that the relation of prices to demand does not depend only on 'consumers' tastes' but also on the census of ownership of inputs, and on technical conditions which govern the interaction between the prices of the commodities and the rentals of inputs. (This seems to vindicate Marshall's one-at-a-time method of treating supply and demand. The world demand for, say, peanuts can be treated as independent of their conditions of production, but, in general equilibrium, supply and demand cannot be treated as independent of each other.)

With the aid of Professor Johnson's simplified model, we can examine the relations of tastes, rentals and technical conditions with prices and the composition of output, in alternative positions of equilibrium. The argument must be conducted, however, strictly in terms of comparisons of specified positions. We cannot say anything about how any position was reached from some other starting point. Nor can we say what would happen if there was a change in tastes. It is not legitimate to introduce an event into a system of simultaneous equations.

On a two-dimensional diagram, time lies at right angles to the plane on which the diagram is drawn, with the past behind it and the future in front. Suppose that Professor Johnson's economy has been living through history on a path passing through one equilibrium point and that, at some date, a change in tastes occurs. Then the position is no longer one of equilibrium. A change in the pattern of production must involve investment and disinvestment, at least in work-in-progress, and windfall losses and gains on stocks that have become inappropriate. To say how long it will take, or by what path, to find a new equilibrium (if there is one) we have to fill in a whole story about the behaviour of the economy when it is out of equilibrium, including the effect of disappointed expectations on decisions being taken by its inhabitants. The Walrasian system is no more capable of dealing with changes in demand than the system of Sraffa or von Neumann.

The theory of markets was in need of a Keynesian revolution just as much as the theory of employment. Keynes himself threw out some hints and anyone who is acquainted with the conduct, say, of trade in primary commodities, knows that it is dominated by *speculation*, that is by guesses about the future behaviour of demand and of supply. Such markets are made by intermediaries (often on several layers) between original producers and final buyers. Uncertainty tends to make markets unstable, since a rise of price is often a signal for buying in stocks and a fall for selling out.

The prices of manufacturers are less volatile. The large powerful firms deal directly with retailers and set prices according to a more or less long range policy. Even they, however, cannot know the future; they work on estimates. The system of so called 'full-cost pricing' means calculating expenses, including amortization allowances, per unit of output on the basis of an assumed average level of utilization and length of earning life of plant and then adding a margin for the level of net profit that it seems prudent to go for. When actual utilization over the life of plant exceeds the standard, net profit exceeds the calculated level, and conversely.

There is a range of small businesses which operate in markets of an intermediate type. Such producers are subject to a large extent to the vagaries of supply and demand but not to the perpetual oscillations of commodity prices. They are an important part of an economy such as that of India, but in the West they are falling more and more under the control of oligopsonists (large retail chains) which administer prices for them. All this is ruled out from equilibrium theory 'which tries to deal with the present by abstracting from the fact that we know very little about the future'.

3

Another major characteristic that Keynes had in common with the classics was that they, like him, were concerned with actual contemporary problems and put their arguments in terms of the structure and behaviour of the economy in which they were living, while the neoclassics enunciated what purported to be universal laws, based on human nature — greed, impatience and so forth. The latter rarely say anything at all about the kind of economy to which an argument is to be applied. The suggestion is that the same laws which govern the supposed behaviour of Robinson Crusoe are equally valid for the conduct of Gosplan, or rather for what its conduct *ought* to be, and for analysing the vagaries of Wall Street.

Marshall retained something of the classical tradition. His world is inhabited by businessmen, housewives, workers, trade union leaders, bankers and traders. His moralizing tone — 'There are many fine natures among domestic servants . . .' sounds comical to modern ears, and he was not above twisting observation to suit his theory — Joint Stock Companies stagnate — but he was studying a recognizable economy in a particular phase of its historical development, in which recognizable classes of the

community interact with each other in a particular framework of law and
accepted conventions.

Pigou emptied history out of Marshall and reduced the analysis to a
two-dimensional scheme. Marshall's argument had created a notorious
dilemma. He believed in economies of scale for the individual firm; as a
firm grows it acquires experience, invests in new techniques and lowers cost
of production per unit of output. But in every market (with a few well
known exceptions) there are enough firms competing with each other to
keep prices in line with costs. Why does not one firm, that happens to get a
start, undersell others, grow, reduce costs further, and finally establish a
monopoly? Marshall's argument was that the life of a firm is bound up with
that of a family; by the third generation, the vigour of the founder has been
lost and the firm ceases to grow. This is certainly true of many actual case
histories but as a universal law it had to be backed up by the remarkably
untrue dictum that joint-stock companies stagnate.

Pigou set out to rescue Marshall from his dilemma by introducing the
equilibrium size of firm. Every week, a firm is maximizing profits by selling
such an output as to make the marginal cost of its product equal to the ruling
price; over the long run, competition forces it to operate at the minimum
point of a U-shaped curve, where marginal and average cost are both equal
to price. There is a rate of interest (somehow connected with the discount
of the future of owners of wealth) at which every firm can borrow as much
or as little as it likes; when it is in equilibrium, its net profit per annum is
just sufficient to cover interest, at the ruling rate on the value of its capital.

This rigmarole was the only legacy from Marshall that has been
incorporated into modern orthodoxy.

Side by side with the Pigovian system, the heritage of Walras has been
very much elaborated; in this sphere the specification of the character of the
economy is not so much unreal as non-existent. Sometimes it seems that
there are no people in the market at all – only prices and quantities of
commodities are mentioned. Sometimes every individual has his own
endowment both of labour power and of physical inputs, so that society
consists of a number of Robinson Crusoes, living side by side and exchanging their products. Sometimes we seem to be in Adam Smith's world where
a man (evidently of independent means) appeals to the self-interest of the
baker and the brewer to get him his dinner.

But then again, society is represented as a pure co-operative, without
distinction of classes or occupations. Society saves, as in Frank Ramsey's
famous theorem, and society enjoys the benefit of the increased income that
accumulation provides.

The leap from Walras to Pigou is made by means of a pun. For Walras, a 'factor of production' is something like a carpenter, a load of bricks, or a meadow. In the system, relayed by Pigou, that Marshall derived from Ricardo, the factors of production are labour, capital and land. Taking the word 'factor' in both senses at once, the argument about the prices of items in the available stock of inputs, established by higgling and haggling in a market, is applied to the determination of wages, interest and rent in long run equilibrium.

This pun, presented in mathematical notation, is the basis of so-called micro-economics offered in the fashionable text books.

4

Keynes pointed out the distinction between interest, which a business has to pay on borrowed finance, and profit, which it hopes to get on an investment. For his strictly short period problem, he did not need a realized rate of profit on capital, only a forward looking, uncertain expectation of profits. This could be formally expressed as the rate of discount that reduces the expected series of future quasi-rents to equality with the capital sum to be invested today; but uncertainty and prospective changes in the value of money make the calculation vague.

Marshall's normal profits and Wicksell's natural rate of interest were supposed to apply to a capitalist economy but their level was never explained. Adam Smith had quite a different story for the pin factory from that of the baker and the brewer; there, the share of profit was higher the lower the wage could be set, but a clear explanation of the determination of the rate of profit eluded him. Only Ricardo laid the basis for a theory of the rate of profit on capital and this was forgotten in the neoclassical era until it was disinterred by Sraffa. The neo-neoclassicals try to substitute the concept of 'the rate of return' for a theory of profits.

For Irving Fisher, the rate of return was the increment of income that a man could get from adding an increment to his wealth. Thus, in a modern economy with a gilt-edged rate of interest of 10 per cent, £10 per annum in perpetuity is the rate of return on a saving of £100. In an artisan economy, the return on saving is an addition to the flow of output, say of horse-shoes, produced with a given amount of work by a blacksmith who puts part of his energy into improving his forge. On Frank Ramsey's growth path, the rate return in terms of utility to society as a whole on further saving varies as wealth accumulates. But the rate of return is connected with the rate of profit in a capitalist economy only by a methodological confusion.

Let us return to the picture of an economy in a static state of Walrasian equilibrium. Now compare it with another economy, with the same tastes and technology, in equilibrium with the same labour force and a larger amount of physical inputs (more of some and no less of any). There is then a larger output of some or all of the commodities being produced.

Professor Johnson could say that the second economy has a larger lump of putty, so that the hire price of putty per unit, taken as a whole, is lower than in the first economy, while the income of a representative worker is higher than in the first economy. The income of a representative putty owner may be less or greater according to the elasticity of substitution between putty and labour. (This follows from the assumptions of general equilibrium; it does not correspond to anything in real life.)

For such a comparison putty may be thought to be an adequate concept. But it does not enable us to say *how much* greater the second set of inputs is as simple quantity (putty is a parable, not to be taken literally) still less, how the additional output in the second position is related to the additional inputs as a simple ratio.

The two lists of inputs and outputs are made up of items in different proportions and there may be some item in the second list that did not appear in the first. All relative prices are different in the two positions. A comparison of wage rates or of the value of stocks of inputs in the two positions would depend entirely on the numeraire chosen, and no one numeraire has more relevance than any other.

The question has been much discussed under the title of the 'measurement of capital'. But, properly speaking, there is no 'capital' in a Walrasian market. There are no capitalists who have invested finance in productive capacity with a view to employing labour and making profits. There is only a list of quantities of various kinds of available inputs.

In a Pigovian stationary state, there is a stock of capital, of which the value, say, in terms of wage units, depends upon technical conditions and the rate of interest. Instead of an arbitrary list of objects, there is a flow of investment going on which is just sufficient to keep the balanced stock of equipment intact as it wears out and to renew supplies of raw materials used up in production. The flow of net output constitutes the income of the economy, which is all being consumed.

The Austrian theory, developed by Wicksell, attempted to 'measure capital' in such a case by the 'average period of production'. As Wicksell found, this is not exact; but even if it were, it would be no help in detecting the 'rate of return'.

We may imagine that we make a comparison between two equilibrium positions, with an identical labour force, one with a higher net output than the other. But it does not follow that the second has 'more capital' or a longer average period of production than the first. If we compare them at a common rate of interest, there is no guarantee that the one with the higher output has the higher value of capital. They are simply two equilibrium positions using different techniques, each with the stock of means of production appropriate to its own technique, and each with its own past history, that led to its present position.

The long wrangle about 'measuring capital' has been a great deal of fuss over a secondary question. The real source of trouble is the confusion between comparisons of equilibrium positions and the history of a process of accumulation.

We might suppose that we can take a number of still photographs of economies each in stationary equilibrium; let us suppose that the 'measurement' problem can be solved by calculating all values in terms of labour time, and that it happens that the economies can be arranged in a series in which a larger value of capital per man employed is associated with a higher net output per man of a homogeneous consumption good, as on Professor Samuelson's 'Surrogate production function'. This is an allowable thought experiment. But it is not allowable to flip the stills through a projector to obtain a moving picture of a process of accumulation.

Before we can discuss accumulation, we must go back to the beginning and deal with the questions which Walras and Pigou left unanswered. In what kind of economy is accumulation taking place? Is it Frank Ramsey's classless co-operative, a collection of peasants and artisans, or a modern capitalist nation? Is it a property-owning democracy in which the rate of saving depends on the decisions of households? If so, by what means is saving converted into additions to the stock of inputs? Or if investment depends on the decisions of industrial firms, how do they get command of finance, and what expectations of profits are guiding their plans? Is there a mechanism in the system to ensure growth with continuous full employment? And if an increasing value of capital per man leads to a prospective fall in the rate of profit, do the firms go meekly crawling down a pre-existing production function, or do they introduce new techniques that raise output per unit of investment as well as output per man?

The data for periods of continuous growth in the industrial capitalist countries generally seem to conform pretty well to Kaldor's stylized facts – a fairly constant ratio both of the value of capital and of the wage bill to the value of output. This entails that the overall ex-post rate of profit on capital was fairly constant. With rising real wages and a constant rate of profit, it follows that each point of observation must have been drawn from a different technology. Even as a thought-experiment, it is meaningless to postulate the existence in a growing economy of a surrogate production function or a pseudo-production function, well or ill-behaved, on which a number of equilibrium positions, with different techniques, co-exist at a moment of time.

Certainly, for a developing country, the choice of technique is an important problem. The choice is not concerned with the ratio of 'capital' to labour or to output. It is concerned with the allocation of investible resources. The increment of future productivity of labour due to creating an addition to the stock of inputs might be called the return to investment (though it is not easy to express it as a rate) but it has nothing whatever to do with the rate of profit or the rate of interest on the pre-existing total stock of capital, or of wealth, inherited from the past.

The problem of the 'measurement of capital' is a minor element in the criticism of the neo-classical doctrines. The major point is that what they pretend to offer as an alternative or rival to the post-Keynesian theory of accumulation is nothing but an error in methodology – a confusion between comparisons of imagined equilibrium positions and a process of accumulation going on through history.

5

The lack of a comprehensible treatment of historical time, and failure to specify the rules of the game in the type of economy under discussion, make the theoretical apparatus offered in neo-neoclassical text-books useless for the analysis of contemporary problems, both in the micro and macro spheres.

13

A LECTURE DELIVERED AT OXFORD BY ·
A CAMBRIDGE ECONOMIST

IF there are any galled jades present they are going to find this lecture very disobliging. (Those whose withers are unwrung will find it just their bag of oats.)

As I am going to give a disobliging lecture I will begin with a disobliging Cambridge joke. In Cambridge we all make them, and, taking one with another, as Marshall says, they come out about fair, but if you make one in isolation, among nice, polite people, it sounds very ill bred.

My disobliging joke is this: when an economist from Oxford comes to lecture at Cambridge he fills up the blackboard with such a lot of equations and diagrams that the audience is knocked out cold. I have come from Cambridge to knock you out cold with this diagram:

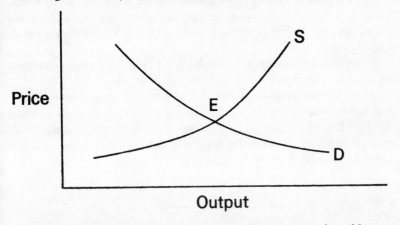

Think of a tutor explaining to a freshman the meaning of equilibrium. The tutor is a neoclassical economist. If the cap fits put it on, and if it does not, no one will be better pleased than I.

The tutor might say to the freshman: 'E is the point of equilibrium of supply and demand,' and if the young man asks: 'What is the equilibrium of supply and demand?' he answers: 'It is the point E.' So he has holed out in one. He has given the freshman a short excerpt from an illustrated dictionary.

Or he may say:

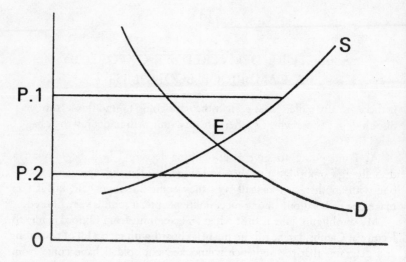

'When price is O P^1, supply exceeds demand and price tends to fall. When it is O P^2 demand exceeds supply and price tends to rise. Price may never actually be in equilibrium, but it is always tending towards equilibrium.'

Now he has gone clean off the rails. Why? He is using a metaphor based on space to explain a process which takes place in time.

Have you ever considered the difference between moving through space and moving through time? A and B are two points in space. If the bodies at A and B are out of equilibrium with each other they move simultaneously in both directions. Some of the A's go towards B, and some of the B's go towards A, and they pass each other *en route*.

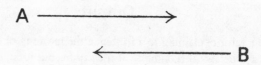

In time, there is an exceptionally strict rule of one-way traffic. You can have

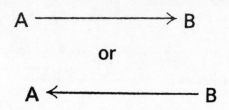

but not both.

The second point about space is that there is none of this stuff about *tending* (which the freshman, poor soul, finds extremely fishy). If you give your bodies time, they actually do get into equilibrium. Time will help you with space. But take as much space as you like – how is that going to help you with time?

The third point about space is that the distance from A to B is of the same order of magnitude as the distance from B to A. I do not say of equal magnitude because of the Trade Winds, and returning empty, and all that. But the distances are of the same order of magnitude.

In time, the distance between today and tomorrow is twenty-four hours forwards, and the distance between today and yesterday is eternity backwards. There is a lot about this written in verse, but the tutor (who never met Keynes) reads poetry, if at all, only in the evening, and does not think of mixing it up with his work.

Now the tutor says to himself: 'This is one of these tiresome logic-chopping points. I will soon fiddle my assumptions and get out of trouble.' All right – go ahead. The only single thing I insist on is that you put in the arrow of time between each pair of points.

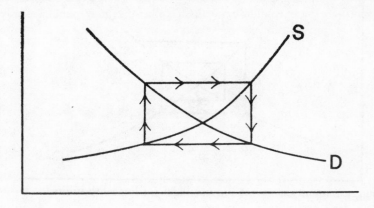

What does that remind you of? The pig cycle, the shipbuilding cycle, and the trade cycle. Now the tutor cheers up a bit. He has heard this one before.

He has two cases — first he says: 'Pigs are an exception. If I drew the picture for peanuts, I would be all right. The cycle would be a damped one.'

Go ahead — I only ask for an arrow for each move.

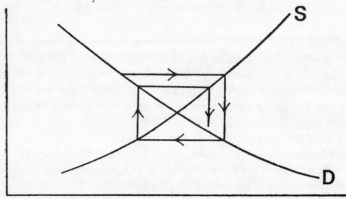

First time round, it looks as if he was on to something. Second time round? His stocks of peanuts have been altering. It would not be the same on the second round if he had started at a different point on the first round. The stocks would have altered differently. This is a kind of *tending* that the freshman cannot be expected to take in so early in his career.

Meanwhile the tutor tries his second answer. If the cycle goes like this:

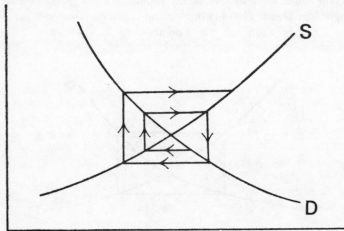

you get to infinity in a week or two, which is a logical absurdity.

But now he has played right into the Keynesian court. Even if he gets a ball over the net once in a while, Samuelson, Kaldor or Kalecki kill his service, so that he never scores a single point. It is a love game to the Keynesian every time.

Who would you say was the economist who best understood the idea that I am trying to explain with these arrows? Certainly not Keynes. He thought that neo-classical economics was a lot of stinking fish, and he threw it out of the window, holding his nose and making very disobliging remarks indeed. He never stopped to examine what it was that made the fish stink. He knew that it was something to do with time, but he could not hold his nose for long enough to find out exactly what.

Keynes got the tutor rattled. He said: 'I honestly have to admit I am a bit high in the short period. But, all the same, the long period is a non-Keynesian world. There I smell quite sweet.' (We will see about that later.)

No. The one who understood it thoroughly well was Marshall. This is not a learned lecture. I will only refer you to Appendix H in his *Principles*. Read it over again, and you will see how right I am.

Now Marshall had a remarkable intuitive genius and he knew by instinct how to find out the one case where you can say something without the arrow getting you all mixed up. The short period supply curve, under strictly perfect competition, when demand always rises, never falls.

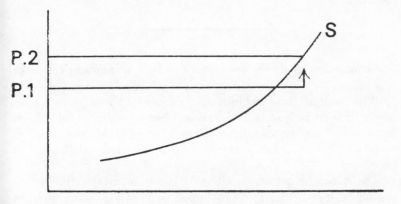

One hop up in time, and you have a position where the arrow will not worry you laterally, so long as you are in the short period.

What did he do? The more I learn about economics the more I admire Marshall's intellect and the less I like his character.

He worked out his short period for forward movements with great lucidity and then he filled the book with tear gas, so that no one would notice that he had fudged the whole of the rest of the argument. Just read Marshall's *Principles* through again with a gas mask on and you will see how right I am.

After Keynes died the tutor recovered his nerve a bit, and began to read the *General Theory* carefully and he found that it was full of the most frightful howlers. (I will explain about the howlers in a minute.) Would you believe it? That tutor was so badly brought up he did not even know the first principle of Aristotelean logic. He argued like this: Keynes says I am stinking fish. Keynes makes logical errors, therefore I am not stinking fish. (The kind of errors in logic that Keynes made were not of that order of magnitude.)

Now I will explain to you about the errors in the *General Theory*.

There is a time arrow in the process of arguing. Here are the assumptions A and here are the conclusions C.

You can start at A, puzzle: find the conclusions. Or you can start at C, puzzle: find the assumptions.

When the argument is correctly worked out (if ever) it is in equilibrium:

$$A \longleftrightarrow C$$

The conclusions imply the assumptions and the assumptions entail the conclusions.

Next I will tell you a fact from natural history. I cannot prove it; I just happened to notice it when I was making observations in the field. If you lurk in a well-constructed machan and look through field glasses you will observe a difference in habits between the tygers of wrath and the horses of instruction.

The horses of instruction always argue from the premises to the conclusion. It just is their nature to do so. So when a horse argument is not finished it looks like this:

$$A \longrightarrow \qquad C$$

Well – good luck to the horse. He will soon be there.

But the tygers of wrath go the other way. Do not ask me why. It is just a fact that I noticed when I was looking through field glasses from a machan.

To hit off a straight line from the assumptions to the conclusions is just what a horse can do, if he has a bit of horse sense, as well as pure horse stamina. But to hit off the line backwards is not at all easy, even for a tyger. Your half-finished tyger argument looks like this:

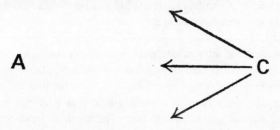

The *Treatise on Money* is a very good example of what I mean, but it takes much longer to read than Appendix H, and is not so rewarding (in this context) as Marshall's *Principles* as a whole, so please do not bother to look it up on my account. Just rely on the memory of the headache you had the first time you read it.

The *General Theory of Employment, Interest and Money* looks like this:

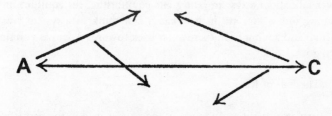

It has got the equilibrium line in it but Keynes did not rub out all the other lines before he published the book.

(You would be surprised if you knew some of the lines that did get rubbed out before R. F. Kahn would allow him to publish. Keynes refers to this in a very handsome manner in the Preface.)

So you see what I mean if I say: When you are doing economics, do not forget your Blake.

Now let us try the long period. The short period means that capital equipment is fixed in kind. You do not have to ask: When is capital not capital? because there is a specific list of blast furnaces and rolling stock and other hard objects, and for Marshall a given number of trawlers.

In the long period capital equipment changes in quantity and in design. So you come slap up to the question: What is the quantity of capital?

I would not like to have to say where the books written on that question would stretch to, if you put them end to end.

This is where my lecture is really very disobliging. All those books are nonsense, in the strict sense given to that word by Wittgenstein: 'What can be thought can be thought clearly. What can be said can be said clearly. What can be shown cannot be said.'

Now, this is pre-eminently true of captial. When you can measure a quantity of capital at all you can measure it exactly, and when it is a list of blast furnaces and other hard objects it can be shown but not be said.

So when you are doing economics, do not forget your Wittgenstein.

Let us apply the notion of equilibrium to capital. What governs the demand for capital goods? Their future prospective quasi-rents. What governs the supply price? Their past cost of production. For hard objects like blast furnaces and rolling stock demand is of its very nature *ex ante*, and cost is of its very nature *ex post*. The tutor cannot find shelter here from the arrows of time.

There is only one case where the quantity of capital can be measured, not shown; that is when the economy as a whole is in equilibrium at our old friend E.

Never talk about a system *getting into* equilibrium, for equilibrium has no meaning unless you are in it already. But think of a system *being* in equilibrium and having been there as far back towards Adam as you find it useful to go:

The Fall of Man   ◀——————   E

so that every *ex ante* expectation about today ever held in the past is being fulfilled today. And the *ex ante* expectation today is that the future will be like the past.

Then you hole out in one. Capital goods are selling today at a price which is both their demand price, based on *ex ante* quasi-rents, and their supply price, based on *ex post* costs.

Who was it who understood this bit? Marshall did, in his wicked way. You will notice, if you re-read his *Principles*, that the thinner is the argument the thicker is the tear gas. But the one who both understood it and played fair was Marx.

He starts to discuss accumulation by setting out a model of Simple Reproduction, which is precisely E, expressed in Marx's language. Then he sends his model moving forward through history and shows how it can never get back to E this side of doomsday.

You remember that Marshall found out the one case where you can say something sensible about the theory of market prices: the short period supply curve under perfect competition. Who found out the corresponding case where you can say something about long-run development? Mr. Harrod, with his *warranted rate of growth*. (You do it by fiddling the assumptions with neutral technical progress and one thing and another.)

Mr. Harrod was rather taken aback when I drew his attention to the fact that his theory was in *Capital*, Vol. II. But he is a thorough Keynesian, and has long ago spewed up every bit of stinking fish he ever ate. So after the shock had worn off he saw how right I was.

In any case it was already in his book. The point of the *warranted rate of growth* is not to show that the model tends towards an equilibrium line of development but that (just as Marx said) once it slips off the line it will never get back between now and doomsday.

It all boils down to a question of playing the game according to the rules. Ricardo established the rules of the game: Fiddle the assumptions as much as you like, but always show what you have done.

I will not say any more about the way Marshall played. Marx, instead of saying in a well-bred manner 'If you would be so good as to give me your attention, I will tell you my assumptions,' falls down on his knees and begs and implores you to *believe* his assumptions, because they are the secret of the universe. Though less reprehensible in a moral light, the result is even more stupefying than Marshall's tear gas. And Keynes often omits to mention a point here or there because (how rashly) he thought that you would see that it is obvious.

Ricardo himself was *too* conscientious. He hated having to fiddle the assumptions. Right up to his dying day he was looking for *the* assumption, that would not need to be fiddled. And that wretched neoclassical tutor took advantage of the obscurities produced by Ricardo's scruples to make out that he meant the opposite of what he said. If you read Mr. Sraffa's Introduction to the *Principles* you will see how right I am.

14

THE PHILOSOPHY OF PRICES

INTRODUCTION

WHY did the hunters in the *Wealth of Nations* exchange beavers for deer? In Adam Smith's forest there were no property rights in territory and no specialized skill (for if there were, the exchange value of the game would have been affected by the relative supply of hunters specialized for each quarry). Any man could catch a beaver for himself with the same exertion that it would cost him to catch two deer and exchange them for a beaver. Trade must have occurred only when there were chance discrepancies between an individual's needs and his catch, to be adjusted by swapping, and unless these exchanges were governed by a moral conception that they ought to conform to labour cost, it would have been impossible to detect any normal price in the occasional swaps that took place.

Regular exchanges presuppose specialization. From the earliest times specialized natural resources were used by mankind and specialized skills were developed in working them.

We do not know anything about the social organization surrounding neolithic axe factories,[1] but it seems obvious that there must have been property, in some form or other, in the right to exploit deposits of flints, and that the flint-knappers were highly skilled operatives whose means of subsistence was supplied by exchanging axes for food and other commodities.

We cannot be certain that there was commerce in axes. In some societies the interchange of products is made by ritual gifts, so that, though necessary to the characters concerned for material welfare, it appears to them as a religious duty or a means of emulation, rather than as an economic activity. But the wide diffusion of the flint axes, cutting across tribal boundaries, suggests trade in some form or other. It suggests, indeed, the existence of

[1] J. G. D. Clark, *Prehistoric Europe*, especially Chapter 9.

This paper covers some of the same ground as 'Some reflections on the philosophy of prices', *Manchester School*, May 1958.

some institution fulfilling the function of a category of merchants, whether as agents of the factories, emissaries from importing tribes or an independent group of middlemen, responsible for buying, selling and transporting both the axes and other wares.

We shall never know what exchange ratios emerged in this commerce, but we can guess with some confidence that the terms of trade between axes and corn varied with the harvest (in a famine year axes would be almost unsaleable and the factory workers in sad straits unless they had had the foresight to accumulate stocks). We can also guess that, taking good years with bad, the normal value of the product of a man-year of work in the factory (whatever share of it the operative received) was much above the value of the product of a man-year in agriculture. Specialized skill combined with limited natural resources must have given axes a scarcity value in terms of corn which would make itself felt under whatever guise exchanges were organized.

There is no need to suppose that any form of money was required for this trade. It is an illusion that barter requires a 'double coincidence' – that I happen to need an axe and have corn to offer when you need corn and have an axe to offer. Any durable commodity in regular demand is a 'store of value', and whenever I have corn to spare I should be pleased to buy an axe whether I wanted one or not, for I could exchange it later for whatever I did want to buy with my corn. The purchaser, again, may be buying it to use, to sell or to hoard for future exchange. The axes themselves could serve as currency as well as being useful tools.

Even if there was no formalized currency, there may well have been credit, for credit arises naturally out of good faith. An offer of axes before the harvest, against a promise to pay later, may have been usual. (Speculation grows fanciful when we inquire whether such promises were transferable, so that a true credit currency was in use.)

I suppose that we shall never know how the flint mines and axe factories were organized. Were the workers serfs of a chieftain? Or were they members of a co-operative, and if so, on what principles were the joint receipts from trade distributed amongst the miners, the flint-knappers and the surveyors who planned the sinking of pits? Or were they employees of capitalists, paid contractual wages? What share of the proceeds did the merchants keep for themselves? The physical evidence shows an elaborate and articulated organization, but cannot reveal what the 'relations of production' were within it. Over the centuries they may have passed through a variety of forms while the physical technique in operation remained unchanged.

The 'natural price' that Adam Smith believed in is a contradiction in terms. The existence of prices entails exchange. Exchange entails specialization. Specialization entails an organized society. Value is a social phenomenon and 'natural' technical costs cannot determine prices independently of the social form in which production is organized.

Two Kinds of Prices

The nature of the price system depends upon what is the basis of specialization. It is possible to distinguish two price systems which are quite different in principle, though they are mixed up and interpenetrate each other in reality and are often confused in theory.

In one type of system the basis of specialization is some natural facility for production of a particular commodity possessed by a particular group of producers — mineral deposits, soil and climate favourable to a particular crop or the inherited lore of a particular manner of manufacture. In the other, the basis of specialization is simply the economies of scale, so that a group of producers can produce any one commodity (or a narrow range of varieties of a commodity) more efficiently if they specialize upon it than if they produce many totally different commodities; any group, given time for adaptation, can produce any commodity, and investible resources can be turned into means of production for any commodity.

In the first case the income of an individual depends upon the price in terms of commodities in general of a day's output of his speciality. This is obviously true where the worker owns the means of production or the exclusive knowledge in which specialization is rooted, as when free peasants, who own their land, are producing a crop for sale or when the secrets of a craft are inherited by a special caste. It is very largely true also in capitalist conditions in the case where a particular district has been developed as the source of supply of a single commodity. The value of output per man employed, and therefore the level of wages which plantation workers or miners can secure, depends very much upon the price of the crop or the mineral being produced.

In the other sector of the economy there is sufficient mobility between different lines of production to ensure that the level of wages is pretty much the same in occupations which require the same amount of training, while the mobility of investible resources is such (apart from distortions due to monopoly) as to ensure more or less the same rate of profit on capital in all lines. Thus the income of an individual depends upon the grade of labour that he can perform (skill being roughly measured by the time required to acquire it) or the amount of capital that he owns, and is not at all dependent upon what commodity he happens to be producing or drawing profits from. On the contrary, it is the relative prices of commodities which are governed by the levels of the incomes of those who produce them.

The two types of price system cannot be identified exactly with agriculture and industry, or with peasant and capitalist production. Economic facts never fit into perfectly clear-cut categories. In capitalist industry there is not perfect mobility even in a fairly long run, and there are elements of natural aptitude or inherited tradition in the supply of particular kinds of skill. Some very important elements in industrial production, such as coal-mining and hydro-electricity, are closely tied to natural resources. Moreover, industrial equipment once in being is often very highly specialized, so that in respect to short-period changes there may be a strong influence of relative prices upon the rates of profit realized in different lines, and this may react upon the levels of wages also. Thus there are large elements belonging to the first kind of price system mixed up with the operation of the second. At the same time, in the first kind of system the attachment of particular producers to particular specialities may not be absolute, and an element of mobility (including actual migration) may set a limit to the extent to which incomes vary with prices.

Neither system is ever found quite free from elements of the other, but in order to grasp the nature of each one we must try to see how it would operate in a pure form.

AN EXCHANGE ECONOMY

To illustrate the operation of the first type of price system, let us imagine an economy, isolated from the rest of the world, composed only of peasants and artisans. Each family has some specialized line of production. One owns a vineyard, one inherits the secret of iron-founding, one has a tradition of weaving in which its children are brought up, and so forth. There are enough families with each speciality to make a competitive supply of each commodity. Once a week they all meet at the market and exchange the goods produced last week for goods to be consumed next week.

In this market it is a matter of indifference whether or not it is customary to quote prices in terms of one of the commodities or in terms of a notional money unit. What matters is the price ratios which are established by exchange. For each commodity there is a price in terms of each other commodity, determined by technical and psychological conditions of demand and supply; that is, the capacity and the desire to produce and to consume each kind of commodity of the families making up the economy. There is a wine-price of horseshoes, a cloth-price of horseshoes, etc., and cross-trading brings them into line with each other, so that when the above two prices have emerged from trading, the wine-price of cloth has also been established. Each family is interested in the price level in terms of its own product and the 'general price level' has no meaning.

In the kind of economy which we are discussing there is one important advantage of the free-market pricing system and four serious drawbacks.

The advantage is that each family, within the limits of the purchasing power provided by its own production, can purchase whatever it pleases and each family is led to specialize upon what it can best produce. No one has to be ordered to do anything and there is no need for any allocation or rationing. Where there are no laws there are no crimes. The system polices itself.

This is a very great merit, and anyone who has had anything to do with an allocation system, whether as an administrator or as a mere recipient, must appreciate the virtues of a free-market system in this respect.

But the drawbacks are very serious. First of all, the distribution of real income between families which comes about in this sort of system is highly arbitrary and fails to accord with what is generally felt to be natural justice.

Certainly there is no reason to expect that the price ratios between commodities will be such as to make the value of the product of a man-hour of labour equal in all lines, for each kind of labour is different from every other and there is no mechanism in the system to bring the values of, say, a blacksmith-hour, a weaver-hour and a ploughman-hour into equality with each other.

The value of a week's output of any particular worker depends upon the market prices of his commodity in terms of the rest, and that depends upon the relation of the amount of productive capacity for that commodity to the quantity of it that the community requires to consume. A family whose specialized property or inherited lore is scarce relatively to demand has a high income, and a family who can produce only something in relatively plentiful supply has a low income. It is a pure matter of luck, and does not appeal to normal human notions of what is just and reasonable.

The second drawback of the free price system is that the day-to-day equilibrium of the market may require perpetual oscillations in prices. Each group of producers brings to market a quantity of their particular product which is to some extent influenced by the prices in terms of other commodities which they expect to realize. It may happen that one group finds that they have brought to market more than will sell at the expected price. The consequent disappointment causes them to bring less next time, and then the high price realized causes them once more to overshoot the mark. Meanwhile, each change in one set of prices is liable to alter many of the rest. When, say, meat is unusually dear in terms of cloth and horseshoes, something else, say fruit, has experienced a fall in price, because the weavers and blacksmiths who continue to buy meat have economized on it. Where this kind of market situation is combined with production that has a certain gestation period (as in the well-known case of breeding pigs and growing maize), complicated interacting cycles may go on indefinetely without any tendency to find a stable position.

Thirdly, and this is the worst, changes in demand or in technical conditions may suddenly cause the equilibrium level of prices for a particular commodity to fall below the level at which it is possible to make a living by producing it. There are many historical examples of the dreadful misery that specialst producers are plunged into when their market disappears. Nowadays this situation is admitted to be intolerable, and is often met by a scheme to restrict output, so as to limit supply to a quantity which commands a tolerable price.

Finally, the situation may be reversed and, owing to a sharp fall in the supply of a particular commodity, the fortunate owners of what remains may be suddenly enriched to an extravagant degree by the famine prices which their wares then command.

Wherever the incomes of groups of individuals depend upon the relative prices of commodities, the evils of a free market system much outweigh its advantages. The search for a 'just price' in medieval theory, and in modern capitalism the proliferation of 'commodity schemes' and 'price supports' in times of glut and of food subsidies and rationing in times of scarcity are both evidence that such a system cannot be trusted to produce tolerable results.

PRICES AND INCOME IN A PLANNED ECONOMY

The major problem of price policy in a planned economy is to arrive at a fair distribution of income between agricultural and industrial workers. The agricultural workers, grouped in cooperatives, own their principal means of production – the right to exploit a particular area of land – and their money income depends upon the selling price of their produce. Their situation corresponds to that of sellers in the exchange economy. The industrial workers (including all the professions except for a few 'free-lance' journalists, etc.) receive money payments for work done, irrespective of what is produced, and their incomes are even more completely insulated from the prices of the particular commodities that their work contributes to producing than is the case in capitalist industry.

It is easier to make a rapid expansion of outlay on industry than it is to increase output in agriculture. At given rates of payment, the total of money income earned in industry is expanding fast in a rapidly developing economy, and the free market price of food rises as demand expands faster than supply. The money income of the farmers rises, and the real income of the industrial workers falls. The agricultural workers cannot be allowed to enjoy the full benefit of the demand price for their produce for, if they were, they would be receiving too large a share in the total income of the economy. The problem is not one of government finance; if the farmers spend their money, the government recovers it as additional profits on sales of goods from the industrial sector, and if they save it, the government can print notes for them to hoard or sell them bonds (though, of course, this may be laying up trouble for the future). The difficulty is not concerned with finance, but with the distribution of income. Both from the point of view of satisfying the general notions of what is fair and from the point of view of the morale of the industrial sector, the distribution of real income which would come about under a free market system would be intolerable. On the other hand, the methods which have actually been used to correct this tendency in the USSR until recently went, it is now admitted, too much to the other extreme, and were grossly unfair to the agricultural sector.

There cannot be any simple criterion to decide what is the 'right' distribution of income between the sectors. The ultimate ideal may be 'equal pay for equal work', but the whole life of an industrial worker is different from that of an agricultural worker, and what constitutes equal pay, taking account of the purchasing power of money over the different kinds of goods and services that each wants to buy, and what constitutes equal work, taking account of the different kinds of jobs that each has to do, can never be obvious and will always leave room for dispute. In any case, the ultimate ideal of justice has to give way meanwhile to expediency, and the distribution of rewards has to be made in the manner most helpful to development. In short, the distribution of income between the two sectors cannot but be a political decision, whether it is made consciously or whether it emerges as the result of expedients adopted from time to time to meet problems as they arise.

Until the supply of foodstuffs is sufficient to saturate demand, it is necessary, in order to establish whatever may be the desired distribution of income between the sectors, to keep the selling prices of foodstuffs on the farm below the demand prices in the consumers' market. This gives rise to very serious problems. In so far as agricultural output is sold to the government and private sales are illegal, there is a great temptation to develop a black market. In so far as private sales are permitted, there is a temptation to deflect both work-time and the use of land away from government sales into the free market. Either way, administrative means have to be used to keep trade in the required channels and market forces cannot be left to operate freely.

Industrial crops, such as cotton, do not give rise to a black market, since the government is the only buyer who has any use for them, but even they are involved in the general problem, for it is necessary to set a procurement price which will make it worth while for farmers to produce them, taking into account the rival attractions of the black or free prices which other uses of land and labour-time might yield.

There is a way out of these difficulties which is quite simple in principle, though no doubt it would involve all sorts of complications in actual application. The way out is to charge the farmers a land tax, assessed in terms of money instead of in terms of crops, and allow them to sell their produce for what it will fetch. In such a system, the yield of the land tax replaces the profit on sale of foodstuffs as a contribution to government revenue; it is apportioned between farms on the basis of potential earning power of the area, not on the basis of actual receipts. In short, it operates like Ricardian rent. The tax is fixed and it is left to the farmers to earn the money to pay it. The larger the part of government outlay which is covered by the receipts from the land tax, the smaller the part which has to be raised by profits and turn-over tax on industrial output. Therefore, given the prices of industrial commodities, money incomes in industry can be higher the greater the yield of the land tax. Thus the over-all rates of land tax can be adjusted so as to bring about any desired pattern of distribution of income between the two sectors.

Such a system would have three very important advantages. First, those aspects of the relations between government and farmers which are liable to give rise to unpleasantness are all concentrated at a single point, the assessment and collection of the tax. It would still be desirable for the bulk of all produce to be handled by government buyers, and it might be useful for those buyers to enter into long-term contracts with the farmers and to operate buffer stocks so as to avoid casual fluctuations in prices, but since the buying prices would be in line with market prices there would be no incentive to evade official dealings, and the government agents would appear in the helpful role of assisting the farmers to market their crops, and to improve their earning power to their own advantage. The free price system polices itself.

Secondly, the farmers would have the greatest incentive to produce energetically and efficiently, since the tax is a lump sum, and all additional earnings due to additional effort are kept by the farm. Moreover, the pattern of production would be as fully as possible responsive to demand (including government demand for industrial crops) for each farm wants the most money income (and so the highest value per labour day) that it can get for its members, and the relative demand prices for different kinds of produce would guide the farmers to produce what the consumers require.

The third advantage is that, since the land tax would be assessed according to an estimate of the money-earning power of the particular areas of land — taking account of soil, climate, situation and the prices of the particular crops obtainable in each district — it would tend to mitigate the differences in earnings between one farm and another which are due to pure accidents of nature, independent of the efficiency or industry of the workers concerned.

Since the right to exploit a particular piece of land is a kind of property, there seems to be no justification for wide differences in earning power due to purely natural factors, and presumably they are allowed to persist in socialist economies today simply because, under the prevailing price system, it is very difficult to do anything about them.

Whatever advantages it may have, the land-tax system is too far from present practice to be considered seriously, and the need for some kind of legal barrier to preserve the difference between prices on the farm and prices in the consumers' market will persist until the scarcity of agricultural products has been overcome. When that time arrives it will probably be necessary to go into reverse and to direct policy (as in the United States) to keeping up farm prices to a level that will ensure a fair income to the farmers.

A WAGE ECONOMY

To see the second type of pricing system in its purest form we may imagine an idealized capitalist economy continually expanding at a steady rate, abstracting, for the sake of argument, from crises and perturbations; abstracting also from monopolistic distortions; and postulating easy and rapid movement both of workers and of investible resources between different lines of production. In such a system, when it is in equilibrium, the level of wages and the rate of profit on capital are uniform throughout the economy, for no one will be content with a lower return in one line than he could get in another.

In such a case there must be a general price level, for wages must be paid in money; that is, generalized purchasing power. The money price of each kind of commodity is governed by its cost of production in money terms, including in costs a proper share of the amortization of plant and of profit at the ruling rate on the capital invested in the productive capacity concerned, for no commodity will continue to be produced unless it yields the same return as the rest.

When these conditions obtain, prices tend to be established at the 'normal long-run level' in Marshall's language, or to correspond to 'prices of production' in Marx's language.

The objections to a profit system are well known – it will not, in fact, be free from crises; it always is distorted by monopoly, and its very basis in the private ownership of means of production is highly irrational – but regarded purely from the point of view of the operation of relative prices, it is free from the objections which we found to the first type of system.

The distribution of income, as between workers and owners of property, is, of course, very arbitrary, but as between producers of different commodities it is perfectly fair. Each unit of work and each unit of capital, in equilibrium, gets just the same return whatever it is applied to producing.

The establishment of equilibrium with a given pattern of demand presents only minor difficulties, for if there has been an over-optimistic estimate of demand in one line, the capital invested in that line will receive less than the expected rate of profit, and will be gradually siphoned off by the oldest plant in the industry not being replaced while its accrued amortization fund is used to build up productive capacity in some other line. The offer of employment goes with productive capacity, so that labour is also shifted gradually out of the over-expanded industry until equilibrium between supply and demand is established. By the same token, so long as overall demand is buoyant, no one will lose his livelihood by a decline in demand for any particular commodity; and, so long as competition is active, no group of producers can hold society to ransom by maintaining famine prices for a commodity whose demand has increased.

Thus, in the postulated conditions, the free market system can claim great merits, not only in allowing consumers to spend whatever income they have on what they fancy amongst given alternatives, but also in steering production into the lines that meet their tastes.

It is to be observed that the whole virtue of the system arises from the process by which competition exercises its invisible discipline over production. The prices of commodities and the rates of wages are given to each seller, and it is his business to see to it that any given output is produced at the lowest cost, and that the selection of commodities to be produced is that which will yield the largest return.

It is obvious enough that the system is vitiated when monopolists are able to keep up the rate of profit that they obtain by preventing new entry into an expanding market, but in a more subtle way the system is vitiated by the power of sellers to fix their own prices, even if they confine themselves to covering costs of production including a 'fair profit' on the capital invested. When demand has expanded relatively to capacity a policy of 'fair profits' means that prices are kept down, there are shortages and unofficial rationing, and the expansion of capacity which should take place under the influence of super-normal profits is delayed.

When there has been a contraction in the demand for a particular commodity (a general decline in demand – a slump – is, of course, quite another matter), its price may be raised to 'cover the overhead' and defend business from the sub-normal profits which ought to be driving investment out of this line into others.

Equally, if total receipts from sales rise with the expansion of demand for a particular commodity but profit is kept down to the normal level by a rise in the money-wage rate of the particular group of workers concerned, the mechanism of the system is inhibited. More workers now would like to be employed in this super-normal-wage trade, but the failure of profits to rise prevents productive capacity from being expanded and so limits the jobs being offered. (Some rise in wages, it is true, may be required to steer labour into an expanding trade, but the whole point of the kind of system we are considering is that labour is highly mobile between uses, so that a very small differential will enable the industry to attract all the labour it can employ.) It is even more harmful to cut wages in face of a fall in demand so as to 'preserve employment'. There should be unemployment of workers now redundant to this trade, so that they will quickly move into occupations where they are needed, and there is no reason why the workers who remain in the shrunken trade should have permanently lower wages just because there were once too many of them.

In short, the proper operation of the system requires that, as between the production of one commodity and another, wage rates should always remain as nearly as possible uniform, while profits swing up and down with the movements of supply and demand – the differences in profits being always in the course of being ironed out by the flow of new investment which is continually adapting productive capacity to the pattern of demand.

It is by concentrating upon the aspect of a competitive economy which concerns its mode of operation as between one commodity and another, while being rather vague about its operation as between workers and capitalists as a whole, that the generally flattering portrait of the system found in the orthodox text-books has been made to pass for a tolerable likeness.

PRICES OF CONSUMERS' GOODS IN A PLANNED ECONOMY

In a socialist economy there are, strictly speaking, no wages. The means of production are owned in common and everyone works, not for a particular employer, but for his fellow citizens. The payment which individuals receive is their share of the whole proceeds of the economy. But in the present phase of socialism, in which shares are allocated in the main according to work done, the incomes received look and feel exactly like wages, and it is convenient to borrow that term to describe money incomes earned in the industrial sector of the economy.

Given the planned allocation of resources, there is a certain physical volume of consumer goods being produced, and given the level of money wages and money incomes in the agricultural sector, there is a certain volume of money demand for consumer goods. Apart from personal saving (which comes to the government as loans) the whole outlay of all the organs of a socialist economy returns to them collectively as taxes or receipts from sales. The greater the proportion of government outlay which produces no saleable commodities – administration and defence, investment and social services – the higher must be the ratio of taxes and profits to costs of production of saleable commodities. What the over-all price level of commodities must be is therefore decided when the general allocation of resources between the sectors of the economy has been laid down.

The problem of pricing policy is concerned, not with the overall level, but with the pattern of prices for different commodities. Social considerations are involved in some prices. It may be thought desirable on general grounds to make tobacco dear and books cheap. In some cases there is such a severe shortage of supply relatively to demand (as during war-time) that a system of allocation is to be preferred to 'rationing by the purse', and in some cases when a shortage is seen to be temporary (as when a new consumer durable, such as a television set, first begins to be produced) a system of queuing may be preferable to regulation of demand by prices.

Apart from such exceptions, there is a strong general presumption in favour of a pattern of prices that equates demand to supply for each commodity in each market. The reason is not to be found in the high claims which orthodox economics makes for the 'maximization of satisfaction' or the 'principle of consumer sovereignty', but in the fact, which we have already noticed, that such a system regulates itself. When legal prices are at the level which equates demand to available supplies there can be no black market (apart from sales of stolen goods), no 'under the counter' sales, no bare shelves and unwanted savings due to the lack of anything to buy.

The case for pricing according to market demand is very much stronger in a socialist society than in a capitalist one, for in the capitalist society the distribution of purchasing power between families depends largely on the distribution of property, which is quite arbitrary from either an economic or an ethical point of view, and the manipulation of prices may be used as a corrective to the maldistribution of income. In the socialist economy every family has the money income (from wages, labour-days earned, pensions, children's allowances, etc.) which it has, on accepted principles, the right to have, so that it seems reasonable to allow money demand to determine prices.

To accept the rule that prices should equate demand to the available supply of each commodity does not settle the question of what the pattern of prices should be. The demand for each commodity of a typical family depends very largely upon how much of the family income has been absorbed by buying other commodities, so that each price depends upon all the rest and there is a great deal of play in the pattern of prices that will establish equality between supply and demand in each market. As between substitutes, say nylon and cotton shirts, it is true that the relative prices that regulate demand are determined by the tastes of the public. When nylon is much less plentiful than cotton, if the public is more or less indifferent between them, nylon must be sold only a little dearer than cotton, whereas if people are very keen on nylon, the price difference will have to be large to get them to take cotton shirts. But as between broad groups of commodities this 'principle of substitution' has much less effect. If clothes as a whole are sold cheaper, people may spend more money on, say, furniture. The same total government revenue could be raised from cheaper clothes and dearer furniture or dearer clothes and cheaper furniture, without any noticeable difference in the fit between supply and demand in each market. There is thus an arbitrary element in the price system at any moment.

The relative prices of different commodities affect the real income of consumers with different tastes, needs and habits. If the pattern of prices happens to be such as to make furniture expensive, the newly married couples find the purchasing power of money correspondingly low. This is certainly arbitrary and may be regarded as unfair, but in a rapidly developing economy it is probably not very important. Groups of consumers who suffer at one time from a pattern of prices unfavourable to them may be the lucky ones a little later.

In any case, even if there is some sense in which one pattern is the fairest, it would take time to discover it, and meanwhile the situation would have changed. The absolute optimum pattern of prices is a mirage. The proper way of approaching the problem is to take whatever situation past history has produced, as a starting-point, and to see what changes in it can profitably be made.

Taking any system of prices that equates demand to available supplies, it will be found that the value of output per man-hour of labour, including the labour providing materials, power, etc. (which we shall discuss later), varies very much between one enterprise and another, and within enterprises, between one line of production and another. Starting from any arbitrary position that happens to have become established, there may be room for very big improvements by shifting labour from low to high money-value-producing occupations. Of course, it is not desirable to do so when the differences in prices are part of social policy. If tobacco is being deliberately kept scarce, its high price is not an indication for more to be produced. But where differences in relative scarcities are purely accidental, everyone gains by reducing them. For some commodities the conditions of demand are such that a considerable increase in sales could be made (if more of the product was available) with a very small reduction in price, and if it is technically possible to draw labour (including the labour required to produce power and materials) into these lines away from low-money-value production, the total surplus of the selling value of commodities over their total costs is increased. This surplus accrues to the government as profits and taxes, but the sums required to finance government outlay remain the same; the average excess of prices over costs can therefore be reduced, and the purchasing power of the public increased.

In other cases it is not possible to move labour into the high-money-value products because the restriction on supply, which causes the scarcity which causes the high price, is due to some technical cause; for instance, that the plant required is specialized and is limited in capacity. The high price must then remain until capacity can be expanded.

All this concerns prices to final consumers. How are these to be related to factory prices to the enterprises which produce the goods? As we have seen, the whole merit of the ideal competitive market system springs from the fact that prices are given to the individual producer, so that it is up to him to produce any given output at the lowest possible cost and to produce the selection of commodities that yields the highest return. To reproduce the good features of this system and to avoid the monopolistic elements that vitiate it in the capitalist world, the responsibility for setting prices must remain with the planners, not be delegated to the enterprises. Moreover, the prices set for the enterprises must not be based upon costs of production, for a system under which the value of output is judged by its cost blurs the distinction between socially necessary costs and the results of slackness and inefficiency. The discipline of the market then has to be replaced by administrative checks, and it is the interest of the enterprises to get the greatest amount of costs allowed as legitimate rather than to strive to eliminate all costs that are not strictly necessary. To enjoy the benefits of the self-regulating market system, prices, costs and the pattern of supply must be brought into harmony with each other by the operation of market forces, not wrenched into line by administrative means.

In order to bring the operation of market forces to bear on the pattern of production it is necessary to make factory prices (received by the enterprises) proportional to market prices. Then, in endeavouring to produce the assortment of products that yields the best return, and to use the methods of production that minimize costs, the managers of enterprises will be helping to get supply into line with demand as far as is possible within the existing productive capacity, while the relative profitability (in terms of tax yield) of different lines of production serves as a guide to the planners as to which should be given priority for expansion.

The proportionality of factory to market prices (allowing for transport costs, etc.) can be secured either by a general tax on the wages bill, which raises all prime costs proportionately, or by an *ad valorem* turnover tax, which reduces all receipts proportionately. A very good case can be made out for preferring the wages tax, but since the turnover tax is more in line with present practice it may be better to conduct the argument in terms of it.

After whatever shuffling that can be done immediately, there are bound to remain large differences in the money value of output per man between one enterprise and another which are in no way under the control of the management. We may suppose that there is enough labour to keep all plant occupied on whatever shift system is in use, and that it is not worth while to try to distiguish between average and marginal cost in the individual enterprise; but, as between one plant and another in the same line, physical output per head varies with the nature of the equipment, and between one line and another money-value (net of material costs, etc.) of the output of a day's working varies with the price of the commodity, which depends upon market conditions.

This variation in the value of output per man in equally well-managed enterprises means that if the whole of the contribution to government funds to be levied on the sale of commodities were raised in a uniform *ad valorem* tax on sales, some enterprises would be making profits and some would have to draw a subsidy to cover part of their wages bill. This is undesirable for a number of reasons. It would be better to fix the rate of tax so that the enterprises with the lowest value of output per man could just cover expenses when working at a reasonable standard of efficiency (exception being made for goods which are intended to be subsidized, or for enterprises which it is desired to keep going in spite of some particular disadvantage; for instance, in respect to geographical position). With such a rate of tax, enterprises where the value of output per man is high (whether because the supply of the commodity being produced is limited and so the demand price high, or because of exceptional advantages in respect to up-to-date plant, etc.) will find themselves earning profits. These must be handed over as a contribution to government funds. Ideally it would be best to assess each enterprise with an annual lump-sum tax, reflecting its special advantages, so that it is equally hard to earn a profit everywhere, and profit reflects only the efficiency of the enterprise. But in practice this assessment would involve precisely the kind of friction which it is the aim of the self-regulating price system to avoid, and a profits tax, leaving the enterprise with whatever share is considered an adequate incentive to efficiency, is probably to be preferred.

Let us now look at the price system which we have outlined. Prices of goods sold to consumers are such as to equate supply to demand in each market (there are no persistent shortages or silting up of stocks). The government is receiving, from taxes and profits, the sums it requires to pay for non-saleable activities. The factory prices are proportional to selling prices. Where it is impossible (for instance, because of limitation on the supply of plant) to transfer labour to lines where the value of output per man is high and so bring down the price of the commodity concerned, the turnover tax absorbs less than the whole surplus over costs, and profits are being made.

The existence of profits is a useful indication to the planners of points at which demand exceeds supply, and therefore serves to guide plans for future expansion, though they cannot be blindly followed.

It is to be observed that there is no use in the above scheme for a rate of interest or any allowance for the cost of capital in forming prices. Indeed, prices are formed solely in the light of market conditions without reference to costs. Yet, in fact, it will be found that the commodities whose production requires exceptionally heavy investment will be yielding a profit; for the heavy investment required to expand output keeps the commodity in question scarce, so keeps up its price and causes the value of output per man in producing it to exceed expenses per man including the *ad valorem* turnover tax.

The proper place for the rate of interest is not in the determination of prices but in the calculation of the relative yields of different investments. This question cannot be discussed here. We may merely remark that in guiding investment plans it is the expected return on the cost of new plant that matters, and the yield of past investment has no relevance except as a rough indication of what to expect. In any case, investment plans have to be integrated and they involve many other considerations besides yield in revenue terms. The pricing system has only a very limited contribution to make to investment planning. Nevertheless, subject to necessary corrections, the revenue yield of different investments (net of depreciation) may be a useful guide to the planners in trying to get the pattern of production into line with the pattern of demand. In so far as they follow this guide, one bottle-neck after another will be broken as time goes by. Outputs of scarce commodities gradually expand and their demand prices come down. Better plant supersedes the least productive, so that the physical productivity of labour is raised where it was lowest. The system is tending towards an ideal state where the value of output per man (net of depreciation of plant) is the same in all lines. This position may never be finally reached, but as the system moves towards it the contribution of profits is gradually reduced and a larger and larger part of the total contribution to revenue comes from the *ad valorem* tax. By the same process the pattern of supplies of goods comes ever closer to the pattern of consumers' wants expressed in money demand.

The indications of the market can never be blindly followed and the planners must take many considerations into account besides the revenue yield of investments, but though the price system is a bad master it can be a very useful servant.

PRICES OF MATERIALS

So far we have discussed the problems of production as though the supply of each commodity could be attributed to a particular group of workers. In reality this is not the case; production is split not only vertically into commodities but also horizontally into stages, and a single material produced at one stage enters into the output of many different commodities at the next stage.

In some respects the most important element in pricing policy for a planned economy is to find the correct prices for materials (including power). They concern only transactions between enterprises and so in one sense are mere book-keeping, affecting no one's real income (except in so far as they are sold to farms), but they are very important because it is in their use that the 'principle of substitution' has most scope to operate. Materials, over all, are scarce relatively to demand and most have a wide variety of uses, while most uses (though not all) can be met less or more efficiently by a variety of materials. It must therefore be the object of policy to see to it that each material is put to the uses where it is most important; that is, the uses in which the next-best substitute for it is least eligible.

The allocation of materials is just the kind of job that the pricing system can do best. The manager of an enterprise, in trying to keep his costs as low as possible, will prefer the material, for any job, which is the best bargain; that is, which is cheapest in relation to performance in that particular job. If the prices of materials reflect their relative scarcity, while the prices of final products are fixed, they will automatically be allocated in the most efficient way.

The demand for materials comes partly from high-priority uses, such as defence, partly from investment schemes and partly for export, which are both controlled by the over-all plan, partly from the consumer-good sector and sale to farms, which are both controlled by market demand. It is, therefore, not a simple matter to organize a simulacrum of a market where each element of demand is given its proper weight in money terms, so that the bids of buyers lead to the establishment of prices that correctly reflect the relative scarcities of different materials. It is probably impossible to escape altogether from the need for direct allocation, at least between the broad categories of uses. But within the consumer-good sector the pricing system could be made to work. The over-all allocation of a material to the consumer sector having been fixed, the authority in charge of it could find out what quantities each enterprise would wish to take at each price, and so arrive at the demand price for the available quantity. These demand prices are derived from the factory prices of commodities which, in turn, are derived from demand in the consumers' market. The factory price has been reduced by the turn-over tax, so that it would not be correct to tax the materials separately, but any profits made on the production of materials must be handed over to the government.

This scheme would be somewhat complicated to apply, but any scheme which makes a rational use of prices takes the weight off direct administration, and the scheme need not be perfect to be a great improvement on allocation as a method of dealing with the distribution of scarce means among a variety of uses.

THE LAW OF VALUE

It is with some hesitation that I suggest an interpretation of the relation of the foregoing argument to the Marxian theory of *value*.

As I understand it, the significance of the Marxian theory of *value* is that, unlike the orthodox neo-classical theory, it stresses the relationship between money prices and the distribution of real income. If this is correct, the law of *value* must appear in a different light in different spheres according to the relationship between prices and incomes in each sphere.

So far as the terms of trade between agricultural and industrial products are concerned, 'prices in accord with *values*' means, I suggest, that prices are such as to give a fair, or in some sense 'right', relation between incomes of farmers and industrial workers. In this sphere, then, *value* has a meaning somewhat akin to the notion of 'the just price'.

In the sphere of consumer-good prices, the over-all relationship of prices to incomes determines the real purchasing power of wages over saleable goods. This is dictated (given the efficiency of production) by the allocation of resources between saleable and non-saleable output. In this over-all sense, the law of *value* merely means that prices both will be and ought to be such as to implement that allocation. As between one industrial commodity and another, prices have no effect on incomes of producers (though they affect the purchasing power of consumers with different tastes and needs). Here *value* has not much to say. Indeed, prices ought not to be in accord with *values*, in the sense of labour-time required for production, until scarcities have been overcome and all labour-time produces equal quantities of net selling value of products. Until that time is reached, the pattern of prices must reflect the pattern of supply and demand. And even when prices are, in fact, in accord with *values*, they should not be directly determined by *values*. Any kind of cost-plus pricing destroys the merit of the market mechanism.

Prices should always be set, at any moment, in the light of demand; then when all supplies have become elastic it will be found that the pattern of demand automatically establishes prices which reflect *values*. There is no short cut to this world, and to try to force a way to it by fixing prices according to *values* before the bottle-necks have been removed is detrimental to efficiency and only puts off the time for reaching it.

The third type of prices, those for materials, do not seem to have any connection with *value*, for they do not directly affect anyone's real income. The market in which they are sold is only the simulacrum of a market, for all the dealers in it are agents of the same principal – the socialist economy. Nevertheless, the simulated operation of a market can be a very useful adjunct to the administration of the plan.

If I am right, the concept of *value* requires a different definition in each sphere, and a good deal of confusion seems to be caused by loading one word with so many different meanings.

15

'IMPERFECT COMPETITION' REVISITED

The Economics of Imperfect Competition was a scholastic book. It was directed to analysing the slogans of the text-books of twenty years ago: 'price tends to equal marginal cost' and 'wages equal the marginal product of labour'; and it treated of text-book questions, such as a comparison of the price and output of a commodity under conditions of monopoly and of competition, demand and costs being given. The assumptions which were adequate (or which I hoped were adequate) for dealing with such questions are by no means a suitable basis for an analysis of the problems of prices, production and distribution which present themselves in reality.[1]

INDUSTRIES AND MARKETS

The assumption that each firm produces a single commodity conceals the distinction between the output of an *industry* — that is, a group of firms engaged in production of commodities alike in their methods of manufacture, and the supply to a *market* — that is, the demand for a group of commodities which are close substitutes for each other. In ordinary language when we speak of the cotton industry, the iron-founding industry, the boot-and-shoe industry (leather) we are thinking of a group of firms engaged in a certain type of production, governed by the kinds of object produced and the materials of which they are made. Sometimes a single firm produces very diverse objects which are complements to each

[1] I should like to take this opportunity of saying that I have never been able to grasp the nature of the distinction between *imperfect* and *monopolistic* competition to which Professor Chamberlin attaches so much importance. (Cf. 'Monopolistic competition revisited', *Economica*, November 1951.) It appears to me that where we dealt with the same question, in our respective books, and made the same assumptions we reached the same results (errors and omissions excepted). When we dealt with different questions we naturally made different assumptions. In many respects Professor Chamberlin's assumptions were more interesting than mine, in particular in connection with oligopoly and with product differentiation as a dynamic process.

Economic Journal, September 1953.

other, and therefore sold together (pens and blotting-paper, low-power electric motors and artificial teeth) and sometimes quite unrelated objects are bound together in production because they are bound together in selling by conventional shopping habits (hair-brushes and medicines). Many of the products of a single industry are extremely remote substitutes for each other. There is no overlap, for instance, between the markets for men's and children's shoes or for drain-pipes and stoves. On the other hand, products of totally different industries may be quite close substitutes – rubber and leather shoes; asbestos and cast-iron drainpipes.

The concept of an industry, though amorphous and impossible to demarcate sharply at the edges, is of importance for the theory of competition. It represents the area within which a firm finds it relatively easy to expand as it grows. There are often certain basic processes required for the production of the most diverse commodities (tennis balls, motor tyres and mattresses) and economies in the utilization of by-products under one roof. The know-how and trade connections established for one range of products make it easier to add different commodities of the same technical nature to a firm's output than it is to add mutually substitutable commodities made of different materials, or made or marketed by radically different methods. Moreover, the members of an industry have common interests and a common language, and feel a kind of patriotism which links them together, even when they are in competition with each other. It is much easier to organize control over one industry serving many markets than over one market served by the products of several industries.

The degree of concentration in an industry, measured by the proportion of its output produced by, say, the three largest firms, or the degree of monopoly in the sense of the closeness of the organization binding the firms, may have little relation to the degree of monopoly in the markets which it serves, in the sense of power to control prices. An unconcentrated and un-organized industry may contain a number of very strong small monopolies over particular commodities, while another, highly concentrated or tightly organized, may be meeting competition in some or all of its markets from the products of rival industries which are substitutes for its own.

Generally speaking, the supply of a commodity (using that term in a broad sense to cover a group of fairly close substitutes) to a market can be expanded much more readily than can the productive capacity of an industry, for to increase capacity usually requires investment in plant and recruitment of labour, while to increase the output of a commodity often means merely switching over from one line of production to another within a plant.

Dropping the fiction of one-commodity firms destroys the simplicity of the analysis of imperfect competition, but enlarges its scope. Cases where the imperfection of markets combined with ease of entry lead to an excessive number of businesses with low turnover occur mainly in special fields (service and bespoke trades, small shops, petrol filling stations), whereas every efficiency expert who comments on British manufacturing industry points out the almost universal prevalence of uneconomically short runs and small batches in the output of individual lines of production.

To provide an analysis of this situation within the framework of the *Economics of Imperfect Competition* it is necessary to combine (with certain modifications) the treatment of polypoly in an imperfect market with the treatment of price discrimination, which shows how prices are fixed by a firm selling in a number of separate markets.[2]

There may be good reasons for the production under one roof of what, from a technical point of view, is an excessive number of separate commodities; there may be genuine economies (in transport, correspondence, etc.) in offering a 'full line' to buyers, as well as commercial advantage to the individual seller, and the principle of gaining on the roundabouts when the swings are slack reduces risk, unemployment and wastage of capacity. Moreover, non-commercial motives, such as pride in covering the whole field, may enter into the matter; but there can be little doubt that the main cause is the imperfection of competition, in the sense that if either buying were rationalized so as to make markets more perfect or monopoly was more complete, productive efficiency would be improved.

The general moral of the *Economics of Imperfect Competition* which points to the rationalizing monopsonist as the best pilot to find a channel between the Scylla of competitive inefficiency and the Charybdis of monopolistic exploitation seems to remain valid when the assumption of one-commodity firms is dropped, though this is not the kind of proposition that can be established by geometry alone.

WHO MAXIMIZES WHAT?

The treatment of the entrepreneur and his profits in the *Economics of Imperfect Competition* is extremely primitive. Clearly, in modern times there is no single universal type of entrepreneur. At the one extreme there is the

---

[2] See Eli W. Clemens, 'Price discrimination and the multiple product firm', *Review of Economic Studies*, Vol. XIX (1), 48, 1951–2. 'Price discrimination and multiple-product production are not exceptions to general practice, but are rather the essence of customary action. . . . The theory of price discrimination must be viewed as the heart of price-cost theory rather than as a peripheral case.'

individual who founds, owns and manages a business, in the Marshallian style; at the other, the great company of the 'managerial revolution', nominally owned by a large and shifting population of shareholders totally ignorant of its workings, and controlled by a self-perpetuating cadre of managers and directors; in between, the type of concern which is legally a public company but in effect a family business, and the type of concern which is controlled by a group of large, permanent shareholders, though it may be more than half-owned at any moment by casual shareholders whose brokers happen to have advised them to put their money into it for a time; there are quasi-independent subsidiaries of other concerns; concerns owned by holding companies; nominally independent concerns linked by overlapping directorates and so on, in bewildering variety. But all have some characteristics in common. A manufacturing business in modern technical conditions requires a high degree of co-operation and continuity. Industry, as opposed to commerce, could not have developed in an economy where the capitalists were all ruthlessly individualistic childless orphans. A successful business has a kind of personality, like a college, with which many, and successive, individuals identify themselves, and the subordination of the interest of casual shareholders, who want immediate profit, to the interest of management, which flourishes with the life of the concern, means that a public company is more like a family business in effect than it is in legal form. I therefore feel that for a first shot at a simple stylized analysis the most useful starting-point is still 'the entrepreneur', regarded as the personification of a 'firm' rather than as a particular individual in a pair of trousers.[3]

What is the aim of the entrepreneur, in this sense? If we neglect the promoter, who starts a business in order to sell it to the public, and the short-lived 'mushroom' who springs up to make a quick profit in a seller's market, it seems to me that the most valid simple generalization is that the aim of the entrepreneur is for the firm first to survive, and secondly to grow. To this end he must pursue profit, but he must avoid action which, though profitable in the present, will damage his future position, and, since this is partly bound up with reputation, his course of conduct will be much influenced by the climate of opinion in which he operates. All this is sadly vague, and the subject needs much more field study of business behaviour. Meanwhile, I am inclined to retort to those who grouse about the assumption that the entrepreneur's aim is to maximize profits in the immortal words of Old Bill: If you know a better 'ole, go to it.[4]

[3] Cf. B. S. Keirstead, *The Theory of Profits and Income Distribution*, p. 40.
[4] See below p. 180.

A more obvious defect is the uncritical acceptance of the idea of a 'normal level of profit' at which the size of a firm is in equilibrium. To discuss the size of firms it is necessary to break up the notion of an industry, and consider its separate stages or branches. In many industries alongside of mass production there is a considerable amount of jobbing or bespoke work (building repairs, electric shop signs, hand-sewn shoes), where the 'little man' has positive advantages compared to the large firm. Since such types of production can be started with a small investment of capital, they are easy to enter for an individual with the requisite know-how, and the rate of profit in them is kept low. An individual who makes a success in such business is more likely to grow out of it than to expand laterally. Here there may be no very definite equilibrium size, but the argument in terms of an equilibrium rate of profit seems to be a useful starting-point for analysis. In other types of manaufacture, where the variegated nature of the material (wool, leather) is inimical to mass production, or where highly imperfect markets impose a very variegated output (fashion trades, publishing), the flexibility of one-man management may give advantages to a moderate-sized firm over a great departmentalized concern, and, in general, there are risks and difficulties and loss of amenities in going through the stage of growth involved by changing from the one type of organization to the other. Once that threshold is passed, there seems no reason to expect dis-economies of scale to be important – certainly not important enough to outweigh the strategic advantages of size.[5]

The rate of growth of a firm is limited by the imperfection of the capital market (here Mr. Kalecki's principle of increasing risk[6] is the best starting-point for analysis, though his formulation, in turn, is over-simplified)[7] and by the need to consolidate and fortify each new position after it has been captured. But, given time to accumulate capital out of profits and to acquire know-how and trade connections, there seems to be no limit to the ultimate size of a firm, until a condition of oligopoly is reached in each of the markets for the commodities supplied by the industry, so that the last stages of the competitive struggle are too costly to be fought out. Even then, firms may continue to grow by crossing the boundary which divides industries and seeking quite fresh fields in which it is possible to expand without challenging too powerful opposition. (Nowadays it is quite common for

[5] Cf. N. S. Ross, 'Management and the size of the firm', *Review of Economic Studies*, Vol. XIX (3), 50, 1952–3.

[6] *Essays in the Theory of Economic Fluctuations.*

[7] L. Wellisz, 'Enterpreneur's risk, lender's risk, and investment', *Review of Economic Studies*, Vol. XX (2), 52, 1952–3.

new industries to be started by large firms already established in a monopoly or oligopoly position in an older industry, rather than by new small-scale firms.)

The profitability of a market is not the same thing as the profitability of an industry. We should expect the profit obtainable in a particular market to be strongly influenced by the difficulty of entering it. Commonly a firm enjoys different profit rates on different parts of its output – less on its 'bread-and-butter lines', which are standardized commodities where the market is nearly perfect and easy to enter, and higher on specialities in which it has individual advantages. But as between industries, and still more as between firms, it is hard to make any kind of simple generalization about profit rates, and the notion of a 'normal level of profits' and an 'equilibrium size of firm' seems to have very little application to reality.[8]

OLIGOPOLY

The reason oligopoly is neglected in the *Economics of Imperfect Competition* is not that I thought it unimportant, but that I could not solve it. I tried to fence it off by means of what unfortunately was a fudge in the definition of the individual demand curve.[9]

FORMS OF COMPETITION

The assumption that price is the main vehicle for competition is a great over-simplification of reality. The very fact that markets are not perfect means that competition may take many forms. The main vehicles of competition may be summarized as: (1) imitation of products; (2) differentiation of products – and these may be in respect of qualities which affect practical usefulness or pleasure to the consumer, qualities which appeal to snobbishness or to pseudo-scientific notions, or simply methods of packing and labelling articles; (3) services of all kinds, prompt delivery, long credit; (4) advertisement; (5) pure salesmanship, in the sense of the persuasiveness of travellers, etc.; (6) higher price – giving the impression of better quality; (7) lower price.

The multi-dimensional nature of competition is illustrated by the fact that rings formed to limit competition, which begin by agreeing only on a

---

[8] Technical economies of scale may, of course, establish a minimum size of plant, and so a minimum size of firm, but they do not establish a maximum size of firm, since, at worst, plants can be duplicated.

[9] Op. cit., p. 21.

price list for their products, often go on to limit terms of sale, permissible types of advertising appeal and the specification of products, so that sometimes competition in pure salesmanship is all that is left unregulated, and rival travellers are found making offers to potential customers which are identical in all respects except the names on the labels of the goods.

In principle, it is possible to set out a system of simultaneous equations showing what combination of price, outlay on production costs and outlay on selling costs would yield the best profit for a particular commodity in a particular market, taking into account the reaction upon costs and sales of other commodities produced by the same firm. Even if he had the data, the business executive would need an electric, not a human, brain to work out from the equations the correct policy in time to put it into effect. And the data are necessarily extremely vague, since the consequences of a given policy cannot be isolated in ever-changing markets. The recent development of advertising of advertisement is a witness to the difficulty which manufacturers have in knowing the consequences of advertisement, for if they knew its effects there would be no scope for persuading them that it is greater than they think. In reality, evidently, an individual demand curve (for a particular product produced by a particular firm) is a mere smudge, to which it is vain to attribute elegant geometrical properties.

It is important to observe that even when competition takes the orthodox form of a lower price charged by a manufacturer there is not necessarily competition in price to the consumer. A common method by which newcomers try to make head against established firms in a particular market is to offer larger margins to dealers to induce them to stock and push the goods concerned. This kind of competition is most definitely seen where the established firms practise resale-price maintenance, or where there are conventional 'price tickets' which settle the retail price of an article of a certain range of (apparent) quality; but it may exist also wherever price competition between dealers is not very sharp.

Product differentiation and advertising, which appeal to the consumer over the head of the retailer, appear to be as much an element in the struggle for strategic advantage between manufacturers and dealers as a vehicle of competition between manufacturers.[10]

Once more the moral of the argument is strengthened rather than weakened by the complications which it is necessary to introduce into the analysis. The wastes of imperfect competition take many more forms besides sub-optimum scales of production, and the benefit of price

[10] N. Kaldor, 'The economic effects of advertising', *Review of Economic Studies*, Vol. XVIII (1), 45, 1949–50.

competition, imposed by perfect markets (provided that it is not at the expense of wage rates), is in putting a premium on technical efficiency, as opposed to cunning salesmanship and strategic power, even more than in defending the consumer from exploitation.

PRICE POLICY

The picture of an entrepreneur finding the most profitable price for a commodity by trial and error, while market and cost conditions remain constant for long enough for the experiment to be carried out, is exceedingly unlifelike. It must be very unusual for an entrepreneur to alter a price in cold blood, just to see what will happen, and even when a change clearly seems advantageous – say a rise in price following a rise in demand – he usually waits for some colourable excuse, say a rise in material costs, before putting it into effect. In many types of market (especially where the firm publishes a price list) overt price changes are avoided as much as possible. It is more common to alter the quality of a commodity at a given 'price ticket', or to offer special rebates to particular classes of buyer, than to make a change in listed prices.

There are a number of situations, however, in which an entrepreneur has to take a decision about price. How far is the kind of analysis suggested by the *Economics of Imperfect Competition* useful in discussing how he behaves?

(*a*) When an entrepreneur has to decide whether to add a new line of production to his output he must consider what gross receipts it can be expected to bring in over a certain period, and compare this estimate with an estimate of costs, including, where it is relevant, the opportunity-cost of displacing some other part of his output. In some cases (a new model motor car, a title in a publisher's list) the idea of elasticity of demand is present to his mind at least in a vague way – he thinks of what quantities are likely to sell at various prices. In some cases he has an idea of 'the right price', given by the prices of similar commodities already in the market; in other cases it is rather a matter of a shot in the dark. Comparing expected receipts with costs, he has to decide whether it is worth while to embark on the new line. In a small firm which cannot carry the overhead of a 'scientific' costing system he may proceed by adding to the prime cost, or the labour cost only, or the material cost only, the percentage margin which his other lines of production carry and then considering if the resulting price 'looks right'. If the resulting price seems too high, he decides that the line in question is not for him. If anyone asks him what he does, he naturally replies that he fixes prices according to costs,[11] but clearly it would be absurd to work out cost, according to some formula, and then cast goods on the market at the corresponding price without consideration of the conditions of demand.[12] Nor does the entrepreneur's idea of 'the right price' mean that he thinks that at a certain price there is an indefinite demand. It means rather that he thinks that a higher price would limit sales very much, and that at 'the right price' a sufficient quantity can be sold to make the venture profitable. It seems to be an over-formalization, rather than a totally misleading approach, to think of his decision as being taken on the basis of some sort of conception of an individual demand curve.

Both demand and costs have to be thought of in three dimensions – a certain rate of sales for a certain length of future time (or rather an uncertain length). The period over which any special investment, or cost of tooling-up, has to be recovered, and the length of time that the commodity will be saleable, are of the greatest importance. This aspect of the matter cannot be adequately dealt with by the concept of the 'long-period elasticity of demand' though the distinction between long- and short-run elasticities is a step in the right direction.[13]

(b) Most firms produce a number of products some of which are sold in more perfect markets than others – these are the 'bread-and-butter lines' where the firm has to meet close competition, and the specialities which are sufficiently different from their nearest substitutes to make demand for them relatively inelastic. In such cases it is often seen that the specialities carry higher gross margins than the more competitive lines. This may be represented as 'recovering overheads' where they can be got, but it comes to the same thing as working on the principle of 'charging what the traffic will bear'.[14]

(c) The entrepreneur has to reconsider prices when costs alter. How do industries react to changes in prime cost, due to changes in wage rates or material costs that affect the whole group of firms? On this question the kind of analysis set out in the *Economics of Imperfect Competition* throws very little light, for here the effect of oligopoly is dominant. The reaction of any one entrepreneur must depend very much upon how he expects others to

[11] See R. L. Hall and C. J. Hitch, 'Price theory and business behaviour', *Oxford Economic Papers*, May 1939.

[12] The 'full-cost theory' seems to imply that this is how entrepreneurs behave, but whenever 'full-cost' is formulated in a precise form it turns out to mean something else.

[13] Cf. E. A. G. Robinson, 'The pricing of manufactured products', *Economic Journal*, December 1950, p. 779, and 'The pricing of manufactured products and the case against imperfect competition', *Economic Journal*, June 1951, p. 432.

[14] Cf. Clemens, loc. cit.

behave. From one point of view it is dangerous to be the first to raise prices when costs have risen, or the last to cut when they have fallen. On the other hand, to be the last, or the first, means an unnecessary loss of profit. It is in this sort of situation that price leadership develops. The rank and file of firms 'wait and see' until a recognized leader reacts to the new situation. Perhaps price leadership should be regarded as a kind of convenient institution, like the monarchy in a feudal society. For when each firm knows that all will follow the leader's signal they are saved from a perplexing choice between raising prices (when cost has risen), debasing quality or submitting to a loss of profit, so that all have an interest in preserving a tradition of 'loyalty' to the price leader. Price leadership may be expected often to operate (from the consumer's point of view) on the system: heads I win and tails you lose. A price leader who is confident of the 'good discipline' of his followers will be inclined to raise prices when costs go up and hold them up when costs go down. But this cannot be an invariable rule. For instance, if the price leader is a strong firm anxious to expand, it may refrain from raising prices when costs go up, in the hope of bankrupting weaker rivals and taking over their share in the markets concerned. Buyers who are aware of a fall in costs may press successfully for a reduction in price. 'Discipline' may break down if the margins maintained by the leader are so high as to tempt some followers to try to increase their share in the market. Or when there is a 'disputed succession' between several strong firms, a fall in costs may set off a bout of violent competition that brings prices down even by more than costs have fallen.

(d) How does a firm react when it has succeeded in reducing costs by technical improvements? We can obtain some light on this question by observing what happens when there is a new invention of a low-cost substitute for an old commodity. In such a case it is open to the entrepreneur to price it at prime cost plus his usual gross margin, or to set its price in line with that of the old variety so that it carries an abnormally high margin. There have recently been one or two striking examples of the latter price policy, which have been exposed to public view by subsequent competition bringing the new commodity down to a small fraction of the original price. Presumably there are other cases which do not come to light because the low-cost commodity is sheltered from competition by a patent, secret technical knowledge or by heavy investment or economies of scale in a preparatory process which it shares with a number of other products of the same firm.[15]

[15] This argument supports Mr. Harrod's view that the main determinant of an entrepreneur's pricing policy is not his own costs but what he believes to be the costs of actual or potential competitors. 'The theory of imperfect competition revised', *Economic Essays*.

(*e*) How do entrepreneurs react to fluctuations in demand? In a seller's market, where demand, even at highly profitable prices, exceeds capacity output, it is often found that powerful firms prefer not to raise prices but rather to delay delivery, thus making an investment in goodwill for the future; whereas in highly competitive conditions, where markets are easy to enter and the number of sellers large, no one can expect to gain in the future by moderation in the present. Thus, we find the apparently paradoxical phenomenon of the imperfection of competition keeping prices below the competitive level.

When a fall in demand has occurred and conditions of a buyer's market set in, prices are likely to be maintained by an oligopoly, for an entrepreneur who supplies a large proportion of a market is strongly influenced by the knowledge that if he cuts price others will follow and he will be no further forward. In highly imperfect markets prices will tend to be sustained by the low elasticity of the shrunken demands for specialities. In fairly competitive markets margins may be held up by a feeling that it is wrong to be the first to cut. Here the famous 'full-cost principle' may play an important part, not as an instrument of analysis for the economist, but as part of the data to be analysed. For if entrepreneurs have taught themselves to believe that prices *are* determined by costs, they will not cut prices when average total costs have been raised by a fall in output, though they excuse themselves from actually raising prices by saying that although it would be *right* to do so, it is unfortunately impossible in the circumstances. In a prolonged slump, margins are cut sooner or later, unless there is a price agreement, and it is usually said to be the high-cost producers who cut first, because they are threatened with bankruptcy unless they can increase sales somehow or other.

It was in connection with slump conditions that the imperfect-market analysis was evolved (and Marshall himself introduced dislike of 'spoiling the market', to account for the maintenance of profit margins after a fall in demand).[16] It now appears much too simple, and oligopoly, price leadership and a feeling for 'playing the rules of the game' have to be brought in to supplement it.

A study of questions such as these, framed in terms of the kind of decisions that entrepreneurs actually have to make, may throw light on the problem of price policy, but it seems clearly impossible to replace the old text-book slogans with any simple generalizations. A debate which consists in defending or attacking 'principles', such as the 'full-cost principle', 'the

[16] *Principles*, p. 375.

marginal principle' or the 'normal-cost principle',[17] and trying to fit all types of situation into one system is obviously foredoomed to futility.

EQUILIBRIUM

In my opinion, the greatest weakness of the *Economics of Imperfect Competition* is one which it shares with the class of economic theory to which it belongs – the failure to deal with time. It is only in a metaphorical sense that price, rate of output, wage rate or what not can move in the plane depicted in a price-quantity diagram. Any movement must take place through time, and the position at any moment of time depends upon what it has been in the past. The point is not merely that any adjustment takes a certain time to complete and that (as has always been admitted) events may occur meanwhile which alter the position, so that the equilibrium towards which the system is said to be *tending* itself moves before it can be reached. The point is that the very process of moving has an effect upon the destination of the movement, so that there is no such thing as a position of long-run equilibrium which exists independently of the course which the economy is following at a particular date.

The most obvious example is the manner in which an industry reacts to large changes in demand for its output. When demand for the range of commodities concerned has risen in the recent past, so that it strains the capacity of plant in existence, or of a supply of skilled workers whom it takes a long time to train, current prices and the prospect of future profits are high, and new capacity is built up. In a text-book argument it is possible to imagine investment being made in continuous small steps, so that prospective profits fall gradually (demand remaining constant at the new level) and come to rest at the original level. But in reality, in an industry supplying markets which are competitive in the broad sense, investment plans are made by a large number of entrepreneurs at the same time, and are carried through while the high profits last, so that capacity is expanded in a long jump, and the rate of profit falls sharply when the new capacity comes

---

[17] Mr. Andrews' *Manufacturing Business* is full of dark sayings, but Miss Brunner ('Competition and the theory of the firm', *Economia Internazionale*, November 1952) makes the 'normal-cost theory' intelligible. Though couched in the form of an attack on imperfect-competition analysis, it seems to come to pretty much the same thing, as far as the hampering assumption of one-product firms permits. The difference is rather in tone and emphasis than in analysis. My generation, brought up on the view that everything in the garden was lovely, concentrated attention on the weeds. A generation to whom our weed manuals were the orthodox text-books naturally react by pointing out that there are after all many splendid blooms to be seen.

into operation. Investment in plant once made persists for a long time (even if it bankrupts its first owners) and firms which have set up in one industry fight to survive where they are, even if the level of profit in other regions is now more attractive. At a date, say, five (or perhaps twenty) years later, whatever the conditions of demand may then be, the level of profit in that industry will be lower than it would have been if this expansion of demand had not occurred.

Similarly, the level of wages and the age composition of a labour force are very different when the present level of employment in an industry is appreciably less than it was five, or twenty, years ago than they would be, with the same present level, if employment in the past had been appreciably less. The irreversibility of the supply curve, which Marshall introduced in connection with economies of scale,[18] has to be extended to all kinds of long-run supply curves, and when it is, the very notion of a long-run supply curve, in its usual simple two-dimensional form, ceases to be admissible.

This kind of difficulty underlies all problems connected with prices, profits and wages, and there seems to be little point in adding more and more subtleties to the superstructure of a theory which is based upon such shaky foundations.

THE CAUSES OF MONOPOLY

An interesting and important question which has received very little analytical treatment (though there is a good deal of historical information about it) is the causes of monopoly.[19]

The chief cause of monopoly (in a broad sense) is obviously competition. Firms are constantly striving to expand, and some must be more successful than others. It is easier to defend a position once gained than to conquer it, so that the most successful firms grow the most rapidly. There is no doubt much truth in Marshall's theory of the tendency (under a régime of nepotism) for old firms to fall into weak hands. But this does not check the process of concentration in industry. On the contrary, it means that at any moment a firm in the prime of its vigour finds itself surrounded by a number of easy victims to swallow up. If in its turn it grows weak with age, it is a large mouthful for someone else. Why did not Marshall think of fish in a pond instead of trees in a forest? An industry which is strongly competitive must be in the course of tending towards a condition of

[18] *Principles*, Appendix H.
[19] An extremely interesting attempt on this problem has been made by L. J. Zimmerman, *The Propensity to Monopolize*, North Holland Publishing Co., Amsterdam.

oligopoly; competition can be permanent only when it is hampered by highly imperfect markets or softened by a spirit of live and let live among the entrepreneurs concerned.

At the same time it is true that monopoly (or powerful oligopolists) at one stage in an industrial structure fosters competition at other stages. Thus, where wholesalers or retail chains dominate a market they foster polypoly among producers by making entry easy to the manufacturing stage of the industry.[20] An exceptional but instructive case is polypoly in the boot-and-shoe trade promoted by monopoly in the supply of machinery. Similarly, an oligopoly in manufacture fosters polypoly in retailing (tobacco is a familiar example).

The second main cause of monopoly is the occurrence of a severe decline in demand, or the failure of demand to continue to expand when an overshoot in investment has occurred in the manner referred to above. So long as a seller's market prevails, the limitation of capacity maintains profit margins, and polypoly is compatible with satisfactory profits even in a fairly perfect market. In a buyer's market when the imperfection of competition, the discipline of price followers or loyalty to the code of the full-cost principle are insufficient to maintain profit margins, firms are driven by the fear of extinction to reinforce them by price agreements, and though some agreements break down again or are eroded by outside competition when prosperity returns, many, once formed, persist permanently.

Such monopolies are produced, in the first place, by the fear of losses; others are due to exceptional hope of profit. Monopolies are relatively easy to form where the boundaries of an industry coincide with the boundaries of markets, as in the case of minerals with particular properties, specialized machinery or commodities such as matches or sewing-cotton which allow a relatively restricted scope for product differentiation. The lure of such victims is all the greater when the demand for the commodities concerned is inelastic.[21] Where there is a natural limitation on supply (as with mineral deposits) or very great economies of scale, or highly specialized know-how (as in many machine-making trades) a monopoly once formed is in a very strong position to maintain itself. Where there is no such 'natural' defence against outside competition, it may defend itself by establishing a hold over retailers, threatening patent actions, using 'fighting brands' to break competitors by localized price competition, and other devices, though it often tolerates the existence of a fringe of competitors, who are useful as a screen provided that they do not threaten to grow too much (small firms in

[20] Kaldor, loc. cit.
[21] Cf. Zimmerman, op. cit., p. 30.

such a situation sometimes make the highest profit rates to be found anywhere).

It is much easier to think of causes for monopoly and examples of monopolies being formed, than it is to think of causes or examples of monopolies breaking down. There seems to be a general presumption, therefore, that every succeeding generation will contain more monopolies than the last.

This is the kind of question which comes into view with the breakdown of traditional theory, but I have the impression that in the twenty years since the Chamberlin-Robinson duopoly first set up in imperfectly monopolistic competition, a great deal of mental energy has been devoted to a theological discussion whether an existing state of imperfect (or impure) competition is (a) beneficial, (b) harmless, (c) a necessary evil or (d) an unnecessary evil, while an analysis (as opposed to historical studies) of the causes and consequences of the process of survival or decline of competition has hardly begun.

POSTSCRIPT

To elaborate on Old Bill's retort, the statement that a firm seeks to 'maximize profits' has no meaning in itself. The firm, in a general way, needs and desires profits in order to be able to continue to exist, but as a statement of policy the slogan has no precise content until it is reduced to particular questions. The struggle of a firm to survive and grow cannot be expressed in terms of maximizing any precise quantity at a particular moment of time.

On the other hand, when it has a certain amount of finance available for investment it may be assumed to choose between various possible projects on the basis of their expected profitability (allowing, however, for considerations about prestige and so forth). When it has to find the price for a new product that 'looks about right' it may be taken to have in mind a price that, on the one hand, will not choke off demand to less than what it hopes to be able to sell and, on the other, will not needlessly sacrifice receipts.

When it has to decide how to react to a fall in prime costs it may be assumed to consider whether a reduction of prices is necessary to defend itself from competition (immediately from existing rivals or a little later from new ones) or, if it is in a fairly strong monopolistic position or is the price-leader for its group, whether a reduction in prices will increase or diminish profits. When the existing price (with the new lower costs) seems to be the most profitable, it may be assumed to leave it alone. Contrariwise, when costs rise, it may be assumed to raise prices unless there is reason to suppose that the old price would be more profitable.

In all these decisions there may be a conflict between higher immediate profits and prudence for the long run; there is bound to be a great deal of uncertainty about the effects of any policy and, partly for that reason, conventional rules may take the place of calculation in making them; and the profit motive may be mixed with many other impulses. All the same, I do not think that any better 'ole has yet been sighted.

16

THE THEORY OF VALUE RECONSIDERED

PRICES are the most obvious surface phenomena in economic life. Every school of economic theory was obliged to give some account of the determination of prices, but each school was concerned with wider questions; a theory of value was merely incidental to a general view of how the economic system operates.

To go back no further than Adam Smith, the concern of theory was to advocate a policy of *laisser-faire*. Adam Smith was maintaining that to release the forces of self-interest would lead to a great increase in material wealth. How right he was ! His theory of prices was very simple. In each neighbourhood there is a certain level of rents, wages and rate of profit. The price of each commodity is determined by the cost of the land, labour and capital required to produce it. He was a bit confused about gross and net output, but otherwise his theory was very sensible and quite adequate for his purpose.

For Adam Smith wages were a cost. The wealth of nations was the surplus. Wages of labour were no more to be counted in net income than the fodder of cattle. Ricardo also was concerned with the surplus of product over wages. He was contemplating the transition from feudalism to capitalism. (I am using feudalism in a loose sense to mean an economic system in which the predominant form of property is ownership of land.) Landlords consumed their share of the surplus; capitalists saved and reinvested profits. His concern was to show that rent was wasted from the point of view of accumulation. His central problem therefore was to find a theory of the distribution of the value of output between the factors of production.

He never quite succeeded in getting it out. Ricardo, with untutored genius, invented the method of constructing a 'model' on simple assumptions. So long as he could assume that there was a single wage good –

A Lecture delivered at University College, London, November 1968. Published in *Australian Economic Papers*, June 1969.

corn – produced by agriculture, and that the subsistence wage was fixed, he could establish a theory of distribution which was quite watertight.

The output of corn per annum per man employed on marginal land is a technical datum. The wage fund required to employ a man is a technical datum, being determined by the weekly needs of subsistence and the number of weeks from harvest to harvest. Profit per man employed is a technical datum – output minus wage. Thus the rate of profit is technically determined – profit per annum, as a quantity of corn, as a percentage of capital, as a stock of corn in the barn after harvest set aside to be paid out as wages over the year. The rate of profit for all other kinds of products must be the same, for the prices of all goods in terms of corn are such as to make it possible for them to cover their corn-wage bill.

This is a very striking conception. We now see from von Neumann that it survives breaking the real wage up into a variety of commodities. So long as the real-wage rate is fixed in physical terms the rate of profit is determined by the technique of production in use.

But Ricardo, in his day, got lost when he tried to bring other commodities into the wage bill. He saw that a difference in the rate of profit produced a difference in the pattern of prices, because the capital to labour ratio is not uniform, so that labour time, through its equivalence with corn, is not an invariable measure of value.

However, it was near enough for his purpose. His main point, that rent is an incubus on society, could be established just as well with this imperfect measure.

Marx took up the argument from Ricardo. Nowadays it is often thought that the Labour Theory of Value was a Marxian idea. This is not the case. To Marx it appeared as the obvious, orthodox theory. The contribution that he made it was the conception that labour power also is sold for its *value*. The wage is necessary to produce labour. The wage is valued by the labour time necessary to produce it. Thus labour has the unique quality of producing more than its own value. This might seem nowadays a rather metaphysical way of looking at things but the simple basic idea is solid enough – it is that by employing labour and other physical inputs it is possible to produce goods that can be sold for more than they cost – that is, to make a profit.

The relative prices of particular commodities were not relevant to Marx's main argument, for it is concerned with the overall division of net product (or value added) of industry as a whole between wages and profits. The overall rate of exploitation – the ratio of net profits to wages – is the clue to distribution.

Prices of particular commodities are determined by the rule that, in competitive conditions, the rate of profit on capital has to be equalized throughout the system. If we know net output in physical terms, and we know that the rate of profit is uniform, then when we know the share of profit in the value of net output, we can find the appropriate pattern of prices.

Marx himself did not get it quite right. He made a slip in working out the relation between prices and labour values. This gave a handle to his critics and confused his followers. The 'transformation problem' became a *pons asinorum* of Marxist theory.

Now that it has been correctly worked out in Sraffa's *Production of Commodities by Means of Commodities* we can see that there is no mystery about it. State your assumptions clearly and do not lose your head. Then the problem solves itself.

Marx's theory is sometimes presented as an attack upon capitalism. This is misleading. Certainly, he regarded capitalism as cruel, unjust and morally repulsive, but so were slavery and serfdom that preceded it. The advantage of capitalism was that it took the surplus and invested it. It ripened the productive power of social labour as though in a hot-house. It would bring itself to an end when it has completed its historical task. Revolutionary activity was to prepare the workers to take over when the time was ripe.

This view of the procession of economic systems was not to the taste of the nineteenth century. In the 1860s, capitalism was flourishing; real wages had begun to rise. Engels complained that the working class was becoming bourgeois.

Orthodox teaching took a violent turn. The neoclassical school came into fashion. *Laisser-faire* was no longer merely a programme. It became a dogma.

To attack the classical view, Böhm-Bawerk and Marshall changed the question. Ricardo had used labour as the measure of value. The neoclassicals pretended that he treated it as the *cause* of value, and advanced the view that capital also causes value. Thus the moral basis of the argument was shifted. The labourer is worthy of his hire and the capitalist is worthy of his profit.

However, the neoclassical school never succeeded in getting out a theory of profits. There are two main branches of the school which we may call for convenience Walrasian and Marshallian.

The Walrasian system is concerned with given physical means of production already in existence – labour, machines, stocks of cement and copper, and so forth. It can be shown that, for any basket of final output, with known techniques of production, there is a maximum quantity of output from the given resources and a set of relative prices which show the marginal rates of transformation between one basket of goods and another. This is a very pretty argument. It embodies the central notion of the meaning of economic efficiency and the nature of opportunity cost. With modern mathematical refinements it has been found to be applicable to a number of problems.

But how can it provide a theory of distribution? Who owns the commodities and receives the prices paid for them?

The weakness of the Walrasian system is exposed when too much is asked of it. Take for instance the refinement of the theory of demand made by Hicks and Allen.

Their question was how demand will be affected when the price of one commodity is reduced. The argument is as follows:

There are two elements in the response of demand, a substitution effect and an income effect. The income effect follows from the rise in real income due to a fall in one price. More of all commodities can now be bought. A negative income effect follows if the commodity whose price has fallen is an inferior good of which less is consumed at a higher level of real income.

This also is a very useful idea. But what is it doing in a theory of prices determined by supply and demand? What about the sellers of the good whose price has fallen? What has happened to their real income? Has it gone up or gone down? And how is it going to affect their demand for other goods?

This is very far from being what it claims – a system of general equilibrium.

Marshall had quite a different approach. If we scrape all the nonsense off it, his theory is much more relevant to the economic system that we know. There is a normal rate of profit on capital which is established where there is competition in the long-period sense that all markets are equally easy to enter. Supernormal profits attract new investment, which tends to bring them down by increasing supply relatively to demand. The prices of commodities are determined by costs, including profit at the normal rate on the capital directly or indirectly required to produce them.

But what determines the normal rate? All we hear about is that, in the ultimate stationary state when accumulation has come to an end, the rate of profit must be equal to the rate of interest which measures 'discount of the future'. If the return on capital were below this level, the capitalists would prefer to consume their wealth in 'present gratifications'. They have to receive the 'reward of waiting' to induce them to continue to own it.

Marshall was not really thinking of a stationary state. He was thinking of investment rolling along through time, normally earning profits at the normal rate. But then there is no theory at all of what the normal rate is.

Orthodox teaching came to a crash in the great slump and was overthrown in the Keynesian revolution. But the neo-neoclassical school, now dominant in the USA and rapidly infecting the profession all over the world, is based on a revival of Walrasian supply and demand.

The neo-classicals evidently had not been told that the neo-classical theory did not contain a solution of the problems of profits or of the value of capital. They have erected a towering structure of mathematical theorems on a foundation that does not exist. Recently Paul Samuelson was sufficiently candid to admit that the basis of his system does not hold, but the theorems go on pouring out just the same.

Why should this be? How do very clever and well educated men allow themselves to become committed to an untenable position? Perhaps the neo-neoclassical theory is acceptable because it *seems* to provide the justification for the profit system that the old neoclassicals were looking for. It renews the justification for *laisser-faire* – what is profitable is right. Don't interfere with businessmen, they always know best.

But for modern capitalism those slogans are useless. Modern governments, even in USA, have to consider the balance of payments, full employment, inflation, and even sometimes the distribution of income and problems of social justice.

This situation leads to a complete gulf between economic orthodoxy and actual problems. The orthodox theory has relapsed into the state from which it was awoken in the 'thirties, dreaming of equilibrium.

The Keynesian revolution brought us down from the neoclassical cloud-cuckoo-land, to here and now, facing the problems that we actually face. Combined with the theory of imperfect competition, the Keynesian theory of value starts from the formation of prices as it actually occurs. Prices of manufactures are set by a gross margin added to prime costs. The main influence on the level of prime costs is the level of money-wage rates. Thus the wage bargain determines the general level of prices.

How are the gross margins formed? From the point of view of the individual producer, they are set by the rule that, at the expected rate of output, receipts should cover the total cost of producing and selling the goods, including whatever seems a reasonable level of profits.

From the point of view of total income for industry as a whole, applying the Keynesian notion of the two-sidedness of income – one man's receipts is another man's expenditure – it is obvious that gross profit overall on goods sold to the public (when the above-the-line budget is balanced, and neglecting foreign trade) is equal to the wage bill for investment *plus* the excess of expenditure out of profits over saving out of wages.

Thus the share of gross profit in the short run and the rate of profit on capital in the long run are governed by investment and the propensity to consume. This is the Keynesian theory of distribution.

Though Keynes himself rejected Ricardo and disapproved of Marx, this theory links up with the classics. The function of profit is to be accumulated. Expenditure out of unearned income is an extra exploitation of the workers that is not justified by its usefulness to society.

This is the uncomfortable element in the generalization of Keynes's *General Theory* that is being smothered by the teaching of the neo-neoclassicals.

Let us apply this analysis to one of the urgent problems of modern capitalism – wages policy.

The Keynesian theory of how the system works is now pretty well accepted except by the most devotedly loyal disciples of the neo-neoclassics. A rise in money-wage rates throughout the economy leads to a more or less proportional rise of prices. The profit margins are roughly proportional, so that the absolute margin rises in terms of money and is more or less constant in terms of purchasing power. Thus the remedy is to ask the workers to limit the rise of money-wage rates so as to keep prices from rising. They are being asked to recognize the justice of keeping gross margins constant. The workers find this hard to accept. Let us consider their case.

What is the gross margin made up of? It covers the following items:

1. Salaries of overhead staff. Let us put the incomes of lower-paid white-collar employees in with the wage bill. This part of the overhead can be regarded as a necessary cost. High salaries of top executives will be discussed below.

2. Amortization of capital. In so far as this corresponds to replacements required to keep equipment in order, it is part of necessary costs.

3. Promotion and advertisement. For the individual firm these outlays are just as necessary as prime costs. There is no use in producing goods which find no market. But looking at the matter from the point of view of the workers, can this be said to contribute to the level of real wages? When you buy a packet of goods, part of the price you pay is the cost of persuading you to buy it. As a contribution to your standard of life it is not much to get your teeth into.

4. Taxes, both direct and indirect. Government outlay enters into the stream of demand which makes it possible for gross profits to be earned. In so far as taxes cover this outlay, they must be held to be part of the necessary

costs of output in general. It would take us too far afield to inquire whether the objects of government outlay are well chosen. The point to notice, however, is that all government outlay, whether covered by profit taxes or not, is at the expense of real wages, since it enters into the difference between money prices and money-wage rates.

5. Net profits. In so far as profits are retained to finance investment they are fulfilling their proper function – to exploit us for our own good. Once more we cannot go into the question of judging the desirability of the content of outlay in investment – we must take it in the round as a necessary cost of development. But we can distinguish between expenditure of profits on investment which increases the productivity of industry and expenditure on take-overs, that is buying up productive capacity that already exists.

6. Finally we come to the heart of the argument – distributed profits. For the firm it is necessary to pay dividends to keep up its credit, but what do the workers gain from it?

It used to be said that income from property is an inducement to accumulation. The rich are useful to society because they save. But nowadays industry does not depend upon saving from individual households. The whole of investment – sometimes even more than the whole – is covered by retentions. This does not mean, of course, that no firm ever goes to the market for funds, but it does mean that by and large, taking them together, the saving provided out of profit margins is sufficient to finance the total outlay on investment. Legally, the firm is saving on behalf of its shareholders but this is legal fiction. The shareholders can realize the capital gains that arise from ploughing profits back into real assets, and when they do so, the same money is being spent twice over.

This is the extraordinary economic system that we are living in. It has been evolved by a historical process; no one thought it out or designed it, and no one has yet been able to give a rational account of it. Workers, managers and research teams bring about technical progress and accumulation, and the capital falls into the lap of shareholders who are not making the smallest contribution to the process which is bringing it into being. Income from property is not the reward of waiting, it is the reward of employing a good stockbroker.

Along with dividends, we can consider the salaries of the top executives. Once more, the individual firm has to pay the going price for the services of good men; they compete amongst themselves for a limited supply. A great part of the level of the high salaries are like selling costs, a phenomenon of imperfect competition, not a necessary cost of production.

When we ask the workers to accept the mechanism which ensures that wages cannot encroach on the share of profits in the proceeds of industry, are we asking something reasonable?

Moreover we cannot even be sure that the mechanism keeps the share of profits no more than constant. When money-wages are kept in check, the more progressive industries, where output per head is rising, experience falling costs. Can we be sure that their prices automatically fall? Profit margins may be fixed on the principle of heads I win and tails you lose. Where costs fall, the first effect is to make the market in question more profitable. Selling costs are often pushed up, each producer trying to catch a larger share of it. Then the higher margin becomes necessary, the more progressive industries find it impossible to cut prices, while the less progressive find it necessary to raise them.

If this is how the system really works, it is no wonder that the neo-neoclassicals do not want to draw attention to it.

17

BEGGAR-MY-NEIGHBOUR REMEDIES FOR UNEMPLOYMENT

FOR any one country an increase in the balance of trade is equivalent to an increase in investment and normally leads (given the level of home investment) to an increase in employment.[1] An expansion of export industries, or of home industries rival to imports, causes a primary increase in employment, while the expenditure of additional incomes earned in these industries leads, in so far as it falls upon home-produced goods, to a secondary increase in employment. But an increase in employment brought about in this way is of a totally different nature from an increase due to home investment. For an increase in home investment brings about a net increase in employment for the world as a whole, while an increase in the balance of trade of one country at best leaves the level of employment for the world as a whole unaffected.[2] A decline in the imports of one country is a decline in the exports of other countries, and the balance of trade for the world as a whole is always equal to zero.[3]

In times of general unemployment a game of beggar-my-neighbour is played between the nations, each one endeavouring to throw a larger share of the burden upon the others. As soon as one suceeds in increasing its trade balance at the expense of the rest, others retaliate, and the total volume of international trade sinks continuously, relatively to the total volume of world activity. Political, strategic and sentimental considerations add fuel to the fire, and the flames of economic nationalism blaze ever higher and higher.

In the process not only is the efficiency of world production impaired by

[1] See below, p. 192, note 5 for an exceptional case.

[2] Unless it happens that the multiplier is higher than the average for the world in the country whose balance increases.

[3] The visible balances of all countries normally add up to a negative figure, since exports are reckoned f.o.b. and imports c.i.f. But this is compensated by a corresponding item in the invisible account, representing shipping and handling costs.

From *Essays in the Theory of Employment*, 1937.

the sacrifice of international division of labour, but the total of world activity is also likely to be reduced. For while an increase in the balance of trade of one country creates a situation in which its home rate of interest tends to fall, the corresponding reduction in the balances of the rest tends to raise their rates of interest, and owing to the apprehensive and cautious tradition which dominates the policy of monetary authorities, they are chronically more inclined to foster a rise in the rate of interest when the balance of trade is reduced than to permit a fall when it is increased. The beggar-my-neighbour game is therefore likely to be accompanied by a rise in the rate of interest for the world as a whole and consequently by a decline in world activity.

The principal devices by which the balance of trade can be increased are (1) exchange depreciation, (2) reductions in wages (which may take the form of increasing hours of work at the same weekly wage), (3) subsidies to exports and (4) restriction of imports by means of tariffs and quotas. To borrow a trope from Mr. D. H. Robertson, there are four suits in the pack, and a trick can be taken by playing a higher card out of any suit.

Before proceeding any further it is necessary to make a digression, for it has sometimes been denied that the restriction of imports will increase home employment.[4] This view appears to arise from a confusion as to the nature of the classical argument for free trade. The classical argument states that (with certain well-known exceptions) the pursuit of profit will bring about the specialization of resources and the distribution of trade between nations in such a way that the maximum of efficiency is achieved. Any arbitrary interference with the channels of trade will therefore lead to a decline in efficiency, and a reduction in the amount of output obtained from a given amount of resources. This argument, on its own ground, is un-exceptionable. But in the nature of the case it can throw no light upon the division of a given total of employment between nations. It tells us that, with given employment, output per head will be higher when trade is free. It cannot tell us that when one country increases its share in world employment, at the expense of reducing output per unit of employment, its total output will be reduced. Still less can it tell us that employment in any one country cannot be increased by increasing its balance of trade. Indeed it is obvious to common sense that a tax upon imported goods will lead to an increase in the output of rival home-produced goods, just as a tax

[4] See *General Theory*, p. 334. Mr. Keynes offers himself as a sacrifice. But (*pace* Sir William Beveridge) it was never the orthodox view that a tariff cannot lead to an increase in employment in the short period; see Pigou, *Public Finance*, p. 224.

upon any commodity will stimulate the output of substitutes for it.[5]

The popular view that free trade is all very well so long as all nations are free-traders, but that when other nations erect tariffs we must erect tariffs too, is countered by the argument that it would be just as sensible to drop rocks into our harbours because other nations have rocky coasts.[6] This argument, once more, is unexceptionable on its own ground. The tariffs of foreign nations (except in so far as they can be modified by bargaining) are simply a fact of nature from the point of view of the home authorities, and the maximum of specialization that is possible in face of them still yields the maximum of efficiency. But when the game of beggar-my-neighbour has been played for one or two rounds, and foreign nations have stimulated their exports and cut down their imports by every device in their power, the burden of unemployment upon any country which refuses to join in the game will become intolerable and the demand for some form of retaliation irresistible. The popular view that tariffs must be answered by tariffs has therefore much practical force, though the question still remains open from which suit in any given circumstances it is wisest to play a card.

Exchange depreciation and a reduction in the level of money wages lead to an increase in the balance of trade, provided that each stands above the optimum level. A subsidy to exports will increase the balance of trade provided that foreign demand has an elasticity greater than unity,[7] while restriction of imports by quotas will increase the balance of trade provided that home demand has an elasticity greater than unity. These four

[5] The argument is backed up by the contention that 'exports pay for imports', see, e.g. Beveridge and others, *Tariffs: the Case Examined*, Chapter VI. It is admitted that in some circumstances imports may be curtailed without exports falling to an equal extent, but this entails an increase in foreign lending, and it is argued that if foreign lending increases, home investment must decline (loc cit., p. 57). Now when the imposition of a tariff increases the balance of trade the increase in foreign lending which is required to prevent a rise in the exchange rate is brought about by a fall in the home rate of interest, and this is calculated to increase, not diminish, the volume of home investment. The flaw in the argument consists in overlooking the fact that an increase in home income will increase saving, so that increased foreign lending is not made at the expense of lending at home.

The classical, as opposed to the neo-classical, argument is usually set out upon the assumption that full employment is the normal state, and in the classical system of analysis the question of a beggar-my-neighbour increase in home employment does not arise.

[6] Beveridge, op. cit., p. 110.

[7] When the foreign demand is inelastic a tax on exports (as in Germany in 1922) or restriction of output (as in many raw-material-producing countries in recent years) will increase the balance of trade, while at the same time reducing the amount of employment in the export industries, and increasing the ratio of profits to wages in them. In these circumstances, therefore, an induced increase in the balance of trade may be accompanied by no increase, or even a decrease, in the level of employment.

expedients are thus all limited in their scope. A tariff reduces the volume of imports, and tends to reduce their foreign price, even when home demand is inelastic. Total expenditure by home consumers upon imports, including tax payments, may increase, but the payment to foreigners must be reduced. Tariffs thus provide an expedient for increasing the balance of trade which can still be used when all else fails.

We must now consider the effect upon home employment of an increase in the balance of trade brought about by each of the four expedients. To simplify the discussion we may postulate that the funds necessary for a subsidy are raised, or the receipts from import duties expended, in such a way as not to interfere with the distribution of income or to alter thriftiness in the home country.[8] Each expedient must be supposed to produce its own full effect. For instance, it must not be supposed that the influence of a fall in the exchange rate on the balance of trade is counteracted by a rise in money wages, or that a tariff leads to a rise in the exchange rate.

A fall in the exchange rate, or in money wages, causes a primary increase in employment in export industries, and in industries producing goods rival to imports.[9] For a given increase in the value of exports (in terms of home wage units) the increase in employment will be greater the greater is the elasticity of supply, and for a given decrease in the value of imports it will be greater the greater is the elasticity of foreign supply and the greater is the elasticity of supply in the rival home industries. It is possible that an increase in the balance of trade may lead to no primary increase in employment. For instance, suppose that the elasticity of home supply of export goods is zero and the elasticity of demand for import goods unity. Then a fall in the exchange rate will lead to a proportional increase in the value of exports, without any increase in their volume, and consequently without any increase in employment in the industries producing them, while the value of imports and the output of rival commodities will be un-changed.

In the case of a subsidy the primary increase in employment is in the

[8] The manner in which funds are raised or receipts expended is, of course, of the utmost importance, but analysis of the effects of changes in fiscal policy on employment can easily be superimposed upon the analysis here set out. For instance if receipts from import duties are paid into a sinking fund, or used to relieve taxation on the rich in such a way as to increase their savings, there will be an increase in thriftiness which will counteract the effect upon employment of increased foreign investment.

[9] If the elasticity of demand for imports is less than unity, there will be a primary decrease in employment in these industries, since additional expenditure upon imports will be made at their expense, but in this case a given increase in the balance of trade must entail so much the greater increase in exports.

export industries alone,[10] while in the case of a tariff the primary increase is in the industries rival to imports[11] and in the industries benefited by the expenditure of the receipts from duties.[12] In the case of quotas the primary increase is in the rival industries alone.

In each case, the increase in incomes due to the increased balance of trade will lead to secondary employment. Thus even when there is no primary increase in employment at all, total employment will increase as a result of the increased balance of trade. The lower are the elasticities of supply in the industries primarily affected the greater will be the increase in profits, relatively to wages, in them, and the smaller the increase in expenditure coming from them. Thus the secondary increase in employment is likely to be smaller the smaller is the increase in primary employment.

We must next consider the effect of the various expedients upon real income per unit of employment. Output per unit of employment normally falls off as employment increases. For a given increase in employment the decline in output per unit of employment will be greater in the case of subsidies, tariffs or quotas than in the case of exchange depreciation or a fall in wages, since advance is being made upon a narrower front. This is merely another way of stating the classical argument that the mal-distribution of resources due to an artificial stimulus of particular industries leads to a decline in output for a given level of employment.

The change in income per unit of employment will also be influenced by the effect of the various expedients upon the terms of trade. An improvement in the terms of trade, that is, a rise in the price of exports relatively to the price of imports represents an increase in incomes, per unit of employment, earned in export industries, relatively to the cost of imported commodities. If the total value of imports and of exports is more or less commensurate an improvement in the terms of trade will therefore bring about a rise in the average real income per unit of employment for the country as a whole.

A fall in money wages which affects all industries equally, is equivalent, as we have seen, to an equal proportional fall in the exchange except in respect to obligations fixed in terms of home currency. Abstracting from

[10] While there may be a primary decrease in employment in industries whose costs are raised as a result of the increase in output of export goods or whose receipts are reduced by the collection of funds for the subsidy.

[11] While there may be a primary decrease in employment in the industries whose costs are raised.

[12] In general, the more elastic is the demand for imports the larger will be the increase in the output of the rival industries and the smaller the proceeds of the duties.

them for the moment, we may conduct our discussion in terms of exchange depreciation alone, the argument being made applicable to a fall in wages by means of reckoning prices and incomes in terms of home wage units.

A fall in the exchange rate, which stimulates the output of export goods and reduces the demand for import goods, leads to a fall in the world price of both types of goods, and a rise in the home price. Since the prices of both types of goods move in the same direction it is impossible to say out of hand what the effect will be upon the terms of trade.

The fall in the world price of export goods in the first instance will be greater the less elastic is the foreign demand for them, and the more elastic is the home supply; while the fall in the price of import goods will be greater the more elastic is the home demand and the less elastic is the foreign supply. It can be seen that if the elasticity of foreign demand for exports is equal to the elasticity of foreign supply of imports, while the elasticity of home supply of exports is equal to the elasticity of home demand for imports, the initial effect of a fall in the exchange rate will be to move both sets of prices to the same extent, so that the terms of trade are unchanged. Further, if the foreign elasticity of supply exceeds the foreign elasticity of demand in the same proportion as the home elasticity of demand exceeds the home elasticity of supply, the terms of trade are unchanged.[13]

In general, each country is more specialized in respect to the goods which it produces than in respect to the goods which it consumes, so that any one country plays a more dominant role in the world supply of those goods which it exports than it plays in the world market for those goods which it imports. In general, therefore, the world demand for the exports of one country is less elastic than the world supply to it of those goods which it imports. So far as the foreign elasticities are concerned, there is thus a strong presumption that a fall in the exchange rate will turn the terms of trade in the unfavourable direction.

Each country imports a large number of commodities which cannot be produced at home, so that the elasticity of demand for imports tends to be low. The elasticity of supply of exports will depend upon the particular types of goods in question, and upon the general state of trade. In slump conditions, such as prevail when the game of beggar-my-neighbour is most

[13] Let p be the home price of imports and q of exports. Let ϵh and ϵf be the elasticities of home demand for imports and foreign demand for exports, and ηh and ηf the elasticities of home supply of exports and foreign supply of imports. Then the adverse change in the terms of trade is $\dfrac{\delta p}{p} - \dfrac{\delta q}{q}$, which is equal to $k\left(\dfrac{\eta f}{\epsilon h + \eta f} - \dfrac{\epsilon f}{\eta h + \epsilon f}\right)$. Thus the change in the terms of trade is adverse or favourable according $\dfrac{\eta h}{\epsilon h}$ is greater or less than $\dfrac{\epsilon f}{\eta f}$.

in vogue, the elasticity of supply of all commodities, except certain agricultural products, is likely to be high. It is thus only in exceptional cases that the home elasticity of demand can exceed the home elasticity of supply to a sufficient extent to compensate for the excess of the foreign elasticity of supply over the foreign elasticity of demand, and in general a fall in the exchange rate must be expected to cause a deterioration in the terms of trade.

An exceptional case would occur if the home supply of exportable goods were perfectly inelastic. There would then be no fall in the world price of exports, while unless either home demand for import goods is perfectly inelastic or the foreign supply of them perfectly elastic, there will be some fall in the price of imports, and the terms of trade will become favourable when the exchange rate falls. Thus for an agricultural country which produces a considerable proportion of the world supply of some commodity, the drawbacks of an inelastic world demand for its exports may be overcome by a sufficiently inelastic home supply. A country for which an inelastic foreign demand is combined with a highly elastic home supply will suffer a serious deterioration in the terms of trade as a result of exchange depreciation.

The importance of the home country in world markets will also affect the result. The change in world prices brought about by exchange depreciation will in general be smaller the smaller is the country concerned, and the narrower will be the range of the possible changes in the terms of trade. A large country is likely to suffer a greater deterioration in the terms of trade, when its exchange depreciates, than a small country, but at the same time it is only for a very large country that a favourable movement in the terms of trade can possibly occur, for it is only a large country which can exercise an appreciable influence on the world prices of the goods which it imports.

The effect upon the terms of trade of a fall in money wages differs from the effect of depreciation in so far as there are foreign obligations fixed in terms of home currency. These are unaffected by a fall in the exchange rate, while a fall in wages raises the cost of payments and the value of receipts in terms of home wage units. Thus, in so far as payments fixed in terms of home currency are an appreciable element in invisible imports, the deleterious effect of a fall in wages upon the terms of trade will be greater than the effect of a corresponding depreciation in the exchange, while a given increase in the balance of trade, in terms of wage units, will require a larger fall in wages, and so entail larger changes in the prices of other imports and exports. In so far as receipts fixed in terms of home currency are an appreciable element in invisible exports, the deleterious effect of a fall in the exchange rate will be greater.

A subsidy to exports leads to a fall in the world price of export goods which will be greater the less elastic is foreign demand and the more elastic is home supply. In so far as the price of import goods is affected at all, it must be raised. The output of export goods is increased, and their price in the home market, in which they are not subsidized, is raised,[14] so that the price of imports which are rival in the home market to exportable goods may be raised. A subsidy to exports therefore causes an unfavourable movement in the terms of trade.[15] In this respect a subsidy is necessarily more deleterious than exchange depreciation or a fall in money wages.

A tariff leads to a fall in the world price of import goods, which will be greater the less elastic is foreign supply and the more elastic is home demand.[16] In so far as it affects the price of exports it must raise them. Raw materials entering into export goods may be subject to duties, while the increase in the output of home goods which are substitutes for imports may raise the price of the exportable goods. A tariff therefore has a favourable effect upon the terms of trade.

Neither a tariff nor a subsidy can normally be applied to the invisible exports and imports (with the exception of shipping services). Where it is possible to increase the invisible balance by means of exchange depreciation without any adverse effect upon the terms of trade (for instance when the main invisible export consists of receipts fixed in terms of foreign currency), the advantage of a tariff, as opposed to exchange depreciation, is *pro tanto* diminished, and the disadvantage of subsidies increased.

The restriction of imports by means of quotas does not have the same effect upon the terms of trade as a tariff, since it leads to a rise in the home price of import goods, while preventing the restriction in home consumption from lowering the foreign price. A quota upon imports has much the same effect as an increase in the degree of monopoly amongst foreign suppliers. It leads to a deterioration in the terms of trade, while the benefit from the raised price to the home consumer, which goes to the exchequer under a tariff, goes to the foreign producers under a quota.

We have so far considered the terms of trade only in the light of the

[14] Services such as transport must be regarded as exports in so far as they enter into the production of export goods.

[15] Income per unit of output in the export trades is not reduced, but real income per unit of output for the country as a whole is reduced by the levy of funds to pay the subsidy.

[16] This is known as 'making the foreigner pay the tax'. If foreign supply is perfectly inelastic, price to the home consumer is not raised by the import duty at all and 'the foreigner pays the whole of the tax'.

elasticities of home and foreign supply and demand. Any increase in the balance of trade, by whichever expedient it is brought about, will lead to an increase in home incomes and activity. It will therefore raise both the demand curve for imports and the supply curve of exports. But the effect of increased incomes in raising the demand for consumable imports, and the effect of increased activity in raising the demand for raw materials, will normally be far greater than the effect of increased home consumption in reducing the supply of goods available for export. Increased activity is therefore likely to have a larger effect in raising the price of imports than in raising the price of exports, and therefore tells in the direction of worsening the terms of trade. The presumption that the terms of trade will deteriorate as a result of a fall in the exchange rate or of wages is therefore increased, the deterioration due to a subsidy or to quotas is enhanced, and the improvement due to a tariff mitigated, by the effect of increased activity.

The effect of changes in the terms of trade upon income per unit of employment must be combined with the effects, discussed above,[17] of the distribution of home activity between different groups of industries. The beneficial effects of a tariff upon the terms of trade may offset the deleterious effects of concentrating output in a narrower group of industries, and in favourable circumstances may even lead to an increase in income per unit of employment. Exchange depreciation and wage cuts occupy the intermediate position on both counts; while subsidies and quotas are the most deleterious, on both counts, of all the expedients for increasing the balance of trade.

The change in real wages which is brought about by the various expedients is not necessarily commensurate with the change in real income per unit of employment, for wage earners may consume goods of various types in different proportions from the average for the country as a whole, while, in the case of a tariff, the benefit to wage earners of the expenditure of tax receipts is not necessarily, or usually, commensurate with the contribution which they make to them. For a given increase in the balance of trade, the rise in the home price of export goods is greatest in the case of a subsidy, and the rise in the price of import goods, and of home goods which are rival to them, greatest in the case of tariffs, while a fall in the exchange rate or in money wages has an intermediate effect upon both sets of prices (prices being calculated in wages units, in the case of a fall in money wages). Thus for a country whose export goods are an unimportant element in the consumption of wage earners the fall in real wages will be least for a subsidy, greater for depreciation, and greatest for tariffs, while for a country

[17] See p. 193–194.

which exports food-stuffs and imports the luxuries of the rich the order of preference is reversed. Quotas, which are commonly applied to agricultural commodities and so raise the price of food-stuffs, and which make no contribution to fiscal revenue, bring about the largest fall in real wages of all the expedients for increasing the balance of trade.

The various expedients have important effects upon the distribution of income and activity between industries within the home country. An increase in the balance of trade is accompanied by a rise in the home price of export goods, or of goods which are rival to imports, or of both together, so that an increase in the balance of trade increases not only activity, but also income per unit of output, in the industries concerned in producing these goods. Now, when the game of beggar-my-neighbour is being hotly played, these industries suffer a decline in incomes relatively to the industries which are not subject to foreign competition,[18] and an improvement in their situation may be regarded as desirable for its own sake, apart from any increase in the total of activity and incomes of the country. This consideration is of particular importance in so far as it affects agricultural commodities, since the agricultural community is in general poorer than the industrial. Any policy which is designed to increase the exports, or reduce the imports, of agricultural commodities has the effect of turning the terms of trade between agriculture and industry inside the home country in favour of agriculture, and so of reducing the inequality in their earnings. Such policies are widely held to be beneficial, in spite of the fall in the average of real wages which they necessarily bring about.[19]

Certain special considerations apply to each of the four expedients. We have treated a reduction in wages as being in general equivalent to a fall in the exchange rate, but there is one difference between the two which is of the utmost importance. Even if obligations to foreigners fixed in terms of home currency are unimportant, internal indebtedness still has to be

[18] Even in a country so greatly dependent upon foreign trade as Great Britain these industries occupy much less than half the working population, while the multiplier appears to be normally something in the neighbourhood of 2. Thus a given decline in employment in the foreign trade industries causes an almost equal absolute, and therefore a smaller proportionate, decline in employment in the home trade industries. This is known as 'the problem of the unsheltered industries'.

[19] A fall in the exchange rate, or an all-round reduction in wages, will benefit the export industries even when they bring about no increase, or even a decrease, in the balance of trade, while quotas will always benefit the home industries protected by them, and subsidises the industries which receive them. These expedients may therefore be resorted to in certain circumstances entirely for the sake of the industries concerned, without regard to their effect upon the general level of activity, while tariffs are often designed for the benefit of particular groups without much regard to their incidental effect in improving the balance of trade.

considered. A cut in wages leads to a redistribution of real income in favour of the fixed-income classes, and an increase in the burden of indebtedness within the home country. For this reason a cut in wages is undesirable so long as any other expedient will serve, even if it can be brought about smoothly without the distress and wastage of industrial disputes, and even if it can be made equal in all industries so as to avoid arbitrary redistribution of income and activity between them.

Depreciation of the exchange rate has the disadvantage of being regarded as a breach of international good faith, while the apprehension of a fall may have serious effects upon the international financial position of the home country.

Tariffs and subsidies bring well-known political evils in their train, from which the more general, automatic and inhuman mechanism of exchange depreciation is comparatively free, while tariffs foster monopoly by violently reducing the elasticity of demand for home goods formerly subject to foreign competition, and so making the gains of monopolization more tempting to the home producers. Tariffs, it is true, have the advantage that they are selective, and may be devised in such a way as to bring about the minimum decrease in real wages for a given increase in employment, but actually they are not always devised with this end in view.

All expedients are subject to the objection that they are calculated to promote retaliation; indeed this is the very nature of the beggar-my-neighbour game. Which expedient is the least dangerous from this point of view will depend upon general political considerations.

When a nation, hard pressed in the game, is determined to take a trick, the decision as to which suit it is wisest to play must be taken in the light of all the considerations set out above, as they apply to the particular situation of the nation concerned at the particular moment when the decision is taken.

From an un-nationalist point of view all are equally objectionable, since each is designed to benefit one nation at the expense of the rest. But there are circumstances in which a limited indulgence in them cannot be regarded as a crime. First of all, they may be justified by the plea of self-defence, and secondly they may be used merely to cancel out a benefit to the rest of the world that would otherwise result from the policy of one nation. An increase in home investment in one country tends to increase activity in the rest of the world, and measures designed to protect the balance of trade when home investment increases merely cause a larger share of the reward of virtue to fall to the virtuous nation, while measures which protect the balance of trade when money wages rise at home merely prevent the rest of the world from gaining an advantage, and leave it no worse than before.

18

THE NEW MERCANTILISM

I BEGAN to read for the Tripos in the last decade in which the doctrine of the universal benefits of free trade was still dominant. It was imposed upon our young minds as a dogma. We were being received into the fraternity of economists, who knew that free trade is right, unlike the silly plain man who supposed that protection might do his country good, and the misguided politician who supported the vested interests of particular industries. In the dark age before the light of Adam Smith dawned, there had been mercantilists who were both misguided, because they thought it proper for a government to operate in favour of the economic interests of its own country, though at the expense of others, and silly because they thought that it *was* in a country's interest to build up a trade surplus by restricting imports. When Keynes attacked the dominant orthodoxy, one of the things that grieved my teachers most was that he should try to rehabilitate the mercantilists, thus damaging the claim of the free-traders to superior benevolence and wisdom.

1

The economist's case for free trade is deployed by means of a model from which all relevant considerations are eliminated by the assumptions. Each country enjoys full employment. There is no migration of labour and no international investment, however great the differences in the level of profits in different countries may be. At the same time there is perfect mobility and adaptability of factors of production within each country. Perfect competition prevails. Fixed exchange rates are taken for granted. Equality between the values of imports and exports of each country is quickly established, in the face even of large disturbances, by movements of relative prices brought about through the international monetary mechanism. All this has to be granted before the argument begins. Yet

---

An Inaugural Lecture, delivered at the University of Cambridge on 15 October 1965.

prescriptions for policy were drawn from it, with great confidence, to apply to a world which by no means conformed to the assumptions.

In practice the policy seemed to work, in the era that ended in 1914, just because the assumptions of the model were not fulfilled. There was enough unemployment to keep money-wage rates in check. There were massive migrations reallocating the supply of labour between countries of low and high economic opportunity; and there was a continuous, though fluctuating, flow of international investment.

Investment was typically made by the enterprise of developed industrial countries looking out (under the guidance of prospective profit) for supplies of primary products. The finance and the imports required in the developing country came in the main from the same source, so that surpluses of exports offset the capital outflow. By the time that loan charges and remittances of profits in the developing countries began to outweigh new borrowing, a sufficient flow of exports to provide for them would be built up (barring errors and accidents) for the object of the investment in the first place was precisely to develop the production of commodities for export to the ever expanding market of the industrial metropolis.

In this way a broad general tendency prevailed to harmony between flows of trade and capital movements.

When perfect harmony did not prevail, discrepancies were not difficult to eliminate. London was the money market of the world; the income account for sterling, taking trade and interest payments together, was always in surplus. When a deficit appeared in the overall balance of payments, causing a loss of gold, it was only necessary to raise the bank rate and cut down lending from London to fit the surplus. There was no need for heavy pressure operating through prices on the balance of trade, in the manner postulated for the economists' model.

On the other hand a borrowing country, when it found capital inflow falling short of its import surplus, was automatically obliged to curtail expenditure until unemployment and falling incomes cut down its imports to what it could pay for. For these countries, eliminating discrepancies was very disagreeable but they were not yet provided with economists to make their complaints articulate.

For England, the general system of free trade, fixed exchange rates, and uninhibited play of market forces was highly satisfactory as long as her economy held the dominant place in the expanding capitalist world. I say England deliberately for Ireland and Scotland suffered in the process.

We ought not to be surprised that what now seems such a flimsy construction as the economists' model should have appeared to hold so much weight and authority, for it did not really have to stand on its own logical base. It was the façade of a dogma with solid interests behind it.

In the 1920s, at the time when I was being brainwashed, the solid interests had already crumbled, for, in the immortal words of *1066 and All That*, after 1918 America became Top Nation, and that was a Bad Thing.

But the façade still stood. It was an eminent economist who persuaded the authorities that restoring the mere mechanism of the gold standard would restore the harmonious international financial relations in which it had been able to operate.

In the 1930s, the façade, along with the whole structure, was thoroughly pulverized in the great slump.

Each country, finding profits falling and unemployment growing, tried to save for itself a larger share in the shrunken total of world activity, by one means or another – tariffs, import quotas, subsidies, exchange depreciation and counter-depreciation – each exporting its own unemployment, as the phrase was, to the rest of the world. International trade was cut down all round relatively to home production, which itself had been drastically reduced. Over three years the total output of manufacturing industry in the capitalist countries fell by 40 per cent while international trade fell by 60 per cent.[1]

Certainly the free play of market forces was not operating, as in the model, to secure full employment and balanced trade for each country.

It was now seen that any one country that could succeed in cutting its imports (relatively to its exports) and substituting home production was so much the less badly off. Since all were trying to do it, none could gain much for long, but any that had refrained from joining the scramble would have found the world's unemployment being dumped upon it.

These considerations caused Keynes to repudiate the free-trade doctrine which he had once preached as fervently as any. We know now that free trade is not an equilibrium state that would be reached if each country individually followed its own enlightened self-interest. It could be achieved only by mutually accepted self-denying ordinances, establishing a code of behaviour that would be good for all if each observed it.

It was found possible to show, even within the terms of the economists' model, that, when each country individually pursues its own individual interests, they will pile up tariffs against each other. In the final position, with trade restricted all round, no one, considered separately, is likely to be better off than they would have been if they had all agreed not to begin, and certainly, taken together, they are much worse off. It follows, within the

[1] See USA Department of Commerce, *The United States in the World Economy*, p. 170.

terms of the model, where full employment is always guaranteed, that they should enter into a treaty which would impose free trade under the sanction of a mutually accepted rule.

But in reality, since full employment is not guaranteed, merely to agree to prohibit beggar-my-neighbour devices for checking imports and pushing exports would not be to the good of all. The same rule would inhibit also constructive remedies for unemployment from being undertaken by individual countries. When one country gives a boost to the world as a whole by increasing its home activity, its imports are liable to rise, while, until the rest of the world follows suit, the market for its exports is not better than before. In short it tends to develop a trade deficit, which it may not be able to finance. To be able to benefit the world by increasing employment at home, it must be free to reduce its *propensity* to import, so that its total *amount* of imports does not rise too fast. Of all bad-neighbourly conduct among trading nations, the worst is to go into a slump, and expedients necessary to prevent it have to be excused.

When the trading system for the capitalist world was being reconstructed after the last war, many agreements, such as GATT and IMF, were based upon the philosophy of mutual undertakings to avoid bad-neighbourly conduct of one kind or another, but it proved impossible to frame rules that would permit the right exceptions while ruling out the wrong ones.

The great slump is now a half-forgotten nightmare. Ever since the war, partly by good luck, partly by good management and partly by the arms race, overall effective demand has been kept from serious relapses. Nowadays governments are concerned not just to maintain employment, but to make national income grow. Nevertheless, the capitalist world is still always somewhat of a buyer's market, in the sense that capacity to produce exceeds what can be sold at a profitable price. Some countries have experienced spells of excessive demand, but this corrects itself only too soon. The chronic condition for industrial enterprise is to be looking round anxiously for prospects of sales. Since the total market does not grow fast enough to make room for all, each government feels it a worthy and commendable aim to increase its own share in world activity for the benefit of its own people.

This is the new mercantilism.

The fact that a section of the world economy has contracted out of the market system and is growing up beside it, is helpful to it to some extent, for the socialist countries believe in the old free-trade doctrine that the purpose of exports is to pay for imports, and they are always willing to buy as much as they can sell. But political hostility and particular vested interests limit the amount of trade that they are allowed with the capitalist world, and so limit the amount of relief that they give.

For the rest, everyone is keen to sell and wary of buying. Every nation wants to have a surplus in its balance of trade. This is a game where the total scores add up to zero. Some can win only if others lose. The beautiful harmony of the free-trade model is far indeed to seek.

It is sometimes argued that the fact that common markets and free-trade areas are now in fashion proves that this is not an age of economic nationalism but just the reverse.

Adam Smith triumphed over the old mercantilists by observing that the division of labour depends upon the extent of the market. This principle has been vindicated beyond his wildest dreams by the economies of specialization introduced by modern technology and the innumerable animal, vegetable and mineral products unknown in his day. For any group of producers, provided that they can be sure of adequate demand, the greatest possible specialization is highly advantageous. And a large nation, with a large internal market within the orbit of its political control, has important economic advantages over a small one. The small nation has to weigh the prospects of gain from specialization against the security of home production for home consumption, while the large nation can enjoy a great deal of both.

A group of nations that can succeed in agreeing to behave as if, for certain purposes, they were one, thus scores a benefit for all of them in competition with the outside world.

The larger and more various the free-trade area in which an economy grows up the more efficient it will be, but it is not at all easy for national economies, once grown, to make the mutual sacrifices required to create a common market. The experiences of EEC illustrate the fallacy of the doctrine that free trade comes about of itself through the operation of enlightened self-interest. Even the East European socialist countries, who accept planning for specialization in principle, having been started off by Stalin on a false track of autarky, are finding it very difficult to move out of it into a rational system of trade.

2

The characteristic feature of the new mercantilism is that every nation wants to earn a surplus from the rest. I have already referred to the distinction between a country's income account and its overall balance of payments. Precise definitions are very tricky; rough and ready categories will serve for now. Expenditure on income account includes payments for imports, visible and invisible, interest and profits due to creditors overseas, and recurrent government outlay abroad on military installations, etc. Receipts are the corresponding items on the other side of the account. Capital outflow comprises loans of all kinds from home citizens and institutions to foreign, government grants, purchases of foreign securities, and finance for direct investment carried out overseas by home companies. These are all included in the general category of foreign lending. The corresponding items on the other side of the account are the capital inflow, or foreign borrowing for short.

When, over any period of time, net lending, in this wide sense, falls short of a surplus on income account, or borrowing exceeds a deficit, the overall balance of payments is in surplus and there is an inflow into the monetary system of the country concerned of internationally liquid means of payment, such as gold or dollar balances. When net lending exceeds the surplus on income account, or net borrowing falls short of the deficit, the country is losing monetary reserves.

Now one of the reasons why countries want to have a surplus on income account is that it makes it possible to have an overall surplus so as to gain reserves. This is partly because an exact balance is not possible, and a surplus is a fault on the right side, and partly because it is highly desirable to have a good stock of reserves available to be paid out in an emergency, especially in these uncertain times when even the most respectable currencies are liable to sudden attacks of adverse speculation.

The free-traders used to mock at the old mercantilists for thinking that a country could grow rich by amassing treasure. The new mercantilists believe that it is not necessarily foolish to prefer to acquire sterile money rather than useful goods or profitable assets.

Apart from new mining, some countries can gain reserves only if others are losing them. (What is in effect a loss of reserves may take the form of accepting short-term liabilities, equivalent, as we used to put it, to an inflow of negative gold.)

At one time the United States was losing reserves quite cheerfully. Having an enormous surplus on income account after the war, American business got into the habit of financing investment abroad and American governments got into commitments of all kinds. The surplus failed to grow as fast as the outflow, till one fine day the United States found itself with an overall deficit and reserves flowing out. The stock of gold acquired from the overall surpluses of more than twenty years was grotesquely huge, and the American authorities did not object to letting it begin to go. This was the correct, good-neighbourly policy. It was a very great benefit to the surplus countries who wanted to acquire reserves. For some time they have been battening upon it. But no stock is inexhaustible to a one-way flow, even the American stock of gold. Over the last few years the authorities have begun to worry, and to cut down overseas payments, and call in receipts. The surplus countries that had become accustomed to an inflow of reserves are worried when it threatens to dry up, and curtail their outgoings in turn, so that a spasm of contraction runs through the world financial system.

There is a lot of talk nowadays about international liquidity; the total stock of the net reserves of all countries taken together has failed to grow with the money value of the total trade that it has to serve. This is certainly a serious problem and it should be solved. But to solve it will not cure us of mercantilism. However great the total supply of liquidity, there will still be a deflationary kink in a financial system in which every country likes to gain reserves and hates to lose them. This complaint used to be made against the old-fashioned gold standard. Our modern sophisticated arrangements are haunted by it still.

The story of the American gold hoard is an illustration of how wrong Marshall was to choose as his motto *Natura non facit saltum* — nature does not proceed by sudden leaps. Economic history creeps in this petty pace from day to day, but over decades it can swing round sharp corners that leave equilibrium analysis gaping.

In the system of the new mercantilism, an inflow of reserves is a rather superficial aim. There are more solid reasons why a surplus on income account is advantageous. For one thing, it permits the home country's financiers to acquire foreign assets. Provided there is no fear of default, foreign assets are eligible from a purely financial point of view, simply because the world is larger and more varied than the home country. Finance can pick out the plums from a bigger pie. Even when default or confiscation sometime is vaguely feared, a profit rate which may be, say, 30 per cent per annum meanwhile, offers a good gamble.

The kind of capital outflow now in vogue is much unlike nineteenth-century colonial investment to supply exotic commodities for which there was a market already in view. Modern lending is largely mere placement — buying up assets that already exist. And when it is implementing real investment it is often investment to supply the recipient's home market, protected by tariffs or monopolistic conditions. For the receiving country this kind of investment may be an embarrassment. The remission of profits will put a burden upon its future balance of payments; and in this age of economic nationalism it is dangerous and disagreeable to be bought up by foreign interests. By the same token, the lending country is gaining something over and above a high return on its money.

The high return goes primarily to the financiers. The most important benefit from a surplus on income account, which affects the whole economy, is that, provided that there are energetic enterprises and thrifty capitalists to take advantage of it, it permits home investment to go full steam ahead, while a deficit country is nervously pulling on the brake for fear of excessive imports. Investment in the strong country brings technical progress which improves its competitive position and makes its balance of trade all the stronger, while the weak country slips into stagnation or suffers distressing spasms of stop and go.

There is another hazard that has been introduced into the game in the post-war period. Partly because of long spells of near-full employment and partly because of a change in the internal balance of political forces, industrial countries have been experiencing a continuous process of rising money-wage rates. In the stagnant country, costs are pushed up, making its competitive position all the weaker, while the strong country can afford a greater rise, because output per head is increasing faster, and yet is subject to less pressure, because its workers' real earnings are visibly growing.

A strong country may find itself only too strong when the energy and competitive advantages of its industrialists give it such a large surplus that, from the point of view of the economy as a whole, home investment would offer a better use for its resources. An excessive surplus could be reduced, by appreciating the currency or allowing money-wage rates to rise faster, thus cutting down the competitive advantage that causes the excess. But this remedy cannot easily be applied in a measured dose. Industrial supply curves are usually horizontal, and the world demand curve at any moment strongly kinked. It is impossible to cut exports a little, by raising relative costs, without cutting them much too much. Even when its surplus is more than the country has a good use for, it would rather keep it than risk losing it.

Thus the authorities in each country, requiring to maintain employment for their own people and growth in their own national income, in the general environment of a buyer's market, have good reason to strive to gain a surplus in their trade and a rising share in world markets. In so far as some succeed, others fail.

Great Britain has been a notorious failure. I am not thinking of the sterling crisis and our troubles with the gnomes of Zurich, but of our continuous, obstinate, unmanageable tendency to run into a deficit on income account. This is not only due to the complacency of our businessmen and the touchiness of our trade unions, which put us into a weak competitive position. It is due to the corner in economic history that we have to go round. The rapid descent from the position of Top Nation, and the pyrrhic victories of two wars, have left us with a propensity to import greater than we can any longer provide for.

From our own point of view, the indicated remedy is to cut inessential imports, and to restrict consumption for a time while devoting research and investment to import substitution, as well as to modernizing industry and education to improve our general efficiency. For us this would not be too uncomfortable and might even be turned to good account. But for the other mercantilist nations it would be a sad blow. Their full employment and their growth depend upon surpluses that, directly or indirectly, depend upon our deficit. Our deficit and our falling share in world markets have been going on long enough for the economies of the rest to become adapted to them. A kind of quasi-equilibrium has been built round them, which will be violently upset when they are reversed. And there is bound to be a formidable back-wash upon our own position, partly from retaliation and partly from the automatic chain reaction throughout the rest of the world of a fall in demand following a fall in sales.

This does not depend on which particular remedies we apply. To cut imports is an immediate blow to the exporters concerned. Exchange depreciation is considered a breach of faith. Various methods of pushing exports were ruled out by mutual agreements to avoid beggar-my-neighbour policies. But suppose that we suddenly became very efficient and began to recapture our market by offering excellently designed goods at eligible prices. Our competitors would suffer just as much from a loss of sales and would be obliged to react just as sharply as if we balanced our own trade by any other means.

The remedy favoured by the monetary authorities of the world, including the gnomes, is the old-fashioned one of a credit squeeze, inducing a sufficient slump to cut down imports and enough unemployment to check the rise in wages. This method maintains the authority of finance over industry. Moreover, we were used, in the old days of free trade, to make deficit nations swallow this bitter medicine, and there is some *schadenfreude* in seeing us drink it now.

But this remedy is not only the most intolerable for us; it is the most dangerous for the others, especially now, when several countries for various reasons have had to slacken their rate of growth, so that an actual recession in any one might threaten the whole regime of near-full employment for all.

The actual sums involved in the British deficit, though serious for us, are not large in relation to the volume of world trade. With common sense and goodwill, it would be possible to limit the damage or even turn it to advantage. But there is no tradition to help us. The free-trade doctrine, ignoring the leaps and twists of economic history, simply denied that such a problem could occur. In the era of the new mercantilism the problem is recognized so well that all the world stands around shouting at us that whatever we do is bound to be wrong.

3

All this concerns the relations between the industrial capitalist nations. The greatest change that has come over the world since the war is the emergence of many new nations, existing at a low economic level, determined to begin to share in the benefits of modern technology. The most striking thing that modern technology has done for them so far is to reduce death rates, while leaving their primitive birth rates unchecked. A terrifying growth of population is making it all the more necessary for them to increase production.

Most were provided by colonial investment with one or two export commodities. This gives them something to start on. All but the most besottedly fanatical free-traders would concede their right to cut down inessential imports and use their export earnings to import know-how and investment goods to lay a basis for development.

Such earnings, however, are far from adequate. Technological developments have limited demand for the ex-colonial products, relatively to supplies available, partly because of the growth of synthetic substitutes and partly because the wealthy mercantilists countries foster their own agriculture, and keep as much of the market as they can to themselves. Commerce in commodities is conducted on competitive principles, while the prices of industrial products are administered on a cost-plus basis, so that they have been drifting upwards with the continuous rise of money-wage rates. The result has been sluggish growth in the sales of the ex-colonial commodities and a downward trend in their purchasing power over manufactures. Moreover, the free play of market forces, which in the economists' model produces an equilibrium beneficial to all, in reality generates unpredictable fluctuations in export earnings, that make consistent planning impossible and turn the choice of investment projects into a gamble.

Export earnings from commodities provide limited ammunition for growth, also, just because they were the product of colonial investment and are still earmarked to pay for it. This is markedly the case in the Latin-American economies, which came into a colonial relationship to the United States after they had won national independence from Spain and Portugal. Nowadays many of these countries are paying back 30 or 40 per cent of all their export earnings as profits and interest to foreign capitalists.[2] These payments are being made, in the main, not for sophisticated know-how and up-to-date equipment supplied by the metropolitan industry, but merely for extracting their own natural wealth from their own soil.

Another legacy from colonialism which impedes development is the tastes and habits of the middle class that grew up within it. Having become accustomed to an imported style of life, these people find it very hard to give up imported consumption goods, so that such export earnings as do come in are not easy to mobilize for investment.

In spite of these limitations, considerable development has gone on and many amongst the new nations are beginning to export industrial products. Now they come hard up against the mercantilism of the wealthy countries, who hate cheap imports.

When England was the leading exporter of manufactures, India, for instance, in the sacred name of free trade, was forbidden to protect her handicraft workers or foster her infant capitalist industry (though protection for infant industries was admitted as an exception in the economists' doctrine). When a duty on imported cloth was imposed for revenue purposes it had to be offset by a corresponding excise to prevent local production from enjoying a competitive advantage.

The free-traders argued that the manufactures from Lancashire were far and away cheaper and better than homespun so that it was a clear benefit to the Indian consumer to allow imports to undercut and wipe out handicraft production. They failed to notice that, while the Indian economy had to bear the whole cost of the imports, the consumer gained only the difference; at the same time the handicraftsman was thrown into agriculture, already over-supplied with labour, and lost his earnings to his rival in Lancashire.

Now the boot is on the other foot, and Lancashire is being undercut by cheap imports. Free trade is no longer in fashion and Lancashire has to be protected. To do ourselves justice, we have gone much further than other well-to-do nations in permitting manufactured imports from developing

[2] See United Nations, *Proceedings of UNCTAD*, v. 87–8.

countries, though by no means going to the whole length of free trade. In general the new mercantilist system is brutally obstructive to them.

It seems after all that the free-trade doctrine is just a more subtle form of mercantilism. It is believed only by those who will gain an advantage from it.

Nowadays the wealthy capitalist nations make a great thing of the aid that they are giving to the new nations. Military aid, intended to steel them against Communism, actually encourages them to go in for cold or hot wars against each other, which is most inimical to economic growth. Much of the civilian so-called aid is made on financial terms which are building up a Latin-American situation for the future in Asia and Africa, though here, once more, we can take credit for starting a line in interest-free loans. Even aid which is really a gift is not unambiguous. Individuals who advocate and administer aid to the developing countries are sincerely concerned to help them to overcome poverty and to establish their independence, but the programme as a whole is based upon a contradiction. Its underlying purpose is to prop up a number of conservative, feudal and fascist governments, which can be relied upon in return to respect foreign property. In short the aim of aid is to perpetuate the system that makes aid necessary.

If the wealthy countries were genuinely anxious to put the new nations on their feet they would use their funds to compensate the capitalists at home, and present the developing countries with the equity in their own resources; and to find alternative employment for the workers at home so as to be able to permit and encourage imports.

But this would be a complete reversal of the new mercantilist system. In each era the rules for international economic relations are moulded to suit the views of the country that is then the most powerful. Therefore it is generally impossible to get the rules altered.

The Russian people have a way of expressing their view about the Soviet régime by passing around extremely acid jokes. There was one after the first manned sputnik. A journalist comes to interview Gagarin's wife: 'And how did you feel when your husband went up into space?' 'I was not there. I was out queueing for milk.' 'Well, how did you feel when he came down?' 'I had not got back yet.' The joke is not really against the Soviets but against the modern world. Considering the fantastic technical mastery and lavish expenditure shown by investment in horror weapons, and supersonic flight, and the moon race, surely with a little common sense and goodwill we could relieve all the housewives of want and discomfort. But it would have to be genuine common sense and genuine goodwill, not a disguise for national interests.

19

THE NEED FOR A RECONSIDERATION OF THE THEORY OF INTERNATIONAL TRADE

THERE is no branch of economics in which there is a wider gap between orthodox doctrine and actual problems than in the theory of international trade.

1

The argument is usually conducted in terms of static comparisons of equilibrium positions of a model which has the following characteristics. There are two countries which represent the whole trading world. Each country is in stationary equilibrium with given 'resources' fully employed. There is perfect mobility of labour between occupations within each country and no mobility between countries. The value of imports is equal to the value of exports.

These characteristics of the model exclude discussion of any question which is interesting in reality.

Even within the terms of static comparisons, it is necessary to consider at least three countries before any general conclusions can be drawn. Propositions intended to show that some change is inevitably beneficial to all concerned cannot be demonstrated for more than two partners. For instance, an increase in efficiency in producing an export commodity in country A, within the conditions of the model, benefits B and C taken together, but if C was exporting the same commodity it is likely to be injured. Furthermore, the model applies only to trade between countries at the same level of industrial development; it was ill-suited to dealing with the importation into an industrial metropolis of primary products from colonial and quasi-colonial dependencies, though this in fact formed the great bulk of trade at the very time when teaching derived for the model was in its greatest ascendancy. (Nowadays the traditional arguments are being used to indoctrinate the intellectuals of the ex-colonial nations.)

Written in 1970. Published in *International Trade and Money*, ed. M. B. Connolly, 1973, Allen & Unwin.

The analysis conducted in terms of stationary states leaves out development, accumulation and technical change. It leaves out the shock effect of change and the process of readjustment. However drastic the change in the pattern of trade, equilibrium has always been restored before the discussion begins.

The assumption of full employment rules out the problems of effective demand. The capitalist world (except in rare moments of strong boom) is a buyer's market. Normally every industry has productive capacity for more output than it can sell. From the point of view of a national economy, exports promote employment and profits; imports reduce them. The comforting doctrines that a country 'cannot be undersold all round' was derived from the postulate of universal full employment. The argument consists merely in assuming what it hopes to prove.

Finally, the assumption that, for each country, the value of imports is necessarily equal to the value of exports rules out the problem of maintaining the national balance of payments which has been the great preoccupation of economic policy from the earliest times.

The aim of the traditional theory was to establish the beneficial effects of free trade. This was eagerly accepted by orthodox opinion in the country which had the most to gain from open markets for its exports. But in fact the case was made out by assuming away all the difficulties and all the aims which in reality give rise to protectionist policies.[1]

The model is usually operated in terms of a comparision between a situation in which each country is isolated, consuming only its own products, with a situation in which trade is taking place, in equilibrium without any difference in the 'resources' or the 'tastes' of the two communities. Since the model was constructed for the purpose of a polemic against protection, the argument focuses on the case where the same commodities are produced in both countries. Protection would not arise unless a country could produce at home goods which others export. The import of exotic commodities did not need to be defended, and in any case, economic geography does not lend itself to the high abstractions of pure theory. Professor Samuelson's remark, that the production of tropical fruit in the tropics is due to the prevalence of tropical conditions there, was not intended to draw the reader's attention to a major aspect of world trade, but rather to dismiss it as uninteresting.[2]

[1] Even within the terms of the orthodox model, they could not succeed even in proving that free trade is necessarily best for *each* country, because of Bickerdike's objection. Cf. Joan Robinson, 'The pure theory of international trade', *CEP*, Vol. I, p. 197.

[2] 'International trade and the equalisation of factor prices', *Economic Journal*, June 1948, p. 182.

2

Ricardo set out the case against protection in terms of two countries, England and Portugal, each capable of producing both wine and cloth. The argument implies that there is a constant amount of labour in each country which can be shifted from one line of production to the other without difficulty or loss. (Even when he takes the example of wine, there is no problem of specialized land. Constant returns prevail for each commodity up to full employment of the whole labour force.) There are different production functions (in modern jargon) in the two countries. Output per head of wine in Portugal relatively to output per head of cloth is greater than in England. Thus total output is increased when trade permits labour to be moved into production of wine in Portugal and cloth in England.

The relative prices of the commodities in each country are proportional to labour cost. (The rate of profit and the value of capital per man, in each country, are the same for both commodities.) Since the relative prices are different, it is impossible for both to rule in a free market. To work out the equilibrium position that the assumptions entail, we have to introduce the conditions of demand. If England consumes more wine than Portugal can export, she must produce some wine herself. The world price of wine in terms of cloth, in the final position, is then set by conditions of production in England. Portugal becomes specialized, exporting wine and importing cloth. She gains on the terms of trade in respect of all her imports. (Portuguese wine sells at the same price as English, which is dearer in terms of cloth.) England gains in respect of the part of her requirements of wine which she can get by exporting cloth, since this uses less labour per unit than wine produced at home.

Contrariwise when Portugal is the country producing both commodities. In the borderline case where each country produces only one commodity, the division of the benefit between them depends solely on the conditions of demand, and relative prices are no longer governed by costs of production.

For Ricardo, the rate of profit on capital depends upon the labour-cost of producing the necessary real wage. Where the imported commodity is a wage good, trade tends to raise the rate of profit. (This was a point of great importance in his campaign against the corn laws.)

He provides a mechanism to ensure balanced trade. In his scheme the rate of profit, in general, will be different in the two countries; if this occurred between districts within one nation, there would be a movement to invest where the rate of profit was higher.

'Experience, however, shews that the fancied or real insecurity of capital, when not under the immediate control of its owner, together with the natural disinclination which every man has to quit the country of his birth and connexions, and intrust himself with all his habits fixed, to a strange government and new laws, check the emigration of capital. These feelings, which I should be sorry to see weakened, induce most men of property to be satisfied with a low rate of profits in their own country, rather than seek a more advantageous employment for their wealth in foreign nations.'[3] It follows that an excess of imports has to be paid for in gold. The surplus country, receiving gold, experiences a rise of prices and the deficit country, losing gold, experiences a fall, until the value of goods traded between them is brought into balance.

Whether convincing or not, Ricardo's analysis is perfectly clear. The model in Marshall's *Pure Theory of Foreign Trade*, expressed in terms of 'offer curves', is not so easy to grasp. He refers to the *Pure Theory of Domestic Values* for the analysis of costs and prices in each country, but this theory is an inextricable mixture of static and dynamic elements. 'Increasing returns' is the result of investment and technical progress going on through time as the output of a particular commodity is growing. How can this be fitted in to the comparisons of static equilibrium? He was aware of the contradiction but did not feel able to deal with it.[4]

To make sense of his system, it seems to be necessary to confine the argument to the case in which each particular commodity is produced 'under conditions of diminishing returns', that is, where labour cost per unit is an increasing function of the level of output, presumably because each requires some specialized ingredient which is in limited supply. (A footnote[5] promises an appendix which will explain the meaning of 'cost of production' but it is nowhere to be found.) On this basis, the analysis can be explained as follows. Two countries (which comprise the world) have different production functions for the various commodities. Each country has at least one commodity for which its productive capacity is limited relative to demand at home and at least one for which productive capacity exceeds demand. In a position of equilibrium with balanced trade, world prices (and the national incomes of the countries) are such that the cost at the margin of a unit of each commodity in each country is equal to its price in the world market (allowing for transport costs). Each country supplies part of its consumption of its high-cost commodity, importing the rest, and consumes part of its low-cost commodity, exporting the rest. The position

---

[3] *Principles*, p. 136–137 (Sraffa's edition).
[4] *Pure Theory of Foreign Trade*, p. 27.   [5] Ibid., p. 2.

of equilibrium is such that if either country were to export a little less, the cost at home of its commodity would be lower and the demand price abroad would be higher. Similarly, if it were to export a little more, its costs would be higher and its demand price lower; the equilibrium volume of trade is determined by the rule that supply price is equal to demand price for each commodity on the world market.

But this argument is completely hollow. There is no mechanism to make trade balance; it is merely assumed that the value of exports is equal to value of imports. Marshall refers to the fact that the rate of profit obtainable in one country must be the same for each commodity, but he says nothing about the rate of profit in the other. He does not discuss what would happen if the rates of profit were different. (Writing in the great age of British overseas investment, he could not very well use Ricardo's argument as an excuse for not discussing the subject.) In his monetary writings Marshall relied on the argument about flows of gold, but in his *Pure Theory* he merely postulates that trade is always balanced. The apparatus of offer curves was intended to elaborate and refine upon the simple system of labour-value prices but Marshall only succeeded in producing a degenerate version of Ricardo's model.

Samuelson's version of the Hecksher–Ohlin theory is still more degenerate.[6] In this model the production functions are everywhere the same; countries differ only in respect to their 'factor endowments'.

It was on this basis that Samuelson produced the theorem that, in equilibrium, with two factors, two countries and two commodities, either at least one country must be specialized, or, if both commodities are produced in both countries, the 'factor prices' must be the same in both countries. (Harrod pointed out that this depends on one more assumption than Samuelson had slipped in – that the production functions are such that the commodity which is more labour intensive at one level of 'factor prices' is so at all levels.)[7]

Samuelson called the factors of production labour and land but the argument is usually developed in terms of labour and 'capital'. Each country is endowed with a lump of 'malleable capital' which can be used in various proportions with labour and the 'factor prices' which are equalized, or not equalized, are the wage rate and the rate of interest. This was the neo-neoclassical system in its hey-day. Recently, this conception of capital has retreated from criticism into a 'one-commodity world'[8] which presumably

[6] Op. cit.
[7] 'Factor-price relations under free trade', *Economic Journal*, June 1958.
[8] Cf. R. M. Solow, *Growth Theory* (Oxford, 1970).

would not allow any scope for trade, though it has been argued that there might be a one-way movement of savings of the commodity from the country where its 'marginal productivity' was lower to be invested in the other where it was higher.[9]

3

Ricardo relied upon adjustments of price levels to keep trade in balance. We can make some sense of this without resorting to the Quantity Theory of Money if we substitute money-wage rates for gold flows as the equilibrating mechanism. If there is near-full employment when trade is balanced, a surplus of exports generates an excess demand for labour which drives up money costs and (with fixed exchange rates) reduces the competitive advantage of the country. In a very broad, long-run historical sweep, this tendency evidently works – high output per head, comparing one region with another, goes with high money-wage rates and therefore high real wages in terms of tradeable goods. But the tendency is weak, sluggish and irregular. At any moment there is certainly not balanced trade between the various areas of the habitable globe that happen to be under separate national governments – there is an ever-changing pattern of deficits and surpluses.

Moreover, Ricardo's doctrine that gold flows in when there is a surplus of exports and out when there is surplus imports, which may have been not far wrong in his day, was quite false when it was repeated by Marshall and Pigou. An inflow of gold (or gain of reserves) occurs when the outflow of finance is less than the surplus in the balance on income account (including interest and dividends as well as visible and invisible trade), or when the inflow of finance is greater than the deficit on income account. The operation of the gold standard mechanism was to keep flows of lending in line with income balances. A centre that was lending too much or borrowing too little raised its interest rate. Since there was perfect confidence in exchange rates, small differences in interest rates were sufficient to redirect the flow of finance. But this mechanism would not have been strong enough to do its work if there had not been harmony in the main between flows of trade and flows of finance.

In the latter part of the nineteenth century, the appearance of equilibrium was maintained just because trade was not balanced. The British economy had a continuous surplus on income account which was matched by an outflow of finance. The borrowing countries enjoyed a surplus of imports while investment was being carried out within their

[9] See below, p. 220.

frontiers and since the main aim of investment was to open up sources of primary products for which there was a profitable market at home, the subsequent development of an export surplus permitted the service of loans to be financed.

Since 1914 the kaleidoscope of economic history has been continually shaken; the pattern today is greatly changed.

We are now in the era of modern capitalism when every industrial country has a national economic policy of near-full employment and growth of GNP. Every industrial country wants a surplus on income account. 'Export led growth' is the most convenient way of running modern capitalism. Who succeeds at any moment is accidental, largely depending upon historical circumstances and political and psychological influences. Success leads to success and failure engenders failure.

There is no longer any underlying harmony between the flows of finance and the pattern of surpluses and deficits on income account. For instance, sterling is weakened by institutions and habits geared to overseas investment while the British economy suffers from a chronic tendency to run into a deficit, and Germany fails to develop a sufficient outflow of finance to prevent her surplus from making the mark exchange rate uncomfortably strong. The British economy goes through agonies to get rid of an unwanted deficit while fear of inflation prevents the German authorities from playing the old rules of the game, that is, to lower interest rates when reserves are accumulating. The new rules of the game – changing exchange rates – are slow, clumsy, and uncertain. The international monetary mechanism is being set problems too hard for it to solve.

There is a further source of discrepancy in balances of payments. Just as the issue of currency notes represents an interest-free loan from the citizens of a country to their government, so the reserves and working balances of foreign and colonial institutions and businesses, held in a metropolitan financial centre, represent loans to that economy. The country whose currency is used as a world medium of exchange is able to support an outflow of finance in excess of its surplus on income account as long as the world's requirement for balances is growing.

The prestige of sterling survived the strength of the British economy; for long periods her deficits were partly covered by loans from her dependencies, and, after 1947, from the so-called developing nations which succeeded.[10] The role of sterling as a reserve currency came to a final end

[10] However, the great bulk of war-time borrowing in the form of accumulated balances was paid off in 'unrequited exports' which made a contribution to the development of the countries concerned.

with the devaluation of 1967. Now sterling balances have to be guaranteed in terms of dollars. The American dollar is effectively the only world currency.

The appetite of the great American corporations for overseas investment is strong; the American economy can support an outflow of finance greatly in excess of its surplus on income account, the difference being offset by an accumulation of foreign-owned dollar balances. This system is known as 'borrowing short and lending long'. It undermines confidence and threatens the stability of the currency so long as there is something to fly into; for the time being the demand for dollars has been propped up by effectively demonetizing gold, but this system somehow lacks the appearance of the solid respectability of the old gold standard managed from London before 1914, and doubts are expressed from time to time as to how long it will continue.

The greatest obfuscation of the orthodox theory was in its treatment of foreign investment. The concept of 'capital' as a factor of production implied that when one country lends to another it is transferring real resources to it.

In the neo-neoclassical revival of pre-Keynesian theory, investment is determined by the desire of society to save, under the influence of time preference. Capital consists of lumps of putty and the rate of interest is determined by the ratio of putty-capital to labour, being equal to the marginal productivity of putty.

In this scheme of ideas, international capital flows consist of exports of putty from one country to another.[11] A rich, high-wage country had a high putty-labour ratio and a low rate of interest. Therefore it exports its putty-savings to a country with a higher rate of interest. Savings of putty, it seems, are put onto a boat and sent to be used as putty-capital in the low-wage country.

Now, it is true that 'capital', in the sense of capital goods, say steel ingots or machine-tools, may be put onto a ship and sent from one country to another, but this is not necessarily associated with a movement of 'capital' in the sense of finance, for the goods may be paid for by visible or invisible exports going in the opposite direction. On the other hand, finance may pass from one country to another to be expended exclusively in employing labour and buying property on the spot, so that there is no movement of capital goods.

A country which receives an inflow of finance is not receiving a supply

[11] Cf. N. C. Miller, 'A general equilibrium theory of international capital flows', *Economic Journal*, June 1968.

of a factor of production called 'capital', it is enjoying the possibility of running a surplus of imports or amassing monetary reserves.

The latter case has been much discussed in recent times. Under the old gold standard, net lending for any country was restricted to equality with its surplus on income account. Nowadays the operation of the international monetary system permits an outflow of long-term lending from the United States in excess of its surplus; it follows that other countries are receiving loans in excess of their deficits. Thus the French complain that the American corporations take over businesses in France or instal branches to compete in their market, while all that the French economy gets in exchange is dollar balances of which they have too much already. Their proper reply, of course, within the rules of the game, would be to set about buying up American industry in return; or like Japan, they might excuse themselves from the rules and keep foreign capital out; since the French do not feel able to do either the one or the other, they complain that the game is unfair.

In the case where borrowing is covering a deficit on income account, there is a certain sense in which savings are being exported from one country to another. The deficit country is absorbing more, taking consumption and investment together, than its own production; in this sense its economy is drawing upon savings made for it abroad. In return it has a permanent obligation to pay interest or profits to the lender. Whether this is a good bargain or not depends upon the nature of the use to which the funds are put. If they merely permit an excess of consumption over production, the economy is on the road to ruin. If they permit an excess of investment over home savings, the result depends upon the nature of the investment. The colonial type of investment, developing animal, mineral and vegetable products to supply the metropolitan market, and transport to move them, was, of course, made in search of profits and was generally handsomely rewarded, but it could, in a certain sense, be said to 'create wealth' which would not otherwise have come into existence. When the colonial regions became independent 'developing countries', the consequent export earnings, minus the profits being remitted, provide ammunition for their development plans; some make bold to keep the profits as well.

The colonial type of investment is still going on (notably from Japan in Australia) – but nowadays (apart from oil) the greater part of overseas investment is looking for markets rather than supplies of materials.

When an American corporation sets up a subsidiary to sell consumer goods say, in Mexico, what does the local economy gain? There is an inflow of finance, which will have to be paid for later by remission of profits. This is a very expensive form of borrowing. The inflow of finance is generally only a small part of the capital acquired, for it is supplemented by borrowing locally. Part of profits may be reinvested on the spot. This may be a benefit to the local economy as far as it goes, but the new capital so created belongs to the parent corporation; it will give rise to additional profits which will increase the amounts to be remitted in the future. Perhaps the corporation supplies know-how and efficient management, so that, while paying the same wages, it can make a higher rate of profit than local industry. This is the point claimed in its favour. But the local economy is charged with the whole profit on the investment, not only with the extra bit due to its embodying foreign methods of production. Legally the local government is free to tax profits accruing within its borders but, for obvious reasons, this power is sparingly used. Moreover, the remission of profits is likely to involve a 'transfer burden' since investments of this type are not directly building up future export earnings to implement the remission of profits. There is a strong presumption that the so-called developing countries would be better off if they financed their investments themselves, even though at a slower rate and with less advanced technology than the foreign firms provide. The doctrine of the advantages of free trade favoured the country which was first in the field with manufacturing industry; the doctrine of the advantage of free capital movements favours the country whose firms command the greatest fund of finance.

Once we have seen through the neo-neoclassical fallacy that 'capital' is a factor of production there is a great deal of rethinking to be done.

20

HAS CAPITALISM CHANGED?

THIS question, posed by Professor Tsuru to a symposium of economists,[1] implies that we knew quite well what capitalism was formerly like. We know, certainly, that it was capable of producing the 1930s. But it was also capable of producing long runs of rapid growth, interrupted by only minor recessions. Ever since the eighteenth century, the industrial revolution has been going off like an irregular string of firecrackers. Taking a long view, we might consider growth to be the most characteristic feature of capitalism. It would be possible to describe the spectacular development now going on in Japan and Germany as a steep climb to make up the arrears of war and defeat; France and North Italy may be seen as catching up on arrears of relatively slow industrialization over a century or more. The present relatively sluggish growth of the United States and Great Britain can be seen as a plateau reached by the leaders in a climb.

More narrowly stated, the question posed for discussion is whether a major depression can occur again.

Certainly the world has changed, in our lifetime, in two relevant respects. The thirties did happen, and some lessons were drawn from that experience. What Keynes called the 'humbug of finance' is extremely tenacious of life (especially in the United States), but it can never be quite what it was. In principle, the doctrine that governments have a responsibility for avoiding slumps is now orthodox. This might prove a broken reed if it were not for the second change – the emergence of a powerful socialist bloc which is itself immune from depressions.

This proves to have a stabilizing effect on capitalism in three ways. First, the extent of fluctuations is limited by the very fact that part of the trading world is excluded from them. This does not operate to any great extent through direct exports from capitalist to socialist countries (though these

[1] *Has Capitalism Changed?* Edited by Shigeto Tsuru. Contributors: John Strachey, Paul Sweezy, C. O. Bettelheim, Y. A. Kronrod, Maurice Dobb, Paul Baran, J. K. Galbraith. Iwanami Shoten, Tokyo 1961.

are quite important for particular industries). It works, and may be expected to do so increasingly, through the support which sales to the socialist world give to the incomes of primary producers, mitigating the vicious spiral of declining trade that follows from a fall in imports from them, with a consequent fall of their power to purchase.

Second, the capitalist world feels itself to be on trial, and the governments which have pledged themselves to maintaining economic stability have been given a powerful motive for trying to keep their word.

Finally, rivalry itself promotes expenditure. The cold war provides an excuse for expenditure on arms – the least harmless way of keeping up employment by 'digging holes in the ground' but the one most acceptable to orthodox opinion. Fortunately, this is not the only form in which rivalry manifests itself. Aid to underdeveloped countries (even if, as Paul Baran argues, most of it goes down the drain in corruption and luxury) is a better way of consuming the surplus. There can be little doubt that more aid is inspired by rivalry with the socialist world than would ever have come from pure benevolence.

The influence of the socialist sector of the world on the capitalist sector is not much stressed in this volume, and most of the contributors are sceptical of the possibility of maintaining employment by government action. All the same, they do not seem to have made out a case that *depression* will come again. There is a general haziness in the whole argument as to whether it is concerned with a slump or with long-run stagnation. Current American experience seems to be that slumps are very mild. The trouble is that booms are mild aso. Each recovery leaves a larger gap between actual and potential output than the one before.

Tsuru regards the rapid rate of technological progress now being experienced as a helpful factor. Here there is a missing link in his argument, which Paul Sweezy picks up. Tsuru, thinking in terms of Keynes and Schumpeter, regards inventions as opening up new profitable investment opportunities and so providing the offset to saving necessary to fend off depression. As Sweezy points out, this misreads the situation. Technical progress is not an occasional 'random shock' that sets investment going but a continuous built-in propensity in the modern industrial system. 'The big corporations have enormous sums of money accruing to them in the form of depreciation quotas which are naturally available for investment in the latest machines and processes. Under these circumstances, it is obvious that a high but carefully regulated rate of technological innovation is compatible with a low or even zero rate of *net* investment and hence with a chronically depressed economy.' Tsuru has put technical progress in on the wrong side of the account. To keep the economy at stretch, output must rise in the proportion that output per man is rising, on top of the proportion in which the labour force is growing. With less technical progress, employment would be easier to maintain.

The other possibility of alleviation that is proposed for discussion is a greater equality in the distribution of income, which (in Keynesian language) might make up for a flagging inducement to invest by a rising propensity to consume. Professor Bettelheim stoutly denies that consuming power can rise even in proportion to productivity (this seems to arise from the usual confusion between a constant rate of exploitation and a constant level of real wages). Professor Galbraith appeals to his theory of countervailing power and Mr. Strachey to the softening effect of democracy upon capitalism. These arguments are good enough to show (as against Bettelheim) that the share of wages need not fall as output per head rises. But to be efficacious, it is not enough for the rise in consumption per head to keep up with the rise in productivity. It has also to rise sufficiently to take over the slack from any reduction in net investment per head.

Merely to maintain effective demand for labour, the demand for commodities has to increase in proportion to output per head. This requires that the overall level of money wage rates should rise, or that prices should be cut. In ideal competitive conditions (such as never existed outside the elementary textbooks), prices fall (relatively to money incomes) when surplus capacity appears, and so stimulate demand till capacity outputs can be sold. Competition was never so perfect, even in 'the good old days', and certainly under the modern regime of administered prices there is no reason to expect profit margins to be cut in the manner that the textbooks case requires. Nor can the trade unions erode margins from below by raising money-wage rates, since there is no better excuse than a rise in wage rates for putting prices up (an excuse often used to raise prices more than proportionately, so that margins actually rise and purchasing power is curtailed).

Moreover, the very progressiveness of taxation, which is the pride of democracy and the vehicle of countervailing power, works against expansion. The great oligopolistic firms, with proper prudence from their own point of view, fix margins which give a 'break-even point' at considerably below capacity — that is, full costs including standard profit are covered by sales when a large margin of productive capacity is idle. An upswing in demand then causes a huge shift to profit, for all proceeds above the break-even point are pure gain. The taxes which the profits attract have to be withheld from distribution by the firms before they are spent by the government. The upswing therefore comes to rest, and it may do so well before capacity is reached. The firms then see no advantage in building up capacity further. It seems as though the built-in stabilizers designed to keep fluctuations within bounds have been only too successful. They work in such a way as more or less to stabilize total output. Meanwhile, technical progress goes on raising output per head, and the manpower required to produce a given output goes on falling.

The problem has slipped out of the framework of Keynesian analysis. It might have been better to pose the question the other way round. Instead of asking whether capitalism has changed for the better, in the sense that it has become immune to short-run depressions, one could ask whether capitalism has changed for the worse, in the sense that it has become incapable of long-run growth.

It would be easy to make a case for an affirmative answer to the latter question. Nineteenth-century capitalism was an expanding system in the literal sense. It did not have to keep itself suspended by the bootstraps of its inner dynamism; it had its feet planted on new lands to be peopled, full of natural wealth to be exploited. There is much force in Rosa Luxemburg's prediction that when capitalism can no longer expand geographically it will not know what to do with itself.

Moreover, for private enterprise the main problem is not to produce, but to sell. Old-style capitalism had a ready-made market. The world was not naked before mills were built in Lancashire. The mill products could undersell the handloom weavers and take the market from them. And they had the handloom weavers of the whole world to ruin before they began to meet competition from their own kind. Even now the spectacular increases of production in Japan and Germany are not all (as we in Britain know only too well) a net addition to the production of the world. Perhaps from the first, capitalism has been sawing off the bough that it was sitting on and all that has really changed is that we have begun to notice how deep the saw has gone.

There is another aspect to the ever-growing productivity of industry that is germane to the discussion. Productivity grows on a narrow front – in physical goods that lend themselves to mass production. Even if incomes grew with productivity, consumers could not be found for the output; they want to spend their growing purchasing power on other things. (Galbraith would have done better to draw upon his *Affluent Society* for a contribution to this volume rather than from his earlier and more soothing work.) This very fact to some extent relieves the situation that it creates. Regular industry cannot find markets to keep output rising as fast as output per head, but the redundant workers can largely find a livelihood in providing services to meet the purchasing power deflected from industry. It seems as though, over the very long run, capitalism reverses the process with which it began, of taking the market from craftsmen and petty traders and absorbing their families into its labour force. Now it is spewing them out again and at the same time creating a market in which they can flourish. The robots of automated industry are eroding the labour force, and small-scale traders and self-employed professionals are proliferating to take its place. Engels' joke about England developing a bourgeois working class is coming true in earnest in the United States.

The argument has slipped out of the Marxist framework also. Capitalism has 'ripened the productive power of social labour' with a vengeance, but what has happened to the proletariat that was to take it over?

Meanwhile socialism has come into being just in those countries that missed the capitalist bus. The tough, disagreeable aspects of socialism, which have so much weakened its idealistic appeal, are due precisely to this fact. Instead of expropriating the expropriators and settling down to civilized ease, the revolutionary governments had to lay upon their people hard tasks and curb their disillusion by bitter means.

It seems that neither the Keynesian nor the Marxian prognosis of the future of capitalism is being fulfilled and we are left without any particular theory as to what will happen next.

The contributors to this volume discuss, with varying degrees of optimism, the prospects of a peaceful transition to socialism within the capitalist countries.

The notion that a new Great Depression is soon to come and that some kind of socialism will emerge from the struggle to fend it off, smacks somewhat of wishful thinking. The slow drift into stagnation that appears to be taking place does not come to a dramatic crisis that calls forth dramatic remedies.

One thing seems fairly clear – private enterprise has ceased to be the form of organization best suited to take advantage of modern technology. Planning of investment to give automated production the long runs that it needs; a high priority for education to raise up a generation which can develop its potentialities; equality of opportunity, to waste no scrap of talent worth training; and adequate distribution of purchasing power to consume the product; increasing leisure to turn redundancy of labour into an advantage – these are what the new technology demands and what socialists economies can supply. There is certainly one way in which capitalism has changed – it is no longer clearly the most effective type of economic system ever known.

In England, we have learned to realize that we are no longer running the world. Given peace and freed from the burden of armaments (for we have no need just yet to dig any holes), it is easy to imagine us muddling through in some kind of semi-planned welfare state – not socialism but capitalism without its claws. Tsuru suggests that something of the kind might be possible also in Japan. But what about the United States? Just at the moment, public opinion in America seems to be taking up the attitude of the wrong mother in the judgment of Solomon – rather blow the world up than allow someone else to lead it.

Until that mood passes, there is nothing else worth discussing, but when it does (I will not write if) a new chapter will begin, and there seems no very clear indication to make it obvious that capitalism will not have a long future as the second best economic system in the world.

21

LATTER-DAY CAPITALISM

THERE was a Soviet joke in circulation some time ago, which gains point with every year that passes – Question: What is the greatest problem facing the President of the United Sates? Answer: Is it possible to have capitalism in one country?

For us the question is, do we really want to continue to keep the United States company? Are we satisfied with latter-day capitalism?

DIGGING HOLES

The strong case for the defence, of course, rests on full employment. Post-Keynesian capitalism *is* different. The generation that remembers the Thirties is constantly, thankfully, amazed at how different it is. To the generation that did not experience the Great Depression, such monstrously stupid, unnecessary misery seems scarcely credible. In 1944, when Beveridge wrote his Keynesian tract, *Full Employment in a Free Society*, it seemed Utopian to proclaim that the British economy could be run, when the war was over, with an *average* unemployment, one year with another, of 3 per cent; that is, with the figure for unemployment fluctuating fairly evenly between 1 per cent and 5 per cent. Since the war, statistical unemployment has barely touched 2 per cent. Whatever our present discontents, this is by no means to be despised. The worst part of heavy unemployment was not the waste of potential wealth (and, as we shall argue in a moment, its removal has not been achieved mainly by avoiding waste) but the rotting of individual lives, the damaged self-respect, the desperate egosim and cringing fear on one side and the smug self-deception on the other. Certainly we live now in a cleaner, more human country. But however thankful we should be for these blessings, it is too soon to claim that full employment vindicates latter-day capitalism.

First of all we must ask how it has been achieved. Keynes' opponents tried to mock him by saying that he advocated curing unemployment by

New Left Review (London), July–August 1962.

setting men to dig holes in the ground and fill them up again. He turned the mockery the other way. If men were paid wages for digging holes, they would spend them on bread and boots – real income would be increased all round. To point up the paradoxes of the system, Keynes even argued that useless investments were more effective than useful ones.

> Ancient Egypt was doubly fortunate, and doubtless owed to this its fabled wealth, in that it possessed *two* activities, namely, pyramid-building as well as the search for the precious metals, the fruits of which, since they could not serve the needs of man by being consumed, did not stale with abundance. The Middle Ages built cathedrals and sang dirges. Two pyramids, two masses for the dead, are twice as good as one; but not so two railways from London to York.[1]

When effective demand falls off as the openings for profitable investment are filled, then:

> Even a diversion of the desire to hold wealth towards assets, which will in fact yield no economic fruits whatever, will increase economic well-being. In so far as millionaries find their satisfaction in building mighty mansions to contain their bodies when alive and pyramids to shelter them after death, or, repenting of their sins, erect cathedrals, and endow monasteries or foreign missions, the day when abundance of capital will interfere with abundance of output may be postponed. 'To dig holes in the ground', paid for out of savings, will increase, not only employment, but the real national dividend of useful goods and services. It is not reasonable, however, that a sensible community should be content to remain dependent on such fortuitous and often wasteful mitigations when once we understand the influences upon which effective demand depends.[2]

Now we do understand the influences upon which effective demand depends, but do we manipulate them in a sensible way?

Effective demand in the capitalist world as a whole is interlinked through trade and finance, and when it flags in one major country, the rest suffer. The United States is more than a major country, it is something like half of the whole. For our full employment we are largely beholden to holes in the ground that Americans dig. In the United States, the declared military budget accounts for nearly 10 per cent of national income, and is equal to 60 per cent of gross investment. It is true, as the United Nations

---

[1] *General Theory of Employment, Interest and Money*, p. 131.

[2] Ibid., p. 220.

Consultative Group argue,[3] that there is no physical, technical obstacle to prevent these resources from being deployed for peaceful purposes. But to do so would involve drastic political changes. Whatever might have been, in fact Keynesian prosperity has been a by-product of the Cold War.

So far as this country is concerned, armaments expenditure of 42 per cent of investment has been a burden rather than a stimulus to the economy. We could have done very well with more industrial investment and less inflationary pressure. But while our relative position in the capitalist world has been damaged by our own armaments, we are beholden, along with the capitalist world as a whole, to the support which the American economy, and so the world market, has received from theirs.

THE POLITICAL TRADE CYCLE

Even so, the Keynesian policy has not worked very smoothly. Michał Kalecki, the Polish economist who discovered the *General Theory* independently of Keynes, predicted, twenty years ago, how it would work out, in an article that it is startling to re-read today.

> In the slump, either under the pressure of the masses, or even without it, public investment financed by borrowing will be undertaken to prevent large-scale unemployment. But if attempts are made to apply this method in order to maintain the high level of employment reached in the subsequent boom a strong opposition of 'business leaders' is likely to be encountered. As has already been argued, lasting full employment is not at all to their liking. The workers would 'get out of hand' and the 'captains of industry' would be anxious to 'teach them a lesson'. Moreover, the price increase in the up-swing is to the disadvantage of small and big *rentiers* and makes them 'boom tired'.
>
> In this situation a powerful block is likely to be formed between big business and the *rentier* interests, and they would probably find more than one economist to declare that the situation was manifestly unsound. The pressure of all these forces, and in particular of big business – as a rule influential in Government departments – would most probably induce the Government to return to the orthodox policy of cutting down the budget deficit. A slump would follow in which Government spending policy would come again into its own. . . .
>
> The regime of the 'political business cycle' would be an artificial

[3] *Economic and Social Consequences of Disarmament*, United Nations, New York, 1962.

restoration of the position as it existed in nineteenth-century capitalism. Full employment would be reached only at the top of the boom, but slumps would be relatively mild and short lived.[4]

The touch about 'more than one economist' is particularly telling. The *Economist* newspaper, and several professors, have often argued for the greater 'flexibility' that would be introduced into the economy by a *little more* unemployment. (Sometimes Beveridge is congratulated on having said that an average of 3 per cent was the minimum to be aimed at.) And they give a sympathetic ear to the industrialists who complain about the workers who 'get out of hand'.

In this country monetary policy, rather than budget surpluses, have been used as the instrument for restriction. For us, 'excessive' activity is generally associated with an adverse balance of payments.

> Restrictive measures are usually called for at times when the country is losing monetary reserves, or having suffered heavy losses is trying to replenish them. This itself calls for dear money, on account of its influence on capital movements, quite apart from its effect in reducing the pressure of demand on the country's productive resources. A favourable balance of payments does not exert the same pressure in the opposite direction in favour of cheap money, because it is far less important to avoid gaining monetary reserves than to avoid losing them. Furthermore, a favourable balance of payments is, up to the point, likely to be taken out in relaxation of import and exchange controls rather than in pushing down rates of interest.[5]

The result has been that restriction in the downward phase of the 'political trade cycle' falls mainly upon investment, while the relaxation in the upward phase goes mainly to consumption. This has contributed to the poor showing of this country in long-run growth, though, certainly, it is not the only cause.

STAGNATION

Even if anti-slump policy were perfectly successful, it would not be sufficient to maintain a healthy capitalist system. Technical progress is continually raising output per man hour in industry, and the labour force is

---

[4] 'Political aspects of full employment', *The Political Quarterly*, October–December 1943.

[5] R. F. Kahn. Evidence submitted to the Radcliffe Committee.

continuously increasing. To preserve near-enough full employment, market demand must expand as fast as potential output; merely to prevent it from falling is not adequate.

In the 'thirties the 'stagnation thesis' came into fashion in the United States, according to which the slowing up of population growth and the 'closing of the frontier' (that is, the completion of geographical expansion in North America) were destroying the need for further capital accumulation, so that there would soon be no useful outlet for the savings that the population desired to make. This, evidently, was a mere confusion. Even the richest country in the world is very far from having completed the useful accumulation of capital in a physical sense. What was lacking was not a public use for investment, but a sufficient prospect of private profit. And it now appears that the lack of prospective profits was not due to the cessation of potential growth, but just to the slump itself. The profitability of investment, for the economy as a whole, is very much a matter of 'thinking makes it so'. When each firm believes that the market will expand, all find that in fact it does, for the activity of each is generating demand for others. But just as there is no reason why there need be stagnation in a private-enterprise economy, there is no reason why there should not be. In recent years the United States economy has been following a mildly fluctuating course around a trend line of growth of around 2 per cent per annum, while potential output must be supposed at the very least to be growing at 4 per cent per annum, and, if the economy were really kept at stretch, at very much more. At each recovery from a mild recession, the gap between the best realized performance and the potential grows greater.

The leading capitalist nation seems to be gradually drifting into the situation of an underdeveloped economy. The characteristic feature of economic underdevelopment is that the system fails to offer jobs to all available workers, not through a temporary *fall* of demand, but for lack of a sufficient increase in the stock of means of production to employ them. This is the situation in which the United States now finds itself.

In his first pronouncement on economic affairs, President Kennedy stated that if industry had been working to capacity in 1960, 'over one-third of all unemployed would have had jobs'.[6] It seems to be calmly accepted that the best boom to be hoped for (and even that was not achieved) would leave a considerable 'reserve army' unemployed.

There are two important mitigations of the tendency to long-run unemployment. The first is the shortening of working hours. This is consciously demanded by Trade Unions as a defence against redundancy

[6] Message to Congress, Feb. 2nd, 1961.

(especially in face of the spread of automation, which is liable to cut sudden swathes through the demand for labour); it is not that the individual prefers more leisure to more income. It is a palliative, not a cure.

The second mitigation is the great growth of service trades which now account for more employment than the whole of industry. Until big business decides to march in (as it has already done into retailing) this provides an opportunity for self-employment for families spewed out from the industrial labour force by the advance of technology. This is one reason why the US Trade-Union movement makes such remarkably little fuss about creeping stagnation.

WAGES

The Keynesian prescription for preventing recessions left an important problem unsolved – inflation. To combine continuous full employment with the traditional wage system of liberal capitalism must be expected to lead to a perpetual 'vicious spiral'. This was an obvious prediction to make: 'The point of full employment, so far from being an equilibrium resting place, appears to be a precipice over which, once it has reached the edge, the value of money must plunge into a bottomless abyss.'[7] The prediction has been painfully fulfilled; but it seems that only during the last year or two has the situation been recognized by official orthodoxy. It seems that the authorities (supported as usual by 'more than one economist') preferred to remain in a fog of confusion in order not to have to face an awkward political situation at the practical level, or to admit, at the philosophical level, that the mechanisms of a 'free' capitalist system are inherently incapable of regulating themselves.

On the other side of the wage bargain the fog is just as great. It is obvious enough, once it is said, that the purchasing power of money depends mainly upon the money price of a man hour of labour, and that when that price is rising faster than output per man hour, the purchasing power of money is falling; but its implications are by no means easy to stomach. The moral is certainly not the simple one that, if only all money-wage rates could be kept from rising, no workers would be any the worse off.

> Trade Union policy is only very loosely co-ordinated, and since the duty of each union is to regard only the interests of its own members, gains and losses are very unevenly distributed between industries. Those unions which are in the strongest position (either because of

[7] Joan Robinson, *Essays in the Theory of Employment*, p. 24, written in 1936.

better organization or because of a more favourable situation in their industries) will secure the greatest rise in money wages when an upward movement occurs, and so secure less than the average fall in real wages. And it is by no means necessarily the case that those Unions which gain the greatest real wages will suffer the largest share in unemployment. Trade union-policy, as it works out in practice, cannot be reduced to terms of even an unconsious decision as to what is in the best interests of 'labour as a whole'.[8]

To agree upon a pattern of 'fair relatives' even amongst the Trade Unions themselves, let alone as between them and the professionals, is admittedly a daunting task. The blind flailing around of the government with the 'pay pause' has certainly not advanced the matter.

Professor Phelps Brown made a useful comment in a letter to *The Times* (22 June 1962):

> I would like to suggest that a main reason why income policy is being brought into disrepute is the failure to distinguish between two sorts of claim. The one sort if met will form part of the next round of rises, the other is meant only to catch up with past rounds.
>
> Underlying the first is the natural wish to do better as time goes on, but this has shown itself to be less peremptory than the resentment of discrimination and the demand for fair play that underlie the second. To restrain both sorts of claim alike is to tar all restraint with the brush of injustice.
>
> In practice most people do seem to believe that jobs of similar requirements should receive similar pay and to decide what rate of pay is fair for a particular job by comparing its requirements with the requirements and pay of others. The principle of 'fair comparison' is not merely one that has to be invoked for lack of the market test in the public service but is being applied continually in all walks of life. When some earnings move up sharply and others are left behind the disparity is usually felt to be unfair. Those who try to catch up are seen not just as demanding 'more for me' but as trying to right a wrong. . . .
>
> A money incomes policy can succeed only in so far as it allows disparities to be redressed. Whenever such a policy is inaugurated some disparities will be outstanding, and others will creep in as time goes on. Redressing then means raising the aggregate of money incomes, very likely by more than the national product warrants at the time. But if

---

[8] Ibid., p. 39. I quote from my own early works, not out of vanity, but in order to show that the problem was already a part of Keynesian theory even while the depression lasted.

the head of resentment is allowed to build up, the rise will be faster before long, and – what is worse – the very idea of a common interest in avoiding too fast a rise will have gone by the board.

The 'pay pause' has evidently damaged the cause of developing a rational wages system.

But even if the problem of relatives could somehow or other be settled, it would settle only relative *earnings*. Is the labour movement ready to accept, and freeze for ever, the pattern of distribution between income from earnings and income from property? From one point of view, it would be perfectly reasonable to do so. The Labour Movement is evidently not in the mood for an all-out drive towards socialism. Then why not accept a junior partnership in capitalism and help it by all means to prosper and pay dividends? At heart, no doubt, this is just what the great majority feel. But to say so openly? To re-write Clause Four? To give up even the name of what their fathers fought for? Much better not to put the question, and just go on pretending that the struggle continues.

The Balance of Payments

Perpetual inflation is a great nuisance from many points of view, but there would be no imperative necessity for any one country to overcome it, if all experienced it to more or less the same degree. The really serious trouble besets a country whose level of money-wage rates, relatively to its productivity in tradeable goods, rises faster than others, when it is not free to depreciate its exchange rate to a corresponding extent. Its costs of production are rising faster than the world level and its competitive position in the world growing weaker. To try to cure this situation by curbing demand, 'creating slack' so as to reduce the upward pressure on wage rates, may do some good for a time, but it makes the long-run position all the worse, for it discourages investment, which, by increasing productivity, provides the only remedy. It is the realization, at long last, of the hopelessness of this policy that has led the authorities in this country to recognize the need for a wages policy (which is not to say that they have found one).

Looking at the picture from the other side, any country that has a relatively rapid rise in productivity in tradeable goods, compared to its rate of rise of money wages, is in a strong competitive position and finds itself developing a favourable balance of trade (an excess of export earnings over payments for imports). The proposition of the classical theory of international trade, that 'one country cannot undersell the others all round' is deduced from assumptions into which the conclusion has been slipped in in advance. In fact one country can undersell others quite far enough round to give itself a large and growing favourable balance at their expense.

Periodic violent reversals of fortunes are a natural and inevitable consequence of international trade between developing capitalist countries, in a regime of more or less free trade and more or less fixed exchange rates. The money-wage level in various industries within each country keeps pretty well in step, but there is nothing to tether the wage levels of different countries to each other. Moreover, many industries, in any one country, share the same climate of technical development and aggressiveness in selling. Thus, at any one time, the competitive position of a whole country is strong or weak compared to the rest.

For some fifteen years after the war the United States was in the strong position, with a chronic tendency to a favourable balance of payments. A sufficient outflow of funds – for military subventions, development loans and private investment – prevented it from seriously upsetting the capitalist world trading system; the position seemed quite right and natural; books and articles were written to explain why it must inevitably be permanent. It was a great shock to discover that the dollar was just as capable of turning soft as any other currency.

The dollar has been embarrassed, primarily by the mark. It is possible to point to a number of reasons for the remarkable performance of the West German economy (especially the fact that her investible resources were used for building up basic productive capacity rather than 'digging holes' in armament production). Certainly, one important element in it was the relation of money-wage rates to productivity. The story shows clearly enough that trade unions who will accept the position of junior partner in a vigorous and technically progressive capitalist economy can do very well in terms of employment and rising real-wage rates. But the success comes precisely from permitting the country to enjoy a competitive advantage in trade over other capitalist nations. It cannot be maintained that the same medicine would work if it were universally applied.

COMMODITY MARKETS

The claim that post-war capitalism has avoided serious recessions is made from the point of view of the industrialized nations. Those whose share in capitalist prosperity depends upon the market for one or other primary product have a different experience to report. For most, a downward trend in relative prices has been overlaid by sharp fluctuations. In spite of much fine talk about wealthy nations aiding the underdeveloped economies to build up productive capacity, insuperable difficulties are put in their way by the 'free market' system, which makes it impossible to rely upon steady and expanding foreign earnings. The one class of primary producers whose markets are regulated for them – farmers inside the industrial nations – provide an exception which strikingly proves the rule.

'BY-PRODUCT OF A CASINO'

There was another hidden snag in the stream of Keynesian prosperity.

Without serious recessions, capital accumulation is continuously going on and a large part of it is financed by undistributed profits, so that the wealth of shareholders, taken overall, is increasing continuously without requiring any contribution from personal saving; moreover in an expanding economy exceptional and chance gains on the average outweigh disappointments and losses over a run of years. The total value of the equity in industry would be rising even if it were not inflated in money terms by the rising price level. Expected future gains are reflected in present stock-exchange prices. To anyone who doubts that the gains will be realized, shares appear over-valued, for their present price contains a value which lies in an uncertain future. The position then is inherently unstable. The instability has not the violent and dramatic character of the South-Sea Bubble or of Wall Street in 1929, but it is of the same nature. When doubt spreads, the market quickly forms the view that prices were too high but it has no means of forming a view as to what level would be just right. Once a fall begins, there is no particular reason for it to stop.

The instability of the Stock Exchange is its own affair. If there were no risks there would be no profits. But if a stock-exchange slump precipitates a slump in industry it is a serious matter for the whole economy. Paper losses cause a drop in private expenditure, and collapse of the money value of capital discourages investment. Real prosperity, as well as money gains, depends on faith that prosperity will continue.

THE POST-WAR RECORD

A run of seventeen years without a serious recession is a unique experience for capitalism. It has undermined the traditions of English socialism by making it seem plausible to argue that 'capitalism has changed'. So, indeed, it has, in that respect.

But how deep does the change go? It has not been proved that recessions can be avoided, except by armament expenditure, and, since to justify armaments, international tension has to be kept up, it appears that the cure is a good deal worse than the disease. It has not been proved that continuous prosperity is compatible with stable prices. It has not been proved that a tolerable system of trading relations can be developed between nations each pursuing its own economic policy. Above all, it has not been found possible to maintain the pace of development without which the system is continually in danger of falling below its stalling speed.

AFFLUENT CHEESEPARING

All this concerns the performance of latter-day capitalism on its own terms. A deeper doubt is raised by the question whether capitalism, even when prosperous, can provide us with what we really want.

The foundation of a comfortable standard life is a decent house. A family requires, above everything, a reliable health service and the best possible education; but growing wealth always leaves us with a greater deficiency in just those things. It is not an accident that it should be so. Capitalist industry is dazzlingly efficient at producing goods to be sold in the shops, and, directly or indirectly, profits are derived from selling. The services to meet basic human needs do not lend themselves to mass production: they are not an easy field for making profits, especially as, with our egalitarian democratic notions, they have to be offered irrespective of means to pay. Consequently they must be largely provided through taxation. To supply goods is a source of profit, but to supply services is a 'burden upon industry'. It is for this reason that when, as a nation, 'we have never had it so good' we find that we 'cannot afford' just what we most need.

22

SOCIALIST AFFLUENCE

HISTORY has seen two methods of carrying out the accumulation necessary to install scientific technology. The first, which has been in operation for two centuries, relies upon individual acquisitiveness; the second, which has been in operation for less than half a century, relies upon socialist planning. Both have reached the stage where, in a number of countries, the fruits of accumulation are now available to be enjoyed in a high level of consumption, but in each the process of accumulation has set up institutions and habits of mind which put obstacles in the way of rational enjoyment.

1

PROBLEMS OF CAPITALISM

In England, the pioneer of private enterprise, the first stages of accumulation were carried out with the utmost brutality. In the later stages, with the evolution of head-counting democracy, and now after the shared experience of two wars, all classes have come more or less to accept the idea of a welfare state – that gross poverty should be eliminated; that there should be equality of opportunity; that the great wealth of the nation should be deployed, for, in some sense, the general good of all its citizens.

The process of accumulation, however, cemented great inequality into the system, and this is now an impediment to realizing the accepted ideal. In principle, a democracy should be able to vote itself into egalitarianism through the tax system, but in practice the legal arrangements favourable to property and the habitual acceptance of the class structure, which were necessary to foster accumulation, now put up a resilient defence of inequality.

The institutions of private property and great inequalities of wealth were necessary to the process of accumulation in the manner in which it was carried out. Universal suffrage and egalitarian ideals in the eighteenth

From *Socialism, Capitalism and Economic Growth*, Essays in Honour of Maurice Dobb, Cambridge University Press, 1967.

century would have inhibited the industrial revolution before it began. But now private property has become otiose. What does the individual share-holder contribute to the operations of a modern corporation? Private saving is a convenience for private families – it is no longer necessary to aliment industrial accumulation. The gross investment that corporations carry out from amortization funds and retained profits is continually installing improved techniques, enlarging productive capacity without requiring 'abstinence' from anyone.

The shareholders and rentiers indeed, make a great negative contribution to industry, for much of the best talent of every generation is engaged, one way and another, in the lucrative business of swapping securities around amongst them and so is kept away from constructive activities. The notion that the Stock Exchange, with all its ancillary apparatus, is the most efficacious means of supplying finance to industry, compared to other available methods, is a fig-leaf which it wears to preserve its self-respect.

After the experience of the 'thirties, full employment is an insistent demand. This, combined with the institutions of private enterprise, which limit the sphere of government expenditure, has led to the ugly situation where democratic opinion accepts the arms race as a useful expedient for maintaining prosperity.

The institutions of private enterprise leave the main initiative in economic affairs to a number of independent corporations which have developed a motivation of their own – a pursuit of *success* which includes but is not bounded by the mere pursuit of profit. It is now generally agreed that the interplay of the policies of these independent corporations cannot be relied upon to secure continuous full employment, a consistent pattern of development, or a viable balance of trade. A national 'plan' is now seen to be necessary to co-ordinate their activities. But their very independence and power of individual initiative, which was the main-spring of the private-enterprise system, now prevents the economy from developing organs to control them in the general interest. So far, 'national planning' at most consists in persuading them to remove gross inconsistencies from their individual programmes.

To direct their behaviour towards a democratically decided programme would be quite another matter. If we think of the nation as a family, how would it wish to dispose its resources? The manner in which the public *does* spend its money is not a reliable guide, for all the arts of salesmanship, direct and indirect, are used to build up in the public a system of wants that provide a convenient outlet for profitable sales. There is a systematic bias in the pattern of production, dramatized in Galbraith's slogan: *private affluence and public squalor*, in favour of goods and services which can be sold piecemeal, so as to provide scope for profit, and against collective consumption which has to be financed by taxation. This bias is unfortunately fostered by economists who, when they purport to measure consumption as an indication of the standard of life, are really measuring only the sale of consumption goods.

Consider a middle class family with an income considerably above the national average but not great enough to saturate all their possible wants, and with sufficient education and self-confidence to resist advertisement and ignore the Joneses. In their notion of a comfortable standard of life beyond the obvious needs of food, clothing and amusement, a decent house ranks highest; the provision of education for the children; retirement pensions for the elderly and good medical help when needed. If a member has some disability, he will be kept as far as possible in the same comfort as the rest. Other wants are sacrificed, when need be, to satisfying these needs. Some scion, perhaps, finds comfort stuffy and goes out of his own free will to test his hardihood in a primitive world, but the family would by no means consider it a benefit to have the test of poverty thrust upon them.

The wealthy capitalist democracies have a great struggle to impose this scale of values upon their pattern of production. Housing, education, the health service are starved of funds. The elderly and the handicapped suffer. Pockets of squalid misery persist. The modern cry for 'growth' is partly an expression of the hope that a sufficient all-round proportionate rise in income will bring the bottom to a tolerable level without the necessity to interfere at the top.

In one respect latter-day capitalism has been remarkably successful – in avoiding serious recessions. This very success creates further problems. With continous near-full employment superimposed upon the system of industrial relations and of wage-bargaining and price-fixing developed in other circumstances, inflation has become chronic and the system is extremely resistant to the institution of an 'incomes policy' designed to preserve the value of money.

Finally, the spread of quasi-planning within each country runs into conflict with international anarchy, so that one government after another has to sacrifice progress towards a welfare state (whether gleefully or sadly) to the requirements of the balance of payments.

2

PROBLEMS OF SOCIALISM

In the European socialist countries, also, the toughest phase of accumulation has been accomplished. They do not have to contend with the heritage of private property and private enterprise. Without unearned income, the objective of equality of opportunity is less hard to attain, and differential earnings can be kept within acceptable limits. The distinction between profits and state revenue does not arise, so that resources can be allocated between industry and social servies according to rational criteria. There can be no question of wilful independence of enterprises which are all organs of the planned economy. Inflationary pressure occurs during the phase of accelerating accumulation, because spendable income is then increasing relatively to the output of purchasable goods; but there is not the same pressure from the mere persistence of full employment to raise money-wage rates and prices. Defence expenditure is a burden to them. They have no need to fear that an 'outbreak of peace' would cause a slump, for the resources involved can be redeployed to useful uses with little delay. They suffer, indeed, like capitalist countries, from insufficient export earnings, but they cut their imports to fit and do not allow the tail to wag the dog.

On the other hand, the socialist method of accumulation has left its own legacy of obstacles to the enjoyment of the potential affluence which it has achieved.

Of these, the most serious is in the political sphere. Whether or not repression is 'necessary' for rapid accumulation, they have in fact occurred together, both in East and West. In England four or five generations passed between the time when trade union organizers were deported to Australia and when they are installed in the House of Lords. The corresponding reversal in socialist countries has occurred within a decade. It is against the background of this disturbing experience that economic reforms are being carried out.

The demand for reforms, which has been rumbling since 1956, has broken out most recently in Czechoslovakia, and is there most sharp and articulate. The following is based mainly upon Czech experience.

The economic system developed for the purpose of rapid accumulation was imitated from the Soviet Union and contained features which were not at all appropriate to the requirements of a small country highly dependent upon international trade. Moreover the Soviet system imposed not only necessary but also unnecessary hardships upon the consumer, for instance, the elimination of individual tradesmen, such as cobblers. The planners were taught to think that only investment goods were 'serious' and neglect of consumer interests became a virtue in itself.

The dogma that, under socialism, the share of investment devoted to Department I, which was identified with heavy industry, must exceed the share of Department II, meant a continous effort to *accelerate* accumulation. The dogma was disputed, for instance in Poland in 1956, but policy in Czechoslovakia continued to be dominated by it. When the rate of growth slackened and actually came to a halt, the authorities could think of no remedy except more investment.

The organization of industry was a system of command from above which deprived the individual manager of authority and initiative. Planning was both rigid and clumsy. The criterion of success was reckoned in terms of gross output. The highest possible degree of self-sufficiency was aimed at. Trade, not only with the capitalist world, but amongst the People's Democracies, was heavily discouraged. The class war was carried to the second generation; children of middle-class parents were debarred from education. Much of this, which may have been unavoidable in the struggle for industrialization in the Soviet Union, was retrograde in Czechoslovakia, where there was a larger professional class and where more subtle methods of accounting and mangement had been developed in capitalist businesses. Even in Czechoslovakia, however, the heavy pressure to accumulate overrode all its drawbacks. It is reckoned that, not only national income, but *per capita* consumption was more than doubled between 1948 and 1960.

The methods which were successful in rushing to full employment and full utilization of resources have now become a fetter upon further progress.

The command system in industry led to inefficiency within an enterprise, both in the details of technique and in the handling of personnel. The method of reckoning in terms of gross output fostered waste of materials. The arbitrary system of prices made cost-accounting useless as a check on efficiency. Dictating the plan to an enterprise in physical terms broke contact with the market, so that it was common for unsaleable goods to be piling up in the cellars of shops while the enterprise was earning premia for plan fulfilment. Foreign competition, as a control upon quality, was cut off, for no imports were permitted of goods which an enterprise could claim to make at home. Innovation within enterprises was inhibited by the exaggerated horror of risk which the command system induces.

Proposals are now being made to overcome these particular drawbacks of the present situation.[1]

The main lines of the central planning system are not to be affected. No one now supports the suggestion that prospective profitability should influence the allocation of investible resources in the central plan; nor, indeed, has anyone succeeded in showing what such a criterion would mean in operational terms. Overall changes that are to be made, for instance greater attention to agriculture and light industry and a relaxation in the general rate of accumulation, are to be made centrally in a coherent manner, but in detail much more autonomy is to be given to the individual enterprise. The enterprise will have control over minor investments and, in the sphere of consumer goods, can choose its own product mix to suit the indications of demand coming from retailers; in some branches it is given authority to vary its prices.

Gradually the system of absorbing the surplus through the turnover tax at various rates on different commodities will be liquidated. Each enterprise will be required to pay a tax of 10 per cent on its wage bill and 6 per cent on a valuation of its installed capital, and will then be instructed to earn its costs from the sales of its output. Management is permitted to dispose of its wage fund as it pleases, so as to introduce incentive schemes.

Between the ministries and the enterprises is to be interposed a system of trusts, each concerned with a particular industry. Efficiency is to be promoted by the trust imposing a system of prices based upon average (or better) performance (taking account of inevitable advantages or drawbacks of the situation of different enterprises), so that its worst managed firms will be penalized unless they can improve, while its best enjoy a stimulating reward.

No doubt these reforms can produce a dramatic improvement. The better performance of individual workers and more efficient deployment of teams, the elimination of wastage of materials, the rationalization of relations between suppliers within a trust, and above all the direction of production towards what consumers actually want to buy, should bring an upward bound in the standard of life that will hearten the reformers.

But it is not easy to see that they have evolved a viable system for continuing development. A great deal of experiment and adaptation still must be to come.

[1] See Ota Šik, 'The problems of the new system of planned management', *Czechoslovak Economic Papers*, No. 5.

These proposals were repudiated in 1968.

3

MANAGEMENT

The much-discussed question: whether there is commodity trade under socialism, is a somewhat metaphysical way of drawing the distinction between principals and agents in economic affairs. The housewife who goes shopping is a principal. She is spending the family's money for their benefit as she judges best. When she buys from a peasant, he also is a principal. (It is commodity trade on both sides of the market.) When she buys in a state shop she is dealing with agents. When the shop replenishes its stock from a socialist enterprise, both parties to the transaction are agents of the same principal.

The point of the distinction is that a principal uses his judgment while an agent is directed by rules laid down for him. A western economist may say that the housewife is maximizing utility under a budget restraint, the advertiser may be studying her motives to get her hooked, but she feels that she is doing what she wants to do; she need not account, even to herself, for why she does it. The distinction is not absolute. An agent must have *some* discretion. A principal is guided by law and tradition. The problem for the reforms in socialist management is where to draw the line. The top management of a capitalist enterprise, though legally agents of the shareholders, act as principals in the interests of the company. They need to make profits, since profits are necessary to secure the survival and growth of the company, but the pursuit of profit does not confine them to a narrow groove; there is a wide range of possibilities between playing safe and adventurous experiment. Moreover, in a world of uncertainty the pursuit of profit is expressed in short-cuts, rules of thumb and conventions of policy. Considerations of reputation and professional honour modify pure money-making. The management of a company feels 'a three-fold public responsibility, to the public which consumes its products, to the public which it employs, and to the public which provides the capital by which it operates and develops'.

When the management of socialist enterprises are given more autonomy, they will have the same three-fold responsibility, with contributions to the national budget substituted for the interests of the share-holders. Merely to instruct them to maximize net profit from the capital equipment with which they are provided is an inadequate guide. From a long-run point of view, a contented labour force and satisfied consumers are essential to profitability – how weigh one against the other when their interests conflict, and each against short-period advantage? One of the evils of the present system is that proper expenditure on upkeep and repairs is sacrificed to short-run plan-fulfilment. An instruction to maximize net profit is no substitute for judgment in weighing the present against the future. Moreover, net profit is an *ex-post* measure. The decisions that have to be taken by management, about day to day operation as well as about long-run policy, are decisions about people and things. At best the instruction to maximize net profit is an instruction to act in a manner that may be reasonably expected to maximize profits over some future term. And what is it reasonable to expect?

In Czechoslovakia the proposal is, not to use net profit as a criterion of success, but to instruct management to recover the wage fund which they have been advanced, along with other expenses, from their annual operations. This is a remedy aimed at the crude evil of fulfilling a plan by producing unsaleable goods at unnecessarily high costs. It seems also to be intended to give the workers an interest in the efficiency and discipline of the enterprise in which they work without going the whole length of giving them the equity in it, on the Yugoslav model. (The wage fund is ensured up to 90 per cent, so that bad management would not be the disaster for a group of workers that a bankruptcy may be under capitalism.)

In practice, it seems, the autonomy of enterprises is to be much less than this scheme suggests. The trusts that have been set up for each broadly defined industry will give instructions to the enterprises in some mixture of physical and financial terms, which, no doubt, will be evolved as experience accumulates, while the overall plan is given to the trusts from above. The analogy, then, will be not with capitalist enterprises, but with cartels. A well-run cartel is by no means the worst form of management that capitalism has produced for its own purposes, but to adapt it to socialist purposes needs some care. The most obvious danger is that the officials of the trusts will develop an excessive patriotism for their particular industry and devote more effort to gaining favours for their enterprises from the centre than to subordinating them to it.

4

THE WORKERS

In China, North Korea and Cuba, where revolutionary patriotism is still warm, the proposal to make greater use of monetary rewards as incentives to the individual worker is regarded with grave suspicion. It seems to them a denial of the moral content of socialism, which should appeal to public spirit and personal self-respect. Capitalist experience suggests that it is dangerous also from a purely economic point of view.

The money motive under capitalism has two sides, fear of loss and hope of gain. The first is far and away more powerful than the second, especially for a worker to whom loss of employment entails total misery. In the post-war era of continous near-full employment, progressive management, to attract labour, to effect improvements in efficiency and to call forth effort from the men, offers increased earnings in various open or disguised forms. Every grievance, every demand, is bought off by offering more pay. It suits the progressive firms to do so, for by setting a level of costs that less efficient firms cannot cope with, they rob their rivals of their market as well as their labour force. But from the point of view of the economy as a whole it is a great nuisance, since money incomes rise faster than *average* output and so generate chronic inflation. When a man has got used to a certain pay packet, it becomes his necessary standard of life; to reconcile him to any change will need another rise. Even under capitalism there is an irresistible demand for fair (that is, more or less equal) relative earnings, so that less progressive industries and occupations have to follow the progressive ones in raising money-wages continuously. Moreover, once it is accepted that the motive for effort, above the bare minimum, is extra income, it becomes perfectly legitimate for individuals or groups of workers to prefer minimum effort with minimum earnings. Hard trades, like mining, become impossible to man.

Let alone morality, the socialist countries should consider the psychology and the economics of money incentives very carefully before they step onto this slippery slope.

5

Prices and Costs

General instructions to the enterprises in terms of net profit or gross receipts make sense only if the system of prices is sensible. One of the sharpest objections to the present system is the arbitrariness of prices.

The Czech proposal is to rationalize the system, gradually introducing prices based on costs, including the taxes on resources used (10 per cent on the wage bill and 6 per cent on assessed capital) which are to provide the fund for accumulation and general expenses of the state. Subject to covering total costs from total receipts, the enterprises have some freedom (in certain lines) to vary prices of particular products – for instance to adjust scales of prices for differences of quality.

So far as consumer goods are concerned, a system of prices based on costs cannot be completely satisfactory. For a long time to come there will be particular scarcities of supply relative to demand. A pattern of supply-and-demand prices has somehow or other roughly been established by differential rates of turnover tax. To move directly to a pattern of prices based on relative costs would fail to maintain a fit between demand and supply. Yet there is no reason why a particular enterprise should benefit (in easier profits) from the scarcity of the type of productive capacity it happens to command. Moreover, since the socialist sector of the economy 'imports' consumer goods from co-operative agriculture, and imports a great deal from capitalist and from other socialist countries, there are bound to be unforeseen changes in supply from time to time, which are more convenient to deal with by altering prices than by rationing. The remedy is for the office of price administration, which is an independent organ of the economy, to set final prices to the consumers so as to maintain an overall balance between sales and expenditure and as close a fit as possible between particular demands and supplies, without upsetting cost relationships by interfering with the prices of productive enterprises.

For the enterprises, to have prices adjusted to costs would bring order into chaos and permit some rational cost-accounting and calculations of efficiency to be undertaken. But is it satisfactory on its own merits? The basis of the proclaimed virtues of the competitive system in the textbooks is that each producer finds himself faced with a price in the market so that his profit depends on keeping his costs below it. In capitalist industry, of course, this situation does not really obtain. Prices are administered on a cost-plus basis, while competition runs into salesmanship and product differentiation. Will the socialist trusts avoid the evils of cost-plus?

6

OPTIMUM SAVING

Czech economists maintain that the cessation of growth in national income in 1963 came about in spite of an exceptionally high rate of investment in the preceding years.[2] To carry out investment faster than the digestive system of the economy can absorb it is a vain sacrifice. But when a proper balance between physical investment, education and research ensures that current saving will increase future production, are there any principles in which the ratio of investment to consumption should be fixed?

[2] J. Goldman, 'Short and long term variations in the growth rate and the model of functioning of a socialist economy', *Czechoslovak Economic Papers*, No. 5.

In practice the capitalist nations have given up the pretence that private enterprise produces either the right amount or the most efficient form of investment (witness the fashion for planning) but the economists still discuss the problem in terms of the desirable rate of saving.

There is no way of judging, from the behaviour of individual families in a capitalist country, what people *really want* to save. The distribution of income between families, the general habits of the various classes, and the reliability of the social security system have a strong influence on private saving. Nor is it possible to judge the effect of incentives to save. It is a fallacy to say that interest is the 'reward' of saving. The reward of saving, in the capitalist world, is owning wealth. The fact that wealth can be placed in assets that yield a return is only one of its advantages. The amount of saving that individuals do to acquire individual wealth cannot tell us anything about the amount of saving they *really want* to do to acquire collective productive capacity. Nor does the reaction of individuals to the return on placements give an indication of what their attitude may be to the return on social investment. The question has been open since Marshall's day, whether the typical family saves more or less from earned income at a higher rate of interest. The question concerns differences, say, between 3 and 7 per cent on gilt-edged placements. Now, it is generally estimated that the incremental capital to output ratio in a developing economy is of the order of 2 or 3. To be on the safe side, and to be sure that it is net, let us put it at 4. This means that saving today yields 25 per cent per annum in perpetuity. How much would you or I save at that offer? How do we know?

There is a more subtle difficulty in passing from individual psychology to social choice. The process of investment cannot be represented simply as sacrificing present for future consumption or vice versa. It is true that a sacrifice in current consumption can always be made, in conditions of full employment, by drafting labour into basic industry, but, after the heroic age of accumulation, such a policy is unlikely to be chosen. Consumption will not be allowed to fall below a level that it has once reached. The other way round, to increase current consumption by cutting investment is generally not possible (except by acting upon the balance of trade). The choice is rather between an increase in consumption in the relatively near future (by directing investment into light industry) and a greater increase in the more distant future (by maintaining investment in basic industry). Any path that is chosen has to be followed consistently and the possible paths are indefinitely various. There is no way in which signalling from the market can direct the choice between them.

This does not mean that the choice must be foisted upon the public by the whim of the authorities. The present revolt is largely a demand (in vague general terms) for consumption to rise as fast as may be. The very inefficiency of the present system provides a hump, so that it should be possible to increase consumption appreciably without cutting basic investment. After that, a wise strategy might be to bring about a further sharp rise in consumption, then to keep it almost stable for a few years while investment was directed to securing another burst later. Such a scheme (in spite of marginal utility theory) might give more satisfaction than a slow steady rise which would scarcely be noticed from year to year.

This is a new problem for the socialist countries. Up till now optimum saving has simply been the maximum possible investment; and in fact they have sometimes done more – imposing abstinence on their people which failed to fructify in increased productive capacity.

7

INVESTMENT PLANNING

The planning of investment is the key to economic control, and the authorities do not intend to relax their grip on it. In Yugoslavia the original conception of the economic reform was that investment funds should be allocated by the central plan to branches of industry and to districts, and that individual enterprises (now under the control of their own workers) should bid for shares. This system has evidently got out of hand, and the authorities instead of trying to get a grip on the plan again, have resorted to a temporary all-round credit squeeze. This has been a useful warning for Czechoslovakia.

Not only the overall rate, but the broad composition of investment must be planned centrally. Long-range decisions, such as the source of power, affect the whole of industry and all elements have to be made consistent with them. (This is precisely what has driven the capitalist countries to accept the necessity for planning.) In this sphere, improvements in methods are being sought, but there is no basic change in contemplation.

So far as the choice of technique for a given output is concerned, the enterprises must have considerable influence, since it is they who have concrete detailed knowledge of the problems involved. The charge of 6 per cent on assessed value of fixed capital is intended to induce economy. Once an installation has been set up, the enterprise ought to use it to the best advantage, and 6 per cent is neither here nor there. The charge is intended to curb demands for unnecessarily lavish extensions and re-equipment, and to affect the design of new installations. Presumably, with experience, the tax charges can be varied to express the scarcity of labour relatively to investible resources, but this could work only if prices are independently given. Cost-plus would make it ineffective.

Hitherto the socialist economies have approached the problem of the choice of technique in terms of the saving of future labour cost to be attributed to an addition to investment – they have had in mind something like a production function, or spectrum of known techniques. Czechoslovakia is the most mature in the sense of having reached an overall scarcity of labour. The amount of progress to be made by pure 'deepening' of the capital structure is presumably not very great. The problem now is to foster technical progress – to find out methods of production that save *both* future labour and present investment cost.

The worst feature of the command system is the timidity which checks experiment. There is considerable danger that mistakes made under the new system will be used by those who flourished under the old to press for a return to rigid planning. There is always a certain superficial plausibility in the argument that it is dangerous to allow a child into the water till he has learned to swim. The problem now is to find a form of economic organization which encourages initiative without being too lenient to wasteful errors.

8

CONSUMER SOVEREIGNTY

In all this what seems to be most lacking is some method to direct the use of the resources now available to 'securing the maximum satisfaction of the constantly rising material and cultural requirements of the whole society'. Now that the emphasis has changed from growth at all costs to raising the standard of life, there is an obvious need for the public to be given some means of saying what their requirements are. It is an illusion to suppose that market signals can guide the planners. Increasing consumption involves not only a consistent path through time, but a consistent composition of output. The goods that represent a rising standard of life are consumed in clusters – housing, electric gadgets and domestic power; sports goods, hotels and travel. The housewife knows what gadgets to buy only after she has been informed what the future price of power will be. Moreover, in a fairly egalitarian society, the demand curves for particular commodities are likely to be highly convex – elastic at small quantities, plunging abruptly to saturation after a certain point. The height of the demand price today does not tell the planners what increase in output would carry supply to the corner. Nor can it tell them anything about the effect of one man's consumption on the welfare of his neighbours. At some stage they will have to face the problems which arise from satisfying the constantly rising requirements of the whole society for motor cars.

The present system is just as much a system of producer's sovereignty as the capitalist system is, and it is even beginning to develop a rudimentary form of sales pressure to get the consumers to take what the producers choose to offer. Under capitalism, the consumers have begun to make some feeble efforts to defend themselves with institutions such as *Which?* Under socialism, surely, the consumer's interest should be defended, by imposing standards of quality and design and by research into needs and desires, not, as under capitalism, to find how to exploit them, but how to give satisfaction.

POSTSCRIPT

In Czechoslovakia the discussion of the above problems was brought to an abrupt end in 1968; solutions still remain to be found.

23

WHAT HAS BECOME OF EMPLOYMENT POLICY?

THE wartime coalition government of the UK published a White Paper, *Employment Policy* (Cmnd. 6527, 1944), which boldly declared that it is the responsibility of government to maintain a high and stable level of employment. Sure enough, from 1945 to 1966 (with the exception of the hard winter of 1947) unemployment in Britain, as represented by official statistics, never rose above 2·5 per cent of the labour force, and in some years hovered around 1 per cent. This was quite a surprise. Sir William Beveridge (Beveridge, 1944) estimated that the attainable minimum would be an average of 3 per cent, varying between 2 and 4 per cent from time to time, and Keynes thought this much too optimistic (Kahn, 1975). The expected post-war slump never came. Twenty years of near-full employment was something new in history. Indeed, in some capitalist countries demand for labour overtook supply and foreign workers flooded in.[1] It seemed that the ghost of the trade cycle of the pre-war variety had been exorcised, apart from accidental disturbances such as the Korean war boom and slump. Continous prosperity began to be taken for granted. Workers came to expect real-wage rates to rise from year to year and shareholders began to look forward to unending capital gains.

Over the period as a whole, annual growth rates in *per capita* income in the rest of western Europe and in Japan ranged between 4 per cent and 10 per cent. Average real consumption per head grew at more or less the same pace but, since inequality was, if anything, slightly reduced, there was probably a greater rise in the level of consumption for the broad mass of the population (see Table 1, p. 265). Even in the poorest third world countries,

[1] For instance, the proportion of foreign workers in the West German labour force increased from less than 1 per cent in the 1950s to some 10 per cent in the 1970s (Böhning and Maillet, 1974).

per capita GNP grew at 1 or 2 per cent per annum, but there it was associated with growing inequality and a great increase in misery.[2]

In the USA *per capita* growth from the early 1950s to the mid-1960s was only 2·5 per cent per annum, but starting from a higher base, mass consumption swelled prodigiously, which made poverty all the more annoying for those who did not get much of it. The UK was at, or near, the bottom of the league table, with a growth rate slightly less than that of the USA, but even so, the general standard of life was indubitably rising. Disgruntled elements in the middle class began to be annoyed to see workers' families encroaching on their former privileges, such as private cars and holidays in Spain, but conservative views were generally supported by the experience of prosperity. The spokesmen for capitalism were saying, in effect: we have to admit that the unemployment that prevailed before the war was a serious defect in the free-market system. Now we are giving you capitalism with full employment, so what have you got to complain of?

In the inter-war period, while capitalism was wallowing in the slump, full employment and rapid growth were being maintained in the USSR. (Perhaps it was the desire to avoid a repetition of this contrast that made conservative opinion accept the Keynesian doctrines, which were formerly considered subversive.) Now the boot was on the other foot; the spectacle of luxury consumption spreading among industrial workers in the West aroused envy and doubt in the socialist world.

In Great Britain, 1966 was disconcerting – a so-called Labour government deliberately causing unemployment in order to maintain the exchange value of sterling (and thereafter failing to do so). But British troubles were put down to special circumstances or to peculiarities in the national character.[3] In the capitalist world as a whole, activity revived after

[2] In the third world countries, during the period 1950–2 to 1964–6, the growth rates of product *per capita* averaged about 1·7 per cent for Africa, 1·8 per cent for America, 1·6 per cent for South Asia, 2·6 per cent for the Far East and 4·4 per cent for the Middle East (as compared with 5·0 per cent in western Europe over the comparable period) (see OECD national accounts). Recent empirical studies have established substantial support for the hypothesis that relative inequality increases in the early stages of development (Ahluwalia, 1976; Chenery, 1974). Ahluwalia's evidence suggests that 'the stronger hypothesis of declining absolute incomes for large sections of the population is not so unequivocally established by cross-country data as to be uncritically accepted as one of the "stylized facts" about development' (p. 135). However, this stronger hypothesis does seem to hold, for example, in the case of the Indian economy, where the percentage of rural people below the 'poverty line' increased from 38 per cent in 1960–1 to 45 per cent in 1964–5 and to 54 per cent in 1968–9 (Bardhan, 1974).

[3] See, for example, Caves (1968), especially Chapters 7 and 8.

a setback, and ran high for another seven years (see Table 1). Belief in perpetual prosperity was restored.

While prosperity ruled, the deeper insights of the Keynesian revolution were lost to view. The bastard Keynesian doctrine, evolved in the United States, invaded the economics faculties of the world, floating on the wings of the almighty dollar. (It established itself even amongst intellectuals in the so-called developing countries, who have reason enough to know better.) The old orthodoxy, against which the Keynesian revolution was raised, was based on Say's law – there cannot be a deficiency of demand. Spending creates demand for consumption goods, while saving creates demand for investment goods such as machinery and stocks. Keynes pointed out the obvious fact that investment is governed by the decisions of business corporations and public institutions, not by the desire of thrifty householders to save. An increase in household saving means a reduction in consumption; it does not increase investment but reduces employment.

According to the bastard Keynesian doctrine, it is possible to calculate the rate of saving that households collectively desire to achieve; then governments, by fiscal and monetary policy, can organize the investment of this amount of saving. Thus Say's law is artificially restored, and under its shelter all the old doctrines creep back again, even the doctrine that a given stock of capital will provide employment for any amount of labour at the appropriate equilibrium real-wage rate. If so, unemployment occurs only because wages are being held above the equilibrium level. (In the third world, it is just too bad, because the equilibrium wage corresponding to full employment is far below the level of subsistence.)

Keynes was diagnosing a defect inherent in capitalism. Kalecki, who developed the same theory independently, went much further and held that without radical change capitalism was incapable of rectifying the defect. But the bastard Keynesians turned the argument back into being a defence of *laisser-faire*, provided that just the one blemish of excessive saving was going to be removed.[4]

---

[4] Thus, typically, Samuelson argues:

 The finding of our macroeconomic analysis rejects both the classical faith that *laisser-faire* must by itself lead to utopian stability and the pre-World War II pessimism that classical microeconomic principles have become inapplicable to the modern world. Instead we end with the reasoned prospect that appropriate monetary and fiscal policies can ensure an economic environment which will *validate* the verities of microeconomics – that society has to choose among its alternative high-employment production possibilities, that paradoxes of thrift and fallacies of composition will not be permitted to create cleavages between private and social virtues or private and public vices.

 By means of appropriately reinforcing monetary and fiscal policies, a mixed

Against this background, the slump of 1973–4 was a considerable shock. We were told, in early 1976, that a revival was gathering momentum and that soon the United States and West Germany would be pulling us all up into a new boom. At best, then, we appear to be getting back into the clutches of the old trade cycle;[5] perpetual steady growth has proved to have been a daydream. The bastard Keynesian economists are quite disconcerted and the spokesmen for capitalism have got their brief muddled up.

The complacency of the age of growth covered up what, in the legal phrase, may be called *inherent vice* in the free-market system, which has now broken out in the unprecedented combination of inflation with unemployment, along with increasing tension in international economic relations and growing distress at the social consequences of unregulated capitalist accumulation.

1

A major point in the analysis of Keynes and Kalecki, which the complacent economists seem to have overlooked, is that there is no meaning to be attached to the concept of equilibrium in the general level of prices. The Keynesian revolution began by refuting the then orthodox theory that there is a natural tendency in a market economy to establish equilibrium with full employment. If men in fact were out of work, on the orthodox view, it must be because wages were above the equilibrium level and profits were too low. Unemployment on this view was 'voluntary' because trade unions could easily get rid of it by accepting lower wage rates. Keynes agreed that a rise in profits would increase employment, but he argued that a general cut in money-wage rates would reduce the price level more or less in proportion, so that neither profits nor employment would increase. If this argument is correct, it must follow that to raise money wages will increase prices, even if there is unemployment.

---

economy can avoid the excesses of boom and slump and can look forward to healthy progressive growth. This being understood, the paradoxes that robbed the older classical principles dealing with small-scale 'microeconomics' of much of their relevance and validity will now lose their sting. The broad cleavage between microeconomics and macroeconomics has been closed by active public use of fiscal and monetary policy (Samuelson, 1970, p. 348).

By 1976, Samuelson's faith in macroeconomic policies (but not in the verities of microeconomics) had been badly shaken. Compare the passage quoted above with the corresponding passage in the tenth edition of his textbook (p. 373).

[5] See Table 1. The old trade cycle was associated with actual reductions in GDP, whereas, as is well known, cyclical downturns in the period since World War II in most industrial countries have merely meant a slowing down of the rate of growth of output.

It was easy to predict that a long run of high employment and high profits, without any change in the mechanism and psychology of wage bargaining, would lead to continuously rising prices. Keynes foresaw that it would be a difficult political problem to prevent free wage bargaining from generating inflation in conditions of continuous high employment (see Robinson, 1973), but he did not suggest how to solve it. Orthodox economists do not like to discuss politics. The old-fashioned monetarist doctrines enabled them to ignore the political causes and consequences of inflation. They held that the level of prices is regulated by the quantity of money. Wage rates are prices like the rest. When there is an excessive creation of money, wages are bound to rise whether trade unions demand increases or not. The simple cure for inflation is to regulate the quantity of money correctly. This theory had a great success with central bankers, but even many bastard Keynesians found it too much to swallow. They prefer to discuss inflation in terms of demand pull and cost push.

The appearance of symmetry between demand and costs is deceptive. A sudden rapid increase in effective demand, with given productive capacity, runs output into bottlenecks and, even if prices do not rise, there is a sharp increase in profits. By itself, this does not cause continuing inflation, though it may set off a rise in wage rates which thereafter continues to feed on itself. A pure cost push – wages being raised, so to speak, in cold blood, without any preceding rise in profits – is logically possible though hard to distinguish in practice.

By the mid-1950s, however, the link between high employment and wage increases had become obvious and Professor Phillips' econometric study (Phillips, 1958) reduced this relationship to a simple formula. His analysis of the causal link between high employment and the rate of wage inflation was widely accepted, despite the doubtful quality of much of his data, and pressure in the labour market was brought to the fore as an explanation of inflation.

This view has now been embodied in a new form of monetarism. According to this doctrine, with non-inflationary equilibrium in the labour market, there is a certain amount of *voluntary unemployment*, of workers who prefer not to work at the ruling level of real wages. If government attempts to lower unemployment below this *natural level* by increasing the money supply, labour market pressures increase money wages. The increased prices which result are built into wage claims via workers' expectations of inflation and the rate of price increase accelerates. To cure inflation the increase in the money supply has to be adjusted so as to raise unemployment to the natural level – even beyond that if there is a large element of expectations in wage claims. When money wages continue to increase while unemployment is rising, this only shows that equilibrium in the labour market has not been reached and that unemployment should be further increased. By emphasizing the importance of voluntary abstentions from the labour market as an explanation for unemployment, the new monetarists have arrived back at the point where Keynes started.[6]

One of the oddest notions produced by bastard Keynesians is that trade unions suffer from 'money illusion' because they do not bargain in real terms. In fact, negotiations about wages can only be conducted in terms of money. When inflation is already going on, the rising 'cost of living' is brought into the argument, but there is no way in which trade unions can operate directly on the level of real wages. Moreover, there is no point in preaching to workers that to raise the general level of money wage rates merely raises prices, so that they get no benefit from it. Any group of workers which secures a rise ahead of others does get higher real wages for some time, and any who fall behind suffer a permanent loss.

A rise of prices normally leads to a demand for a compensating rise in wages and a rise in wages leads to rising prices again. However, the ability of any group of workers to maintain their standard of life in an inflationary period depends on collective action. In industries where workers are strongly organized, trade unions are effective in protecting their members' interests and every rise in living costs quickly leads to increased wages. In other sectors, where organization is weak or trade union leaders complacent, wages lag behind prices, so that real wages fall.[7] For a time, this helps to slow down inflation, since the rise in the aggregate wage bill for industry as a whole is less than proportionate to the rise in the level of prices. But for this very reason, organization grows stronger and rank-and-file pressure on leaders grows more insistent. Soon, wages are following prices more quickly and inflation accelerates.[8]

[6] For example, 'In one sense all employment could be regarded as voluntary because there is some wage level at which almost any individual could price himself into a job' (Brittan, 1975, p. 30). Brittan's list of reasons for voluntary unemployment includes trade unions, minimum wage and equal pay legislation and social benefits. It is worth noting that this list is remarkably similar to that in Pigou (1933), the book singled out by Keynes as 'the only detailed account of the classical theory of unemployment which exists' (Keynes, 1936, p. 7). See also Laidler (1975).

[7] However, in some relatively unorganized sectors, such as domestic service and shorthand typing, wages have risen sharply, apparently in response to demand for labour.

[8] Research being undertaken by one of the authors indicates that the upsurge in militancy among important groups of workers, e.g. hospital ancillary workers, local government manual workers, teachers and, particularly, the miners in the late 1960s and early 1970s, was preceded by a period in which real take-home pay fell sharply. Moreover, a fairly common

It is commonly said that trade unions cause inflation: however that may be, it is quite clear that inflation causes trade unions. In Britain for the last decade, organization has been spreading not only among previously ill-organized manual workers and among the clerical grades, but also among the professional classes. Now respected servants of the public, physicians and judges, have to struggle, just like dustmen, to prevent their living standards from being undermined by the successful struggles of others.

There is, however, another aspect of wage bargaining which certainly does cause inflation. The trade union movement regards itself as charged with the right and duty to maintain for its members a proper share in the growing productivity of industry. In prosperous times, it is performing a useful function for capitalism. In the absence of trade union pressure, real wages would not rise in line with the increasing productivity due to technical progress, and stagnation would be induced by the failure of mass consumption to rise in step with productive capacity. The struggle over the relative share of wages in the product of industry interacts with the struggle over the relative wage rates of different bargaining groups. The strong technically progressive firms do not much object to granting money wage increases as real wage-costs fall. Prices for their products may remain more or less constant. Additional purchasing power from their wage bill tends to raise the demand for other commodities. Workers in the less progressive industries and services are now at a double disadvantage. Their share in consumption has been reduced and their relative position in the hierarchy of wage rates has been pushed down. They must demand rises and, to defend profits, their employers must put up prices.

Though this is the effect of their traditional function, trade union leaders bitterly resented the accusation that they were causing inflation and for a long time refused to admit that rising wage rates had anything to do with it. After all, they were behaving quite correctly in trying to keep wage rates, each for their own members, from falling behind the cost of living. The British trade union movement had inherited a proud tradition and its central principle was the demand for freedom in wage bargaining. It was hardly their fault if modern capitalism could not accommodate itself to their using the strength that they had managed to build up over two centuries.

---

pattern of development of this militancy emerges; a rapid increase in unofficial strikes and other forms of industrial action was eventually followed by official strike action. The situation, therefore, is the opposite of the popular image of the militant leaders pushing the silent, and often reluctant, majority; in fact the militant majority tend to push the silent, and frequently reluctant, leaders (R. J. Tarling and S. F. Wilkinson, 'Wage Differentials and Incomes Policy: an Inter-industry Study', *British Journal of Industrial Relations*, forthcoming).

Moreover, it is not fair to say that trade unions have always ruthlessly followed their sectional interests at the expense of everyone else. Both leaders and members have demonstrated from time to time their willingness to co-operate with government policy, particularly when the Labour party is in power. In 1948, the trade union movement accepted a wage freeze and maintained it more or less intact for two years. Again in 1966, the movement broadly accepted the need for wage control. Both these efforts succeeded in securing their short-term objectives of improving the balance of payments and mitigating inflation for a time, but both soon collapsed into rapid inflation, mainly because of the government's inability to provide an adequate quid pro quo.

The violent inflation of 1974, running up to an annual rate of 27 per cent in 1975, gave everyone a fright. This time the efforts of the trade unions to co-operate with a Labour government to check inflation have been more convincing than before. But, so far, union involvement has been largely confined to tinkering with the process of wage determination; in other spheres of government policy it has been narrowly limited. It was this failure to extend the influence of the unions beyond wage control that proved fatal to previous attempts at co-operation.

In 1943 Kalecki, looking forward, sceptically, to the possibilities of the post-war world, wrote:

'Full employment capitalism' will have, of course, to develop new social and political institutions which will reflect the increased power of the working class. If capitalism can adjust itself to full employment a fundamental reform will have been incorporated in it. If not, it will show itself an outmoded system which must be scrapped (Kalecki, 1943).

2

Class war was not the only element of inherent vice in the free-market system to disturb the age of growth. There were also the problems generated by the unevenness of development amongst various capitalist nations and the economic and political relationships between industrial countries and primary producers, particularly those in the third world.

The pre-Keynesian theory of international trade required the balance of imports and exports for each country to be maintained by movements in relative price levels. After experiencing the attempt to return to the gold standard in 1925 (see Keynes, 1972), Keynes adopted the view that depreciating the exchange rate was much to be preferred to attempting to depress the price level. At the end of his life, feeling obliged to defend the Bretton Woods agreement against his better judgement (Kahn, 1976), he lapsed into arguing that, *in the long run*, market forces would tend to establish equilibrium in international trade (Keynes, 1946). He had forgotten his old crack, that in the long run we are all dead.

As it turned out, market forces generated disequilibrium. Differences in competitive power, whatever their origin, set up a spiral of divergence. A country such as West Germany, with growing exports, could maintain a high rate of investment and therefore of growing productivity, which enhanced its competitive power, and allowed real wages to rise so that workers were less demanding. In the United Kingdom, any increase in employment caused an increase in the deficit in the balance of payments so that every hopeful *go* had to be brought to an end with a despairing *stop*. Thus strong competitors grow stronger and the weak, weaker.

Because of the size and strength of the United States and its overseas economy, trade plays a small part in national income, but not a small part in the world market. The USA can move from deficit to surplus without much disturbance at home, but with a great deal of disturbance to the other trading nations. Moreover, it was able to take advantage of the dollar being the world currency to run an ever greater outflow on capital account with an ever growing deficit on income account, until President Nixon, with the dollar devaluation of 1971, suddenly tried to reverse the position with a stroke of the pen. All this laid great strains on the international monetary system.

Keynes worked out the structure of the *General Theory* mainly in terms of a closed economy. When it is extended to take in the operation of international economic relations, a missing link appears in the argument. The rate of interest was to be used to regulate home investment, and Keynes believed that a secular fall in interest rates was both necessary for this purpose and desirable in itself. Exchange rates were to offset differences in relative labour costs. Then nothing would be left to regulate short-term capital movements. Traditionally this was the function of relative interest rates. Britain, and other countries with chronically weak payments balances, could not indulge in cheap money however much home conditions required it, and had to follow the interest rates of other countries up whenever they happened to rise. This was one more turn in the spiral of weakness weakening itself.

Over and above the strains set up by the uneasy relationships amongst the industrial nations themselves, there were the strains involved in the relations of the industrial countries as a whole and the third world. The formation of prices in the free-market system is in two parts – cost-plus in manufacturing industry and supply and demand for primary products.[9] A rise in the level of production and consumption in industrial countries normally increases demand for all kinds of primary products. When prices of materials rise, while money wage rates are constant, real wages fall and so generate a demand for rising money wages, which adds to the original rise in costs. Thus favourable terms of trade reduce class conflict in the industrial countries and unfavourable terms exacerbate it.

Commodity prices responded sharply to the pressure of demand during the Korean war boom, but this was soon over and during the 1950s the terms of trade moved in favour of industrial countries. However, the long boom, swollen by the Vietnam war, financed by the USA on the principle of guns *and* butter, caused an acceleration in the rate of increase in commodity prices and finally sparked off the great inflation of 1973.

In an economic model, it is possible to analyse the consequences of any one change by keeping other things constant. In real life a lot of things happen at once. During the long boom, an excess of demand over growth of capacity led to shortages of one commodity after another. The demonetization of the dollar in 1971 drove speculative funds into commodity markets. The Moslem oil producers, temporarily bound together by hostility to Israel, suddenly realized the extent of their monopoly power. Inflation at what now seems a mild and acceptable rate had been going on for years all over the capitalist world, setting up expectations that inflation would continue and undermining the conventional belief that a dollar is a dollar. Injected into this situation, the sudden rise in the costs of materials, especially oil, blew the inflation sky high.

This concatenation of circumstances has been described as a historical accident. But it is the inherent vice in the free-market system of international trade which creates the setting for such 'accidents', from which it has no means to defend itself except by destroying prosperity and depriving the primary product sellers of their favourable terms of trade.

3

The hopes which accompanied the Keynesian revolution, of reforming capitalism so as to ensure continuous prosperity with full employment, are

[9] See Robinson (1962); K. J. Coutts, W. A. H. Godley and W. D. Nordhaus, *Industrial Pricing in the United Kingdom*, Cambridge, CUP, forthcoming.

now all but extinguished. The slide into crisis in the capitalist world has re-established the pre-Keynesian orthodoxy as the conventional wisdom in economic policy-making at both national and international levels. The inevitable consequence of this is a much higher general level of unemployment and recurrent crises, involving a massive waste of resources and considerable human misery.

Important changes in the world economy have taken place over the last two decades, which have ended the era of near-full employment and exposed the inadequacies of the conventional Keynesian analysis. One of the most important of these developments has been the relaxation of tariffs and exchange controls and the resulting large increase in international trade[10] and capital movements; this has increasingly exposed national economies to the ravages of uncontrolled capitalist competition, in the way that they were exposed before the 1930s.

While the USA remained the predominant world economic and political power, and effectively acted as the world central bank, some semblance of order in international economic relations was retained. The use of the dollar as a reserve currency and the eagerness of the USA to lend abroad allowed international liquidity to expand to meet the needs of the growing volume of trade and facilitated post-war reconstruction and structural adaptation in the capitalist world. But with the emergence of Japan and western European countries as strong competitors to the USA, and the deterioration of the USA's balance of payments, unhindered capital movements became a major destabilizing force. The IMF proved totally inadequate to its appointed task of protecting national economies from external shocks and assisting the correction of more permanent imbalances in payments. In fact, by establishing rules which threw the burden of adjustment mainly onto deficit countries, the IMF institutionalized an important element in the process of unequal development among capitalist countries.

Faced with growing international pressures, the governments of debtor countries have been obliged to adopt the deflationary policies acceptable to their creditors (including the IMF); policies which conflicted with the avowed aim of maintaining full employment and with the real-wage demands of the working class. Thus democratically elected governments of debtor countries, where the working class is well organized, have walked a knife edge between the international and internal disapproval of their economic policies. But the frequently imposed deflationary policies

[10] Exports of OECD countries as a whole increased from 11 per cent of GDP in 1954 to almost 17 per cent of GDP in 1973.

progressively weakened the competitive position of such economies, increasing their indebtedness and reducing the opportunities for advances in real wages. Unable to meet either internal or external demands, economic policy vacillated wildly; consequently growing economic crisis has been accompanied by increasing political instability and further destabilization of the international economy.

The world market system has run into a second, and much more general, impasse, caught between two interlocking conflicts – the demands of workers in the industrial countries for higher real wages and the demands of the third world for improved terms of trade.

So long as unemployment and slow growth continue, the relative prices of raw materials are kept down and this somewhat mitigates inflation in industrial countries. As soon as a revival begins, prices of raw materials and foodstuffs begin to go up and real wage demands become harder to resist; the authorities nervously pull back and the revival is checked. The orthodox economists, still repeating incantations about equilibrium, encourage the authorities to pursue these deflationary policies – the very same that Keynes in the thirties used to describe as sadistic.

It is ironic that after the great technical achievements brought by the age of growth, all we are offered is a return to large-scale unemployment and poverty in the midst of plenty, in an age of frustration. Kalecki was right to be sceptical; the modern economies have failed to develop the political and social institutions, at either domestic or international level, that are needed to make permanent full employment compatible with capitalism.

Table 1. *Rates of growth of* per capita *Gross Domestic Product and consumption, OECD and selected OECD countries, 1954–75 (constant 1970 prices and exchange rates)*

Annual compound rates of growth	Gross Domestic Product			Consumption		
	1954–66	1966–73	1973–75	1954–66	1966–73	1973–75
USA	2·5	2·7	−2·7	2·6	3·1	−0·7
Canada	2·6	3·5	0·4	2·5	3·8	3·6
Japan	8·4	9·1	−0·6	7·2	7·4	2·4
Germany	5·5	3·9	−1·5	5·6	3·9	n.a.
France	4·3	4·9	0	3·8	4·6	n.a.
UK	2·3	2·5	−0·5	2·3	2·5	−0·7
OECD Total	3·2	3·7	−1·6	3·1	3·7	n.a.

Sources: National Accounts of OECD Countries 1953–69 and 1962–73, OECD, Paris
Main Economic Indicators, OECD, Paris, 1976
Manpower Statistics, 1954–64, OECD, Paris, 1965
Labour Force Statistics, 1963–74, OECD, Paris, 1976
Note: GDP growth rates were adjusted to a *per capita* basis using population statistics from OECD sources.

Bibliography

Ahluwalia, M. S. 1976. 'Income Distribution and Development: Some Stylised Facts', *American Economic Review* (Papers and Proceedings)

Bardhan, P. K. 1974. 'On the Incidence of Rural Poverty in India in the 1960's, in *Poverty and Income Distribution in India*, ed. P. K. Bardhan and T. W. Srinivasan. Calcutta, Indian Institute of Statistics

Beveridge, W. 1944. *Full Employment in a Free Society*, London, Allen & Unwin

Böhning, W. R. and Maillet, D. 1974. *The Effects of the Employment of Foreign Workers*, Paris, OECD

Brittan, S. 1975. *Second Thoughts on Full Employment Policy*, London, Centre for Policy Studies

Caves, R. E. and associates 1968. *Britain's Economic Prospects*, London, Allen & Unwin

Chenery, H. *et al.* 1974. *Redistribution with Growth*, Oxford, OUP

Cmnd. 6527, 1944. *Employment Policy*, London, HMSO

Kahn, R. 1975. 'Unemployment as seen by Keynesians', in *The Concept and Measurement of Involuntary Unemployment*, ed. G. D. N. Worswick, London, Allen & Unwin

Kahn, R. 1976. 'The Historical Origins of the IMF', in *Keynes and International Monetary Relations*, ed. H. P. Thirlwall, London, Macmillan

Kalecki, M. 1943. 'Political Aspects of Full Employment', *Political Quarterly*, Vol. 14

Keynes, J. M. 1936. *The General Theory of Employment, Interest and Money*, London, Macmillan

Keynes, J. M. 1946. 'The Balance of Payments of the United States', *Economic Journal*, Vol. 56

Keynes, J. M. 1972. 'The Economic Consequences of Mr. Winston Churchill', in *Collected Writings of John Maynard Keynes*, Vol. 9, *Essays in Persuasion*, London, Macmillan

Laidler, D. E. W. 1975. 'The End of "demand management". How to Reduce Unemployment in the late 1970s', in M. Friedman, *Unemployment versus Inflation?*, London, Institute of Economic Affairs

Pigou, A. C. 1933. *The Theory of Unemployment*, London, Macmillan

Phillips, A. W. 1958. 'The Relationship between Unemployment and the Rate of Change of Money Wage Rates in the UK, 1861–1957,' *Economica*, Vol. XXV, no. 100

Robinson, J. 1962. 'Philosophy of Prices', in *Collected Economic Papers*, Vol. 2, Oxford, Blackwell

Robinson, J. 1973. *Collected Papers*, Vol. 4, Oxford, Blackwell

Samuelson, P. A. 1970. *Economics*, 8th edition, New York, McGraw-Hill

24

BEAUTY AND THE BEAST

ONCE upon a time there was a great and successful merchant who lived in the prosperous commercial state of Urbania. He filled with success the role of trader and organizer of production, for he invariably dealt thoughtfully with the difficult and vital problems of his business, studying the broader movements of the markets, the yet undeveloped results of current events at home and abroad, and contriving to improve the organization of the internal and external relations of his business. By his bold and tireless enterprise, he had reaped a rich harvest of that material reward which is the steadiest motive to ordinary business work. Yet in the accumulation of his wealth he was, like many traders, often stimulated more by the hope of victory over his rivals than by the desire to add something to his fortune; moreover, like everyone who is worth anything, he carried his higher nature with him into business, and there, as elsewhere, he was influenced by his personal affections, by his conceptions of duty, and his reverence for high ideals.

The business to which he had devoted so much toil, energy and foresight, was located in the capital of Urbania, but the growth of facilities for living far from the centres of industry and commerce had enabled him to take up his residence in a suburb, where an excellent system of drainage, water supply and lighting, together with good schools, and opportunities for open-air play, afforded conditions at least as conducive to vigour as are to be found in the country.

These considerations had been of particular importance to him, as he was the parent of a family of three daughters. This number may appear unduly small, but although in early days he had often reflected that members of a large family are more genial and bright, and often more vigorous in every way than members of a small family, it was yet true that the additional benefit which a person derives from a given stock of a thing diminishes with every increase in the stock which he already has. That is to

---

This paper was compiled in my undergraduate days, in collaboration with Dorothea Morison (afterwards Mrs. R. B. Braithwaite).

say, that the marginal utility decreases, and the merchant had observed that the marginal utility of daughters decreases with surprising rapidity.

To the education of these three daughters he had always devoted the utmost personal attention, for whereas he himself was brought up by parents of strong, earnest character, and was educated by their personal influence and by struggle with difficulties, he was anxious lest his children, who were born after he became rich, might be left too much to the care of domestic servants, who were unlikely to be of the same strong fibre as the parents by whose influence he was educated; for he was conscious that though there are many fine natures among domestic servants, those who live in very rich houses are apt to get self-indulgent habits, to over-estimate the importance of wealth and generally put the lower aims of life above the higher. The company in which the children of some of our best houses spend much of their time is less ennobling than that of the average cottage, yet in these very houses no servant who is not specially qualified is allowed to take charge of a young retriever or a young horse.

In the determination that his household should not be such as this, he had been careful so to regulate his business that he was able to spend his leisure hours amongst his family, and by example and precept to build up a strong and righteous character in his children.

A time came, however, when his daughters were approaching maturity, and it became apparent to him that an opportunity offered for pushing his trade into new and more profitable channels; for, taking account of his own means, he had already pushed the investment of capital in the home trade until what appeared to his judgment to be the outer limit or margin of profitableness had been reached, that is, the gains resulting from any further investment in that particular direction would not compensate him for his outlay.

In other words, the principle of substitution prompted him to invest capital and personal effort in pushing the sale of his goods into a field where the reward seemed to him greater than that which he would receive by any enlargement of the particular branch of trade in which he was at that moment engaged.

He therefore called his daughters together, and communicating to them his intentions, he addressed them as follows. 'My children, as a merchant I have pursued my own interests, but I have generally benefited my country; my personal connections, as well as my patriotism, have hitherto inclined me to give a preference to home goods, other things being nearly equal. A promising opportunity has now presented itself, and I propose to go myself to Baghdad, there to superintend the expansion of my business.

'In view of this new venture, I would have you remember that business men in the past who have pioneered new paths have often conferred on society benefits out of all proportion to their own gains, even though they have died millionaires. A close and careful watching of the advantages and disadvantages of different courses of conduct has led me to anticipate considerable profit from the adventure upon which I am now embarked, but as it has never been my custom to allow the exigencies of commerce to override the dictates of my higher nature, I intend to purchase for each of you a gift, and this I am the more willing to do when I reflect that the sacrifice will be relatively small owing to the decrease in the marginal utility of money which will attend upon the increase in my income.

'I will therefore ask you to inform me after due reflection the nature of the presents which you desire.'

He then departed to make preparations for his journey, and his daughters were left to the discussion of their momentous choice.

The decision of the first daughter was influenced by the knowledge that total satisfaction is maximized when marginal utilities are equal, and her choice fell upon jewellery, for she was animated by that desire for display which is enhanced among the upper classes by custom and emulation, and though jewellery may be considered a luxury, the demand for it among such persons tends to be strong.

But the second daughter, casting an eye upon her existing stock of possessions, concluded that a more urgent need in her case was for clothing, and that the marginal utility of jewellery would therefore be less for her than that of clothes. Consequently she decided to ask for a beautiful and serviceable gown. We may also assume from this that she discounted the future at a higher rate than her elder sister, for it will be generally admitted that the income of satisfaction to be derived from a gown will be yielded over a shorter period of time than that to be anticipated from jewellery.

When the turn of the third daughter came round, she considered various gratifications which she might obtain for herself, and her desires turned now towards one and now towards another; but she remembered after a time that gifts on so lavish a scale would be likely to reduce her father's stock of available purchasing power, and she realized that her choice lay between personal satisfaction and obedience to the dictates of filial affection. We may here note that the economist does not claim to measure any affection of the mind in itself or directly, but only indirectly through its effects, and he studies mental states rather through their manifestations than in themselves, he does not attempt to weigh the higher affections of our nature against those of our lower, he does not balance the love of virtue against the desire for agreeable possessions, he can only estimate their incentives to action by their effects.

When, therefore, the youngest daughter finally chose not such extravagant gifts as her sisters, but a simple rose, we are justified in assuming that she estimated her father's well-being of higher account than any possible gratification which she might obtain for herself.

The choice of all three being thus determined, the merchant set out to pioneer the way for his new markets in the Orient, taking advantage of that growing rapidity and comfort of foreign travel which has induced so many business men and skilled artisans to carry their skill near to the consumers who will purchase their wares. Let it suffice to say that his efforts were amply repaid, for his rare ability and rare good fortune, both in the particular incidents of speculative enterprise and in meeting with a favourable opportunity for the general development of his business, led him to succeed abundantly. Not only did his commerce afford him that increment on his capital which would just have induced him to continue in business, but over and above this, brought in a surplus which he regarded as a payment for the bearing of risks and the earnings of exceptional ability. On the return journey, not unmindful of the claims of family affection in the midst of the manifold cares of commercial enterprise, he sought for the most suitable market in which to purchase for his daughters the presents which they had desired him to bring home.

He was able, on the further side of the Mediterranean, to find jewellery for his first and garments for his second daughter, at a price which, having regard to the undertaking which he had made and his present income, did not appear to him excessive. But in regard to the rose for his third daughter, he had in mind not only the preference due to home products (other things being nearly equal), but to the difficulties and cost involved in the transport of perishable goods.

Therefore it was not until he arrived at the shores of Urbania that he commenced to entertain serious thoughts of his purchase. Upon inquiry, he discovered that the production of roses was subject to seasonal fluctuations, and that during the current month, although employment was provided in certain preparatory processes, the final product was unprocurable. In the commercial papers, roses were quoted at a scarcity price, but the figure was merely nominal, as there were, in fact, no roses on the market. In view of the dissatisfaction (to him) which would attend his failure to procure a rose, he would have been willing not only to offer a very considerable price, but to undergo a certain amount of fatigue in the search for the desired article.

In this sense the disutility of labour may be regarded as entering into the price that he would be willing to pay.

Doubting whether the rose market was so highly organized that communication between the surrounding localities was complete, he set out in the hope of finding some secluded market to which the scarcity demand for roses had not yet been transmitted. In this, however, he was not successful, finding that in those few cases where a small number of roses had been produced at this season, the producers had been able speedily to profit by the high prices ruling elsewhere. Eventually, however, he arrived at a locality where intelligence reached him of a certain landowner who was in possession of a garden of roses. He proceeded thither, and his observation confirmed his information with regard to roses.

He was contemplating the respective quality of various blooms, when the owner of the garden appeared. His aspect was unusual, as he bore the semblance of a beast. The merchant became conscious that he was committing an act of trespass, and attempted to mollify the indignation manifested by the owner by inquiring the price of roses. The beast, knowing that he was in the position of a monopolist, thereupon took unusual steps in maximizing a monopoly profit. Instead of asking a high money price, as might have been expected in the circumstances, he demanded that the merchant, in exchange for the rose, should yield him whatever object first met his view on returning home. The merchant, conscious that his demand for the rose was unusually rigid, and his bargaining position weak, thereupon accepted the somewhat unusual offer. Trained in the course of his business to judge cautiously and take risks boldly, he determined that the certain reward was not out-balanced by a loss which might prove negligible. In this, he displayed that courage and confidence which has by degrees established an upright and honourable tradition in the conduct of business throughout the civilized world; but it must be remembered that while some men make their way by the use of none but noble qualities, others owe their prosperity to qualities in which there is very little which is really admirable except sagacity and strength of purpose. Of such a nature was the beast, who, unknown to the merchant, was in possession of a detailed knowledge of the future, and did not scruple to reap a reward which he had earned neither by constructive work, nor by that function of risk bearing which is the characteristic of speculative activity. For it has been well observed that the speculator who by intelligent foresight anticipates the future, and who makes his gains by shrewd purchases and sales, renders thereby a public service of no small importance, but when to a normal degree of foresight is added supernatural information, the speculator is in a position to enhance his own gains at the expense of less enlightened members of the community. Such malignant forms of speculation are a grievous hindrance to progress.

The merchant, however, was unconscious of the special circumstances which rendered the case a somewhat unusual example of speculative activity, and thereupon concluded the bargain, and entered into immediate possession of the rose. Having thus acquired the object which had caused him such great expense of energy and labour, he proceeded homeward along a route made expeditious and convenient by modern developments of communication.

His arrival in his own city inspired the merchant with that sensation of pleasure which all men of fine feeling must experience after a prolonged absence from the familiar surroundings of their native land, and he looked forward with pleasurable anticipation to those comforts and luxuries of home life which brighten men's lives and stimulate their thoughts.

A certain anxiety which he experienced as to the possible issue of his most recent speculation detracted somewhat from his sense of satisfaction, but he reflected that great progress can be attained only by bold daring, and security may be purchased at too high a price.

As he approached his home, however, this feeling of anxiety gave place to one of positive alarm when he perceived his youngest and best-loved daughter issuing from the house to meet him. He was not slow to realize that this was the price which he would be required to pay for the rose, in fulfilment of the contract which he had made with the foreign landowner. He had never been accustomed to regard his daughters either as capital or as stock-in-trade, and this payment would be in every way as unusual as it was exorbitant. He was therefore for a moment in some doubt as to the advisability of repudiating his obligations – but, reared in that school of honourable tradition which has peopled the world with merchants distinguished for upright dealing and the strictest integrity, he reflected that the structure of modern industry could only be maintained by that rigid observance of contracts which is the essential basis for all commercial progress; for he had always been of opinion that the marvellous growth in recent times of a spirit of honesty and uprightness in commercial matters and the progress of trade morality had been achieved, and could only be maintained, by the scrupulous integrity with which every member of the business community must refrain from yielding to the vast temptations to fraud which lie in his way. But the evils of reckless trading are always apt to spread far beyond the persons directly concerned, and this truth was immediately realized by his youngest daughter when the merchant revealed to her the part which she was called upon to play in the consummation of the transaction which, in obedience to the dictates of his higher nature, he felt himself compelled to fulfil.

With that courage and cheerful determination which had been so carefully inculcated in her by the discipline of a truly liberal education, she instantly proceeded to consider her situation. After much careful thought, an analysis of the position revealed that the disutility of the labour she was called upon to perform was hardly outweighed by the satisfaction of assisting her parent, which would be her reward. For the discommodity of labour may arise from bodily or mental fatigue or from its being carried on in unhealthy surroundings or with unwelcome associates, and the employment which she was contemplating presented undoubtedly the latter, with possibilities of the former characteristics.

Indeed, connubial relations with the beast appeared to her employment of so unpleasant and distasteful a nature that the satisfaction of filial affection hardly appeared to her sufficient remuneration to represent an effective supply price. For the price which is sufficiently attractive to call forth a given expenditure of effort is the effective supply price for that amount of effort, and in the case of employments which are degrading, distasteful, or irksome, the number of persons who are willing to enter them may be so small that a low price is often inadequate to induce the exertions required.

The issue, therefore, seemed to depend on the degree of undesirability represented by the employment under consideration, and she ended her reflections with the following inquiry:

'Father, did you ascertain whether the beast was hairy?'

The merchant who had always cultivated the faculties of observation and memorization to a high degree, was able to assure her that the degree of hairiness was not above the normal for that class of person.

Quickly balancing the factors relevant to the situation in the light of this additional information, she finally replied: 'In these circumstances, I am just willing to accept the bargain'. At this moment they realized simultaneously that she was on the margin, for they did not omit to notice that an additional (small) increment of disutility would have outweighed the satisfaction to be obtained from obedience to filial duty.

The contract was thus ratified by all parties concerned, and when the day of maturity arrived, the daughter of the merchant presented herself punctually at the residence of the beast. As he came forward to meet her, she compelled herself boldly to face the stern fact that she was about to enter into the service of an employer who was likely to prove both harsh and exacting. No sooner, however, had he taken her by the hand than he became transformed into a beautiful prince.

Such sudden transitions are rare in nature, and though she had been accustomed to the contemplation of the astounding progress of scientific achievement and the innumerable marvels which human invention have rendered possible, she yet was filled with astonishment at such an unusual phenomenon. It became instantly apparent to her that the bargain, far from being the marginal transaction which she had supposed it to be, was one from which she would reap a large producers' surplus. The situation was, indeed, exceptional, for the disutility of labour had now sunk to a negative quantity. It was, indeed, a case parallel to that of intellectual pursuits, where, after the painful effort involved in starting has been overcome, the pleasure and excitement, after they have once set in, often go on increasing until progress is stopped, either by necessity or prudence.

With mutual pleasure, they then proceeded to discuss the bargain which had yielded to both of them so large a degree of satisfaction; for he entered into the enjoyment of a large consumer's surplus by the acquisition of a beautiful and useful wife at the price of a single rose, while she, at the cost of an effort which now promised to be pleasurable, had secured a prize for the attainment of which she would have been willing to undergo irksome and unpleasant labour.

With this happy union of producer's and consumer's surplus, they then lived happily ever after, constantly keeping in mind their higher ideals and maximizing their satisfaction by equalizing the marginal utility of each object of expenditure.